EXPERT BUZZ FROM THE BUFFET LINE

"*The Business Buffet* isn't just food for thought—it's a full-on leadership tasting menu. Funny, wise, and genuinely empowering, it delivers real-world strategies every leader needs to succeed. If you are hungry for essential career skills not taught in business school, this book is for you."

Jon Gordon, 18x best-selling author of *The Power of Positive Leadership* and *The Energy Bus*

"A delicious leadership read. *The Business Buffet* packs a powerful message for raising your leadership to new heights in a delightfully entertaining and very digestible package. Once you get a taste of it, you won't want to put it down."

Douglas Conant, retired CEO of Campbell Soup Company, *NYT/WSJ* best-selling author, founder of ConantLeadership

"A no-fluff guide to the real skills your career expects you to know—but no one ever taught you. Think bite-sized business wisdom, served with humor, heat, and just the right amount of seasoning."

Ankur Warikoo, founder of WebVeda.com (and best-selling author of some pretty EPIC books!)

"*The Business Buffet* is the career handbook today's professionals have been waiting for—relatable, research-informed, and refreshingly honest. Matthew Tedesco cuts through the corporate noise to offer bite-sized insights that stick. If you want to lead with impact and navigate the modern workplace confidently, this book belongs on your desk."

Dan Schawbel, author of *Back to Human,*
Promote Yourself,* and *Me 2.0

"A Fortune 50 CEO once told me, 'Leadership is 90% communication.' In that case, *The Business Buffet* is the book every leader needs. It's an insightful, pragmatic, and funny (yes, funny!) guide to help today's leader apply their trade with true impact and clarity. It breaks down the overlooked essentials of leadership to help readers build trust, navigate challenges, and show up better every day."

Scott Mautz, 2x best-selling author of *The Mentally*
Strong Leader* and *Leading from the Middle

"*The Business Buffet* is the rare business book that's equal parts brilliant and bingeable. With sharp insights and hilarious wit, Matthew serves up the leadership and career guidance we all wish we'd gotten years ago."

Rachel DeAlto, communication expert and author of
The Relatable Leader: Create a Culture of Connection

"Imagine a mentor who truly understands the strengths of quieter personalities and wants to help you shine without asking you to change who you are. Each chapter is a fresh plate, ready for you to try at your own pace, whether you are preparing for a big presentation or navigating everyday team moments. With friendly stories, simple exercises, and honest advice, *The Business Buffet* is designed for busy professionals who want real-world insights with a side of humor. You can return again and again, picking up new skills whenever you need them."

Steven Claes, Global Leadership & Career Insights Influencer |
CHRO | founder, A+ Introvert Newsletter

"Smart, funny, and genuinely useful. *The Business Buffet* serves up the essential career skills they never taught you—told by a leader who's lived them and succeeded at the highest level. For anyone who leads, aspires to lead, or just wants to feel a little less lost at work, this is the guide you didn't know you needed."

Chris Schembra, best-selling author of
Gratitude Through Hard Times

"Matthew Tedesco knows that leadership isn't about titles, it's about who people follow. *The Business Buffet* reveals unspoken truths about the importance of effective communication on the job and in real life. It's more than food for thought, it's a recipe for success."

Kevin Budelmann, author, professor, president of Peopledesign

"Reading *The Business Buffet* felt like being privately coached by someone who's walked the talk—with humor, humility, and hard-earned perspective. As a communications and people leader, I found myself nodding, highlighting, and laughing (sometimes all at once). Tedesco gets what leadership is really about: how we show up, communicate, and support one another in the messy, human reality of work. This is a must-read for anyone who cares about leading with intention, empathy, and lasting impact."

Craig Annis, chief communications officer, A&O Sherman

"Look, he's no Malcolm Gladwell… but he's got charm, clean sentences, and a surprisingly strong analogy game. Will he change your life? Quite possibly. Will he be home for dinner? Absolutely not—he's rewriting Chapter 4 for the umpteenth time, and he hasn't lived at home since 2004."

Definitely not my mom

THE BUSINESS BUFFET

THE BUSINESS BUFFET

15 Career Must-Haves They Never Teach—But Still Expect You to Know

MATTHEW TEDESCO

THE BUSINESS BUFFET
15 Career Must-Haves They Never Teach—But Still Expect You to Know

Copyright © 2025 by Matthew Tedesco

Cover Design by Rachel Royer
Interior Layout and Design by Alice Briggs
Editorial Team: Andrew Blackburn, Mandi Reed

ISBNs:
E-book: 979-8-89165-299-6
Paperback: 979-8-89165-300-9
Hardcover: 979-8-89165-301-6

Published by:
Gordon Publishing
gordonpublishing.com

GORDON
PUBLISHING

To me. I really did it.

You go, gurl.

LE MENU

"The single biggest problem in communication is the illusion that it has taken place."

— George Bernard Shaw

THE AMUSE-BOUCHE

Before the feast of ideas begins, here's a bite-sized preview to warm up your mental taste buds... oooh, yummy!

Burnout:

A state of physical, emotional, or mental exhaustion, often accompanied by reduced motivation and performance.

Constructive Conflict:

An approach to disagreements that focuses on finding solutions and fostering understanding, rather than escalating personal attacks or hostility.

Diplomacy:

The skill of navigating complex interpersonal situations with tact and understanding, fostering positive relationships and resolving conflicts effectively.

Do Hard Better:

The practice of approaching tough challenges not just with grit, but with strategy—treating pressure-filled moments as training grounds for resilience, clarity, and growth.

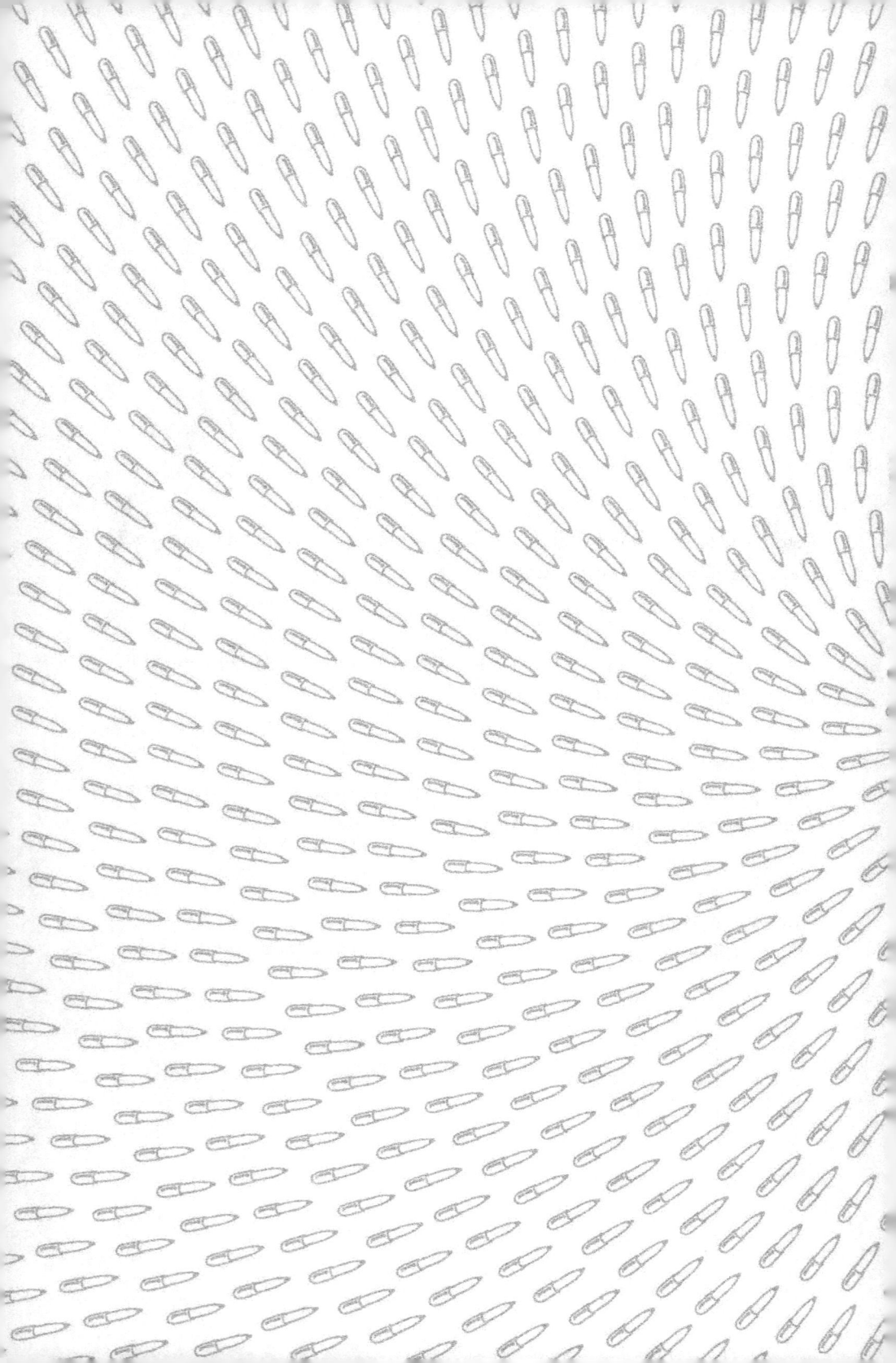

Effective Communication:
The ability to convey ideas clearly, authentically, and persuasively—whether to oneself, to others, or to the world at large.

Energy Management:
Understanding and optimizing one's physical, emotional, mental, and spiritual energy levels to sustain high performance and prevent burnout.

Fixed Mindset:
The belief that intelligence and talent are fixed traits—often leading to avoidance of challenges and fear of failure.

Glimmer:
A small, often overlooked moment of joy, connection, or beauty that sparks a sense of calm or appreciation. Glimmers are the opposite of triggers—they cue your nervous system toward safety and positivity.

Gratitude:
In a professional context, the practice of recognizing and appreciating the positive aspects of one's work and experiences, leading to enhanced well-being and performance.

Growth Mindset:
The belief that abilities and intelligence can grow through effort, feedback, and persistence—encouraging people to embrace challenges, learn from mistakes, and keep improving.

Humility:
Recognizing one's limitations and knowledge gaps, fostering a mindset of continuous learning and collaboration, and building trust through authenticity.

Humor:

The intentional use of wit and levity to build trust, defuse tension, and enhance communication. In leadership, humor helps humanize authority, foster connection, and spark creativity.

Kaizen:

A Japanese business philosophy of continuous improvement through small, incremental changes.

Listening (Active Listening):

Fully engaging with a speaker to understand their words, emotions, and intent—not just hearing, but interpreting and responding with empathy.

Mentorship:

A relationship where an experienced individual provides guidance, advice, and support to a less experienced person.

Mindfulness:

The practice of paying attention to the present moment without judgment, which can improve focus, reduce stress, and foster creativity in the workplace.

Momentum Mirage:

The frustrating-but-true pattern where progress looks invisible… until it suddenly isn't. It's a lesson in patience, compounding, and trusting the work when results lag behind.

Neural Coupling:

A phenomenon where two people's brains sync up during storytelling or deep conversation—turning words into shared experience.

Neuroplasticity:

The brain's ability to reshape itself by forming new neural pathways—proving we can keep learning, adapting, and evolving at any age.

Personal Branding:

The process of defining and communicating one's unique skills, values, and attributes to create a consistent and authentic professional identity.

Power of Three:

A communication principle suggesting that messages structured in sets of three are more memorable, impactful, and satisfying to the human brain.

Psychological Safety:

An environment where individuals feel comfortable taking interpersonal risks, voicing opinions, and making mistakes without fear of negative consequences.

Sponsorship:

A relationship where a senior leader advocates for a more junior professional, providing visibility, opportunities, and support for career advancement.

Storytelling:

The art of presenting information and ideas in a narrative format to engage an audience emotionally, enhance understanding, and make the message more memorable.

Toxic Positivity:

A concept referring to the detrimental effects of an excessive or inauthentic focus on positivity that dismisses genuine struggles or negative emotions.

Yutori:

A Japanese concept referring to the space between things, allowing for renewal, growth, and a more balanced approach to work and life.

Welcome to the Business Buffet

WELL, HELLO THERE! Thanks for picking up this book. I am totally sure you 100% bought this book on purpose with your own hard-earned cash, but even if you accidentally clicked "Buy Now" while doom scrolling your way through an 8 a.m. forecast call, welcome aboard! This is your Michelin guide to transforming good professional instincts into exceptional performance—except instead of pretentious plating and foam reductions, you're getting real-world experience and research that matters, delivered in bite-sized pieces that won't give you indigestion.

So, what exactly have you gotten yourself into? Think of this book as the illegitimate love child of a business textbook and *The Great British Bake Off*—minus the British accents and actual baking parts. It's your insider's guide to all those professional skills they don't teach you in business school, during onboarding, or in the boardroom, but somehow still expect you to know. It's packed with insights that'll make you say "Why didn't anyone tell me this before?" and "Oh, that's why Stacy keeps getting promoted" and "Did I actually pay for this book?". It's for anyone who's ever wanted the TL;DR version of business success and needs the highlight reel before committing to the full game.

Now, before we dive in, let's get three things straight.

First, this isn't your typical, linear, "read from cover to cover or the business gods will smite you" kind of book. Nope. This is more like a literary buffet (hence the title). Feel free to sample a bit of everything, go back for seconds, or focus entirely on the *favorites* section. I won't judge. (Well, maybe a little.) We consume information in bites, snacks, and meals. Bites are the quick hits—a sharp tweet, a viral TikTok, or a meme that delivers an insight in seconds. Meals are the deep dives—full-length books, case studies, or research papers that require time to digest. This book? It's a snack—substantial enough to be satisfying, but digestible enough to keep you moving. Take what you need, skip what you don't, and come back for more whenever you're hungry for it.

Second—and this is important—you'll notice frequent references to "leaders" and "leadership" throughout these pages. That's intentional. Leadership isn't about titles, seniority, or how many people report to you on the org chart. It's about how you show up every day, through your thoughts, actions, and perspectives. Whether you're managing global teams or just trying to manage your inbox, you have the ability, opportunity, and responsibility to lead. So when you see these terms, remember: this buffet is open to everyone ready to make an impact, no matter where they sit in the corporate cafeteria.

Third, and this one will come as a surprise, so I hope you are sitting down and maybe even surrounded by loved ones: I am not an expert. On, like, anything. But I am curious and dedicated to my craft. Two decades of leading global teams, turning around business units, and wearing out countless passport pages between Shanghai, London, and New York has taught me what actually works and what's just business buzzword bingo. And whether it's been in a corporate office, on a factory floor, or from the United Polaris Lounge in Newark, I've read and listened to lots of business books. Like over 150 of them.

What I've learned through all that reading and over the past 20+ years of corporate life is that most business books could be easily condensed into a single chapter. And that, sadly, most aren't that much fun to read. At least not for my Insta-level attention span, which has somehow survived key roles in multiple mergers and acquisitions, managing teams across three continents, and trying to remember which time zone I'm supposed to be in today.

There are, of course, exceptions. If Daniel Pink penned an alarm clock instruction manual, I would read it cover to cover. Malcolm Gladwell could write a treatise on the socioeconomic implications of forgetting why you walked into a room, and I'd pre-order the hardcover. The Brené Browns and Adam Grants of the world make learning feel like binge-watching your favorite show. And for the love of perfectly timed comedic prose, give me Tina Fey or David Sedaris any day. It's great to have authors you cherish and topics that truly inspire you. Who knows? Maybe I could be that for you one day. (Is it just me or are we, like, already vibing?)

There is also value, and frankly necessity, in being a deep expert in a certain field. Expertise drives proficiency and market value, and it naturally requires a high level of content consumption to get to that level. Want to master quantum computing? Get ready to befriend Schrödinger's cat. Diving into financial derivatives? Hope you like Greek letters more than a fraternity recruitment officer. Looking to lead in AI? Prepare to dream in algorithms.

This book is not that.

Don't get me wrong: the world definitely needs experts. But does it really need more experts with no humility, bad storytelling skills, and a complete lack of gratitude? (I'll let you insert your favorite tech billionaire here.) While deep expertise is absolutely critical in specific fields, there's one skill that's universally undeniable, regardless of your specialty. It's the difference between being the smartest person in the room and being the person everyone wants to—and actually can—work with.

So, let me ask you a question: *What do you think the most important human skill is?*

If you said the ability to convincingly fake-smile while internally screaming, I will give you half credit.

I, and many other IRL experts, would argue it's ***effective communication***. Not just the "please circle back with your thoughts" kind, but the real, human-to-human connection that turns good professionals into great leaders. It impacts every aspect of our lives, and yet, if we're being honest, most of us do not spend much, if any, time really investing in becoming better communicators.

Think about it this way: Name a sport or hobby. It could be literally anything, but let's say golf, because apparently that's where all the "real" business happens anyway.

If you wanted to be great at golf, you would invest in lessons, practice until your hands blister, and probably buy pants that shouldn't exist outside of a circus. You could recite *Ben Hogan's Five Lessons* religiously; you would watch *Bryan Bros Golf YouTube* videos and listen to the *Rick Shiels Golf Show* podcast; you would go to the range daily, and even spend more on clubs than your first car.

The point? When something matters, you invest time, energy, and resources.

Not all of us want to be great at golf, but I would hope most of us would want to be great at our chosen profession. So where is the investment in effective communication?

Well, it's here. That's right. You've been tricked. This book is all about effective communication disguised as a spoof white elephant gift disguised as your next favorite business read. The famed double-masquerade!

This isn't just another book on effective communication. It's a buffet of 15 interconnected but distinct snacks on how we communicate to ourselves, to the colleague across from us, and to the world all around. It's about the inside and outside stories we tell, about better understanding our audiences, and about leveraging some key insights and proven methodologies so we can do a little less internal screaming and a lot more external smiling.

It's your insider's guide to the professional kitchen—from mastering your own knife skills to handling that one sous chef who insists on 'deconstructing' every recipe.

Whether you're working to master difficult conversations or navigate office politics, this book provides practical tools for workplace success. Master all 15 skills or just pick up enough to get through your next performance review without breaking a sweat—the journey is yours.

But be warned: this book won't turn you into a corporate communication superhero overnight. Trust me, I've collected enough meeting faux pas to fill another book entirely! (Do I hear sequel?)

What this book offers is more like having a skilled chef mentor you in the kitchen. The results come from showing up, practicing the techniques, and occasionally burning the sauce. Each chapter is your personal test kitchen. These aren't recipes dreamed up in some ivory tower—they're battle-tested strategies that have survived countless meetings, mishaps, and management changes.

As we dive into this buffet of business wisdom, remember: the magic isn't in the knowing. It's in the doing, the failing, and the doing again. And again. And maybe one more time, just for good measure. Your journey won't be about perfection; it'll be about progress toward building better habits while navigating the chaos of corporate life, like when you're on your fifth Zoom call and can't remember if it's Tuesday or February.

So, grab a knife and fork and dig in—before someone else gets the good stuff!

Section 1: The Prep Station

Before diving into external communication strategies, we must first master our own internal dialogue. Like a chef perfecting foundational techniques, these five chapters build the essential skills that drive all professional interaction. Here, we're diving into the stories we tell ourselves, those personal recipes that can either fuel our success or leave us simmering in mediocrity. Think of it as learning to control your burners: too hot and everything burns, too cool and nothing transforms. We'll be exploring:

1. Gratitude: Authentic appreciation that drives connection and performance
2. Mindfulness: Practical techniques for clarity and focus
3. Growth Mindset: Building resilience through continuous learning
4. Do Hard Better: Strategies for embracing and overcoming challenges
5. Navigating the Momentum Mirage: Understanding and pushing through performance barriers

Section 2: The Cooking Line

Every kitchen runs on communication—from rapid-fire exchanges to understanding the order to the delicate art of giving feedback on an over-salted soup. In this section, you'll learn how to read the room, build trust, and handle difficult conversations with the same finesse you'd use to plate a delicate dessert. Whether you're managing up, down, or sideways, these tools will help you turn workplace chaos into coordinated collaboration. We'll look at:

6.   Humor: Leveraging appropriate levity to build trust and connection
7.   Humility: The power of authentic leadership and continuous learning
8.   Listening: Mastering active engagement for better outcomes
9.   Energy Management: Optimizing performance through sustainable practices
10. Psychological Safety: Creating environments that foster innovation and growth

Section 3: The Perfect Plating

Now we're turning up the heat and focusing on how you communicate your value to the world. This section is about transforming your professional presence from "meets expectations" to "who is this person and how do they make it look so easy?" We'll talk about the kinds of skills that make people wonder if you've been secretly attending some elite leadership academy on the weekends. (Spoiler: you have—it's called this book.) Here, we'll explore:

11. Storytelling: Crafting compelling narratives for business impact
12. The Power of Three: Framework principles for effective communication
13. Personal Branding: Developing and managing your professional identity
14. Sponsorship: Building strategic relationships for career advancement
15. Diplomacy: Navigating complex organizational dynamics

What to Expect: Format, Flavor, and Feast

This isn't another one of those single-course business books that stuff you with one big idea and a lot of empty calories. It's a full tasting menu, designed to deliver maximum flavor with zero filler—just practical, proven approaches served in bite-sized portions that fit your schedule and appetite.

Here's what's on the menu:

Three Main Dishes: These are the main courses, the juicy steaks of knowledge that you'll want to sink your teeth into. They're the concepts that'll make you go "Aha!" or possibly "Oh no!" and occasionally "What the F?"

Five Taste-Test Recipes: These are some optional practice exercises—small plates you can try whenever you're ready to expand your palate. Like any good recipe, you might not nail it on your first attempt, but that's part of the fun. Sample them today, perfect them next week, or add them to your "I'll definitely get to that someday" cookbook collection.

10 Quick Bites: These are your quick takeaways that you can easily digest and keep in your pocket for later. They're perfect for those moments when your boss asks, "So, what did you learn from that book?" and your brain flatlines harder than the office Wi-Fi during a critical Teams call.

Also included in this cornucopia of digestible content:

- A customer profile that brings concepts to life.
- Thought-provoking *Cerebral Sous Vide* questions.
- A *Sweet & Savory Shout-Out* of an industry leader and personal fave.
- A *Prep Card* for common challenges.
- Five curated deep dives from the *Self-Serve Station*—for those craving more of a meal after this delicious snack.

Each chapter can stand alone, so feel free to jump around. Got a big presentation coming up? Flip to Storytelling. Just had an embarrassing moment in a meeting? The Humility chapter is calling your name.

Fair warning, though—you might notice some ideas popping up more than once. That's not because I forgot what I wrote (wink, wink). Nope. 100%

intentional. These concepts are unique but interconnected, working together to serve a greater good.

It's just like your favorite recipe, where garlic, olive oil, and basil are great on their own, but create something magical when combined. Gratitude feeds into humility, which enables better listening, which creates psychological safety, which gives people permission to tell better stories... you get the idea.

Each chapter gives you a new lens to look through, a new tool to work with, and a new way to think about how you show up in the workplace. You might benefit from all 15 working together like a well-oiled machine, and other times you'll just need to dial up one or two to get through that tough meeting or difficult conversation.

Whether you're still figuring out where the good snacks are kept, or you're the person who approved the snack budget, there's something in here for you. So, let's dig in! Your journey to becoming a better, brighter, and significantly less bewildered professional starts now.

EFFECTIVE COMMUNICATION IS ALL ABOUT TALKING LOUDER.

ONE

The Prep Station—How You Communicate With Yourself

PANTRY PARTY! BEFORE we dive into the external stuff—the presentations, the tough conversations, the office politics—we need to stock our professional kitchen with something more fundamental: the ingredients that transform the voice in your head from harsh critic to helpful coach. We're filling your shelves with personal growth essentials that'll amplify every dish you create—from the zesty kick of gratitude to the slow-simmered wisdom of resilience.

These aren't just fillers; they're potent, concentrated elements that'll elevate your entire professional recipe. Remember, in this kitchen, it's not about having every spice on the shelf—it's about knowing which ones transform the whole dish.

In this first section, we'll master the five fundamental ingredients that transform your inner critic into your greatest advocate:

1. **Gratitude—The Foundational Stock**: Learn how authentic appreciation can boost everything from team morale to your own career trajectory. We'll explore why "thank you" is more than just good manners—it's good business.

2. **Mindfulness—A Measured Pour**: You can't slice through workplace chaos with a scattered mind and a dull blade. Discover how to sharpen your mental focus without trading your office chair for a meditation cushion.

3

3. **Growth Mindset—The Ultimate Leavening Agent**: Time to upgrade "fake it 'til you make it" to "I haven't mastered it... yet." We'll explore why some people bounce back from setbacks while others stay stuck, and how to join the bouncers.

4. **Do Hard Better—The Searing Method**: Success isn't about avoiding challenges—it's about handling them with style. Learn to stay cool when the pressure's high and the stakes are higher.

5. **Momentum Mirage—The Slow-Cook Method**: Sometimes progress feels like watching a pot that won't boil—lots of energy, no visible change. But just like a great stew needs time to develop its flavors, breakthrough moments often follow periods of seemingly stalled progress. We'll explore why these quiet stretches aren't roadblocks, but stepping stones to lasting success.

These fundamentals aren't garnishes—they're the difference between a microwave dinner and a masterpiece. Conquer them, and everything else in your professional kitchen becomes possible. The presentations land better, the tough conversations flow more easily, and the daily grind transforms into daily growth.

Time to whip up a career that's not just palatable, but absolutely delicious. LET'S GOOOOO!

GRATITUDE

APPETIZER

Ever wonder why some workplaces feel like a vibrant farmers' market, while others have the charm of a gas station bathroom? The key ingredient might just be gratitude! We're diving into how a dash of appreciation can transform your professional kitchen from bland to grand.

MAIN COURSE

Brain Chemistry: How gratitude rewires your neural pathways (and makes Monday meetings survivable!)
Team Dynamics: Transform colleague relationships from frozen TV dinner to home-cooked feast
Performance Boost: Turn everyday tasks into career-accelerating opportunities

DESSERT

The Glimmer Hunt: Your ten-minute appreciation acceleration
The Thank You Challenge: Five days, five colleagues, infinite impact
The Appreciation Station: Create your gratitude highlight reel without sounding like a greeting card

PAIRS WELL WITH

Your morning cup of Joe
That gratitude journal collecting digital dust on your phone
Your "crush this workday" playlist

CHAPTER 1

Gratitude—The Foundational Stock

I'S 9:47 A.M. on a rainy Wednesday, and you're staring at an email that begins with "Per my last request." Your coffee has already gone cold, your Slack is pinging like a pinball machine having an anxiety attack, and your project deadline just got moved up "to create a sense of urgency." In this moment, gratitude probably isn't your first response. Slamming your laptop shut, definitely. Updating your résumé, maybe. But gratitude? Not so much.

Before you light your laptop on fire, consider this: gratitude isn't about putting on a fake smile or pretending everything is okay. But it is about perspective and personal well-being. It's a powerful agent of transformation in how you experience and influence your mental, physical, emotional, and spiritual workplace.

One way to train your brain for gratitude isn't by forcing appreciation, but by spotting *glimmers*. Think of these as the opposite of triggers: the tiny, unexpected moments of joy that make the chaos of work feel just a little lighter. And once you start noticing them, they'll start to multiply.

On the most basic level, practicing gratitude can boost your job satisfaction, reduce your stress levels, and even enhance your mental health. It's like a professional development course and therapy session rolled into one! It's the hot sauce in your business burrito that can change your workday from a monotonous grind to a fulfilling journey.

And it's good for your company's bottom line, too. According to a 2024 Gallup and Workhuman study, employees who feel appreciated are 45% less likely to resign than disengaged workers.[1] Additionally, companies with structured employee recognition programs experience significantly lower voluntary turnover than their peers.[2] Another study published in the *Journal of Personality and Social Psychology* found that gratitude at work improved motivation and engagement.[3] And increasing engagement leads to a whole slew of great things, including a 21% increase in profitability compared to less engaged companies.[4] Again, no expert here, but that seems pretty good.

Now, for all my naysayers working in what we'll politely call "challenging environments" (you know, the kind where "work-life balance" means answering emails from both your phone AND your laptop at midnight), I hear you. Some workplaces are more pressure cooker than slow cooker, and trying to sprinkle gratitude into a shit stew might feel as effective as bringing a spork to a knife fight.

I get it. There are some real shit stews out there. Though ironically, it might be those very places where you need gratitude the most. I also get that too much of anything is not good. While gratitude practices have shown numerous benefits, some critics argue that overemphasis on gratitude in the workplace can lead to toxic positivity, potentially suppressing valid concerns or criticisms and leaving employees feeling pressured to maintain a positive facade, potentially hindering authentic communication.

Here's the thing: building a gratitude practice can be like learning to cook in a poorly equipped kitchen. Maybe your stove only works on high, your measuring cups are all missing, and that weird smell from the break room fridge is gaining sentience. That's okay. Start small. Maybe really small. We're talking George Foreman Grill small. The goal isn't to become the Dalai Lama of gratitude overnight—it's to develop a deliberate practice of finding light in darkness, training your mind to recognize value even when everything feels worthless. Like building any meaningful skill, it happens through consistent small efforts that gradually transform how you experience the world.

Even in high-stakes environments, gratitude can prove its power. Let me take you to Shanghai, 2014. I was managing a team across five countries, juggling multiple time zones, and trying to realign an entire business model. At that point, my idea of gratitude was celebrating every time my VPN connected without a meltdown. Then came a massive deal-breaker—a joint venture bringing two lightly warring companies together. We're talking countless late nights, endless conversations, and enough coffee to keep Colombia's economy afloat. And by coffee, I mean crack. And by crack, I mean gelato.

One particularly brutal night, after what felt like my 400th meeting where someone said "let's take this offline," my global CEO sent me an incredibly specific thank you text about how my handling of this particularly complicated situation had made sense for the company and had helped the organization save face with the local team.

That simple text hit differently. In that moment, I realized I'd been so focused on what wasn't working—the personalities, the drama, the cultural clashes—that I'd completely overlooked what was working: a team about to pull off something remarkable.

Did that one moment of gratitude suddenly transform me into a Zen Master of appreciation? Heck no. But it cracked the door open. Maybe, just maybe, there was something real to this whole gratitude practice.

In this chapter, we're going to simmer up a gratitude reduction that'll concentrate your potential and elevate your entire work life. We'll explore how a *Brain Boost* can rewire your neural pathways for success, how *Team Chemistry* can transform workplace relationships from bland to bold, and how *Performance Plus* can turn appreciation into measurable results. The goal: make your workplace feel less like Office Space and more like Ted Lasso's locker room. Gratitude isn't about fake smiles when your project's on fire; it's about recognizing the good alongside the bad. It's a practical tool that enhances problem-solving, resilience, and measurable performance outcomes. Think of it as the foundational stock that flavors everything—from your daily interactions to long-term career success. Master this, and every other aspect of your professional kitchen will taste better.

Now, let's dig in and see what's cooking.

THREE MAIN DISHES

Brain Boost

1 THINK YOUR BRAIN'S wiring is set in stone? Think again. Just like a master chef developing muscle memory through repetition, your brain physically transforms with every act of gratitude. It's literally re-wiring your brain for success.

Neuroscientist Dr. Alex Korb, author of *The Upward Spiral,* explains that gratitude activates the brain's reward system, releasing dopamine and sero-tonin—neurotransmitters that enhance your ability to focus, learn, and make decisions.[5] Even something as small as noticing a *glimmer*—your favorite song coming on the radio, an unexpected compliment from a colleague, or the smell of fresh coffee—can create a positive neural shift. After all, *a glimmer a day keeps the simmer at bay.*

A 2019 systematic review published in *SciELO Brasil* evaluated the effects of gratitude interventions on mental health. The results? Higher life satisfac-tion, reduced anxiety, and increased altruistic behaviors.[6] In the workplace, gratitude was linked to stronger team dynamics and lower stress levels. This isn't just feel-good fluff—it's neuroscience-backed fuel for better work and better relationships.

Essentially, gratitude is CrossFit for your brain—it builds mental muscles you didn't even know you had (and even helps you look great in spandex). A 2016 study published in *Social Cognitive and Affective Neuroscience* by Kini et al. found that practicing gratitude activates the medial prefrontal cortex, a brain region linked to emotional regulation and decision-making.[7] In other words, training your gratitude muscle rewires your brain to focus on solutions instead of spiraling into frustration.

The payoff? Better performance! By training your gratitude muscles, you're not just feeling better—you're turning those positive vibes into actual pro-ductivity. Insights shared in a 2019 *Sustainability* journal found that different forms of gratitude—individual, relational, and collective—significantly predict higher job satisfaction and improved job performance.[8] What do you think: any room for you to actually like what you do more?

As Dr. Robert Emmons, a leading gratitude researcher, notes throughout his book, *Thanks!*, gratitude blocks toxic emotions such as envy, resentment, and regret, which can destroy our happiness. It allows us to celebrate the present and be an active participant in our own lives.[9] And I can tell you, this stuff works. I start all of my leadership meetings with "Gratitude Share-outs" and my team barely hates me.

So while you're sharpening your technical skills and mastering your market knowledge, remember: sometimes the most powerful tool in your professional kitchen isn't what you know or who you know—it's how well you notice and appreciate what's already on your plate.

And gratitude's power extends far beyond individual brain chemistry. When we bring this practice into our teams, something even more remarkable happens. Let's explore!

Team Chemistry

2 "NONE OF US is as smart as all of us," says management expert Ken Blanchard[10] (allegedly—but let's give Kenny the credit). While *Brain Boost* explored how gratitude rewires your personal operating system, here we're looking at something equally powerful: how appreciation transforms team dynamics from a collection of individual ingredients into a perfectly balanced dish.

Research by Dr. Lisa Williams and Dr. Monica Bartlett indicates that expressions of gratitude can enhance social affiliation by increasing perceptions of interpersonal warmth, suggesting potential benefits for fostering positive relationships in various settings, including the workplace.[11]

Essentially, gratitude in the workplace can create a cycle of prosocial behavior, where one act of kindness or appreciation leads to another. Prosocial behaviors—like helping, sharing, and cooperating—fuel trust, strengthen relationships, and create a culture where people actively support one another. Think of it as compound interest for workplace relationships. Small deposits of appreciation grow and grow over time and multiply with even more and more deposits (unlike, say, my crypto account #HODL).

This culture of appreciation doesn't just make you happier—it boosts the company's bottom line. Simon Sinek puts it bluntly: "Customers will never

"Customers will never love a company until the employees love it first."

— Simon Sinek

Zappos: Where Gratitude is Always in Stock[12]

The Challenge: Turn online shoe retail into a customer service powerhouse when e-commerce was still finding its footing (circa 2000).

The Approach: Zappos flipped the script by building their entire culture around customer happiness. Don't believe me? Google "Zappos 10-hour 43-minute call" and prepare to be amazed. Their "Wow" program empowered employees to go off-script to create legendary customer experiences, while their famous $2,000 "quit bonus" ensured only the truly committed stayed. It was like a dating show—but for company culture!

The Result:

- Acquired by Amazon in 2009 for $1.2B.
- Consistently made Fortune's "100 Best Companies to Work For" list from 2009-2015.
- Net revenue grew from $1.6M in 2000 to over $1B in 2008.

The Take-Home Recipe:

- Culture drives performance.
- Empower people to make decisions.
- Values need action, not just words.

love a company until the employees love it first."[13] And the data is backed by Adam Grant's research at Wharton, one of the world's top business schools, showing that companies with strong appreciation cultures consistently out-perform their peers in both employee satisfaction and customer loyalty.[14] Net-net: When people feel valued, they don't just clock in—they bring their best selves to the table.

Whether you're leading a team or part of one, remember that gratitude starts with you. Like a pinch of salt that brings out the best in every ingredient, your consistent appreciation of others can create ripples that transform rela-tionships, boost performance, and build resilience. In a world of quick emails and virtual thumbs-ups, genuine gratitude might just be the strongest—and cheapest—team-building tool you have. When everyone in the kitchen knows their contribution matters, magic happens. One genuine and specific "thank you" today could transform your team's entire menu tomorrow. Who better than you to start that chain reaction?

Now, while the personal and team benefits of gratitude are compelling, there's another layer to explore. Let's look at how gratitude impacts the bot-tom line—because let's be honest: Cash Rules Everything Around Me. (Am I right, Killa Bees?)

Performance Plus

3 WHILE WE'VE EXPLORED how gratitude rewires your brain and strengthens teams, here's where it gets really interesting: it's also a performance powerhouse. Think of it as transforming appreciation from a mere adornment into a profit-generating main course. And the num-bers? They're sizzling.

According to a 2024 Gallup-Workhuman report, employees who receive high-quality recognition are 12.2 times more likely to feel connected to their organization's culture, nine times more likely to be engaged, and 45% less likely to leave their jobs within two years. Additionally, these employees report greater daily well-being, are 66% less likely to experience loneliness, and are 4.4 times more likely to say their job gives them purpose.[15] Translation: gratitude isn't just feeding good feelings. It's feeding the bottom line.

Leaders who get this right create an environment where appreciation fuels risk-taking and innovation. When people feel valued, they take bolder, smarter risks—exactly the kind of innovation every company is chasing like a corporate white whale.

But without gratitude, the opposite happens. Employees play it safe, withhold ideas, and disengage. Fear of failure replaces creative problem-solving, and the workplace shifts from a space of possibility to one of quiet compliance. Over time, this lack of recognition breeds resentment, stifles collaboration, and turns once-promising teams into a collection of individuals just trying to get through the day.

The difference is measurable. According to Deloitte, organizations with recognition programs had 31% lower voluntary turnover and were 12 times more likely to have strong business outcomes.[16] And the impacts reach across industries. A study by Adair et al. found that a single-exposure gratitude letter-writing intervention significantly reduced emotional exhaustion and improved well-being among healthcare workers.[17] Even in high-pressure environments like hospitals, where burnout is practically part of the job description, gratitude can make a measurable difference in performance, engagement, and resilience.

This is where gratitude graduates from personal practice to business strategy. We've seen how it rewires your brain, builds stronger teams, and now how it drives organizational success. It's the rare ingredient that works at every level: personal, team, and enterprise.

So while your CFO might be skeptical of "soft skills," the ROI of gratitude is anything but soft. It's basically a legal money-printing machine—one that transforms appreciation into innovation, engagement into excellence, and recognition into revenue. It's one of the rare business investments that requires no budget, just intention.

Now *that's* a recipe worth sharing!

FIVE TASTE-TEST RECIPES

Gratitude is like seasoning—small doses can be completely transformative. Here are five ideas to spice up your day with some gratitude. Try one recipe, a few, or mix and match. These are simply ways to help you savor appreciation at work.

1 **The Glimmer Hunt:** Set a timer for 10 minutes during your workday and challenge yourself to notice three glimmers—small moments of joy, connection, or beauty. Maybe it's the sunlight hitting your desk, the way your coworker made you laugh, or the satisfaction of crossing something off your to-do list. Write them down. The more you look, the more you'll find.

2 **The Thank You Challenge:** For the next five workdays, send one genuine "thank you" message to a different colleague each day. Be as specific as possible about what you're thanking them for. It's like a corporate version of Pay It Forward.

3 **The Gratitude Flip:** Reframe challenges as opportunities by identifying three positives in every problem. It's like being a corporate alchemist, turning problems into gold (or at least into slightly shinier problems). See Jocko Willink's "Good" philosophy.

4 **The Appreciation Station:** Create a physical or digital space where team members can publicly acknowledge each other's contributions. It could be a bulletin board, a Slack channel, or a dedicated time in team meetings. Build a team habit of celebrating contributions in real time. I do mine at the start of team calls.

5 **The Gratitude Time Machine:** Write a weekly gratitude note to your future self, then revisit it one month later for perspective. It's like sending a postcard to your future self, reminding them not to take the present for granted.

LAST CALL

Gratitude isn't about mandatory appreciation sessions or forced thank you notes—it's about transforming workplace interactions into meaningful connections. Like a master chef who seasons throughout the cooking process (not just at the end), effective leaders understand that gratitude must be woven into daily communication, not treated as an afterthought.

In this chapter, you've seen how gratitude impacts workplace dynamics through three essential elements. *Brain Boost* revealed how appreciation physically rewires our neural pathways for enhanced performance. *Team Chemistry* demonstrated how gratitude strengthens collective bonds. *Performance Plus* showed how appreciation fuels engagement, innovation, and bottom-line results.

But here's the real takeaway: gratitude isn't just a feel-good practice. It's a communication strategy. When done consistently, it transforms how teams collaborate, solve problems, and push for innovation. The best leaders don't just express appreciation; they communicate it in ways that inspire action.

So, as you move forward, make gratitude your daily special, not just a seasonal offering. Your workplace menu is always better when seasoned with genuine appreciation. Because in the grand banquet of work life, gratitude just might be the most satisfying dish of all.

And let's be real—if your only seasoning is cynicism, that's just bland.

CEREBRAL SOUS VIDE

- When did I last feel genuinely appreciated at work, and how did it affect my motivation?
- How can I express gratitude today to strengthen an important relationship?
- What lesson can I learn from practicing gratitude during challenges?

THE SELF-SERVE STATION

Not buying into gratitude just yet? That's fine—skepticism is healthy! These resources will show you why appreciation is more than hugs and high-fives—it's the secret sauce for meaningful work and happier teams:

- *Thanks!: How Practicing Gratitude Can Make You Happier* by Robert A. Emmons (2007) – The definitive guide to gratitude research from the field's pioneering scientist. Emmons doesn't just tell you gratitude works—he shows you exactly how and why it rewires your brain for success.

- *The Gratitude Effect: How Embracing Thank You Can Change Your Life* by Dr. John Demartini (2007) – A practical blueprint for turning appreciation into achievement. Perfect for skeptics who want hard evidence that gratitude can transform both bottom lines and team dynamics.

- TED Talk: "Remember to Say Thank You" by Laura Trice (2008) – In under 15 minutes, Trice delivers a masterclass on why those two simple words might be the most powerful tools in your professional arsenal. Think of it as your gratitude quick-start guide.

- *Harvard Business Review* article: "The Neuroscience of Trust" by Paul J. Zak (2017) – Here we go! The brain science behind why recognition builds stronger teams. Zak connects the dots between gratitude, trust, and organizational performance with research you can actually use.

- Podcast: WorkLife with Adam Grant—Episode: "The Science of Gratitude" (2022) – Grant brings his signature blend of research and real-world application to show how gratitude transforms workplace dynamics. A must-listen for anyone looking to build stronger teams.

A SWEET & SAVORY SHOUT-OUT

On July 19th, 2021, Chris Schembra and I became friends. The old-fashioned way—on LinkedIn. The relationship has blossomed since then into one of genuine appreciation and admiration for my pasta-loving gratitude guru. Chris has cooked up a feast of insights on thankfulness with his books Gratitude and Pasta: The Secret Sauce for Human Connection and Gratitude Through Hard Times. Through these vessels, he serves up a hearty helping of wisdom on how saying "thanks" can transform relationships faster than carbs can expand your waistline.

Schembra's famous "7:47 Gratitude Experience"—a dinner party where appreciation is the main course—demonstrates how breaking bread and sharing thanks can create bonds stronger than Nonna's homemade spaghetti. It's team building, but with better food and fewer trust falls. Imagine if your last corporate retreat had been at an Italian trattoria instead of that weird ropes course. That's the Schembra effect.

For leaders looking to spice up their organizational culture, Schembra's gratitude recipes offer a way to transform the workplace into an Italian family dinner—warm, welcoming, and full of people talking with their hands. By folding gratitude into daily interactions, companies can whip up a batch of increased morale and belonging that's more satisfying than a perfect tiramisu. Because at the end of the day, a culture built on appreciation isn't just good for business—it's what makes work feel like home.

So, whether you're navigating smooth sailing or choppy waters, remember: a dollop of gratitude can make any situation more palatable. In business as in life, a little appreciation goes a long way—it's the parmesan cheese on the pasta of success. And who doesn't want more parmesan? Buon appetito!

10 QUICK BITES

- Employees who feel appreciated are 45% less likely to resign than disengaged workers, significantly improving retention and workplace morale.

- Companies with strong appreciation programs experience 31% lower turnover and are 12 times more likely to achieve strong business outcomes.

- Research shows that gratitude activates the brain's reward centers, releasing dopamine and serotonin, enhancing focus, learning, and decision-making.

- Employees who receive high-quality recognition are 12.2 times more likely to feel connected to their organization's culture and 9 times more likely to be engaged.

- Employees who feel valued are more likely to recognize and uplift their colleagues, fostering a workplace culture of engagement and support.

- Gratitude strengthens workplace relationships and fosters prosocial behaviors, reinforcing a culture of appreciation and teamwork.

- A 2019 systematic review showed gratitude interventions significantly increase life satisfaction, reduce anxiety, and increase altruistic behaviors.

- Gratitude practice activates the medial prefrontal cortex, a brain region linked to emotional regulation and decision-making, rewiring the brain to focus on solutions.

- In challenging work environments, small acts of appreciation build resilience and improve problem-solving.

- Companies with strong appreciation cultures consistently outperform peers in both employee satisfaction and customer loyalty.

PREP CARD

Common Obstacle:
"Gratitude feels fake in our tough work environment."
Quick Fix:
Start with private gratitude journaling
Long-term:
Share small wins in team meetings until it becomes natural

Common Obstacle:
"I'm too busy for gratitude practices."
Quick Fix:
Pair gratitude with existing habits (coffee break = gratitude break)
Long-term:
Build 5-minute gratitude blocks into your calendar

Common Obstacle:
"Our team is resistant to gratitude exercises."
Quick Fix:
Start with one-on-one appreciation
Long-term:
Share measurable positive impacts of recognition

MINDFULNESS

APPETIZER
Is your mind feeling like a chaotic kitchen during dinner rush? Join the club! We're talking the art of mental organization, where we'll transform your scattered thoughts into a perfectly prepped professional workspace.

MAIN COURSE
Focus Fortune: Moving from distracted to centered (and actually remembering why you walked into that meeting room)
Stress Less: Turn workplace pressure into a personal power-up
Breakthrough Brew: Where great ideas come to life (no meditation cushion required!)

DESSERT
The Morning Amuse-Bouche:
Your 60-second brain-clearing ritual
The Pomodoro Mindfulness Technique:
Master the art of focused sprints
The Mindful Meetings:
Start gatherings with intention, not indigestion

PAIRS WELL WITH
Your favorite quiet corner
Those noise-canceling headphones you splurged on
A "Do Not Disturb" sign (that people actually respect)

CHAPTER 2

Mindfulness—A Measured Pour

YOU'RE IN A high-stakes meeting, trying to look intelligent while your laptop sounds like it's auditioning for an EDM festival. Every ding is another distraction. Notifications are popping off, your boss keeps tapping her pen, and your focus is evaporating faster than your coffee.

Sound familiar? Sure it does! This is the modern workplace—where distraction is the default and focus feels like a luxury.

The constant pings, alerts, and interruptions have become the soundtrack of contemporary work life, pulling your focus in a dozen directions at once. But what if there were a way to reduce the noise, sharpen your focus, and boost your performance—without becoming a mountain-dwelling monk? (Because let's be honest, not everyone can pull off the bald look.)

In the midst of this chaos, mindfulness offers a way out.

At its core, mindfulness is about fully engaging with the present moment, without judgment. It's not about chanting mantras or achieving a blank mind; it's about creating space to respond thoughtfully, rather than reacting impulsively. (Like when you impulsively bought this book because all of your friends and life's heroes recommended it!)

Why is that mental clarity so important, you ask? Great question! It comes down to one word: burnout. The World Health Organization (WHO) officially defines burnout as a syndrome caused by chronic workplace stress that has not been successfully managed. In a 2019 report, WHO recognized burnout as an occupational phenomenon, linking it to exhaustion, reduced effectiveness, and increased mental distance from one's job.[18] You may not be into deep breaths or unlocking your third eye, but chances are, you know workplace burnout all too well. And if you've felt exhausted, cynical, or like your performance is slipping, you're not alone.

The good news, though? Mindfulness is a proven antidote.

Mindfulness transcends the individual, impacting teams and entire companies. When organizations implement mindfulness programs, they see real results. A 2020 study published in *The Journal of Occupational Health Psychology* found that mindfulness practices in the workplace significantly improved attention, cognitive flexibility, and emotional regulation—all of which enhanced job performance and decision-making.[19] In fact, organizations implementing mindfulness programs even report saving money. In *Mindful Work*, David Gelles reports that Aetna's mindfulness program led to healthcare cost savings of approximately $2,000 per employee, along with improvements in employee well-being and job satisfaction.[20] Money well spent.

What's more, research from the University of Western Ontario found that after an eight-week mindfulness program, participants experienced a 32% decrease in stress, a 30% decrease in anxiety, and a 29% decrease in depression.[21] Those aren't just numbers—they represent real people finding their way back from the brink of burnout, that all-too-familiar state of chronic exhaustion, detachment, and mental fog.

And the best part? Getting started doesn't require a meditation retreat in Tibet with those monks from earlier.

Of course, all the science in the world won't mean much until you *need* mindfulness to survive. For me, that moment hit me during a personal—and global—crisis. Like many leaders navigating uncharted territory, I faced unprecedented challenges during those harrowing months of COVID-19.

Late in 2020, I had just taken on the role of Commercial VP for Canada, and I found myself 47 hours deep into crisis calls with major clients from the Great White North. My desk resembled a Post-It-covered crime scene, and my brain felt like an overheated food processor stuck on purée. I've never been one to quit, but between team vent sessions and partner yell-a-thons, the thought crept in more than once: *How much longer can I keep this up?*

That's when a mentor introduced me to mindfulness—not as some mystical practice, but as a survival strategy. I'll never forget his most poignant message: "A dull blade is dangerous—not because it can't cut, but because it forces you to hack away instead of slicing cleanly. Your mind works the same way. If you don't keep it sharp, every decision, every challenge, takes more effort, more stress, and more damage in the long run."

At first, I was skeptical. Meditation? In the middle of a crisis? It felt like bringing a yoga mat to a gunfight. But as I practiced pausing and focusing, something shifted. Instead of my brain playing pinball with every crisis, I found myself calm, clear, and capable of leading through the storm. I went from panicked reactions to purposely planned actions. I showed up better for my team and actually managed a few quality nights of sleep. The supply chain was still a mess, but now, I wasn't. And that made all the difference.

Specifically, sharpening that blade meant starting small: five minutes of deep breathing before my first meeting, stepping outside between calls to reset, and learning to sit with discomfort instead of reacting to it. I swapped doomscrolling for guided mindfulness apps, kept a notebook handy to jot down anxious thoughts instead of letting them spiral, and practiced focusing on just *one* task at a time—radical, I know.

Those tiny changes added up, and I finally felt like I had control over my own headspace again. With a clearer mind, I communicated more effectively—first with myself, then with others. Mindfulness didn't just quiet the noise; it gave me the space to think, listen, and respond with intention.

In this chapter, we're *intentionally* cooking up a mindfulness menu that'll transform your work life from chaotic to controlled. We'll explore how *Focus Fix* can sharpen your mental prep to laser precision, how *Stress Less* can turn down the heat on workplace pressure, and how *Breakthrough Brew* can turn your everyday thoughts into game-changing innovations. You'll learn how mindfulness provides the mental clarity to actually hear what's being said, both by others and (most importantly) by yourself.

So, no more dull blades—deal? Let's sharpen yours so you can cut through the chaos of this crazy, upside-down work world.

THREE MAIN DISHES

Focus Fortune

1 **THINK YOU'RE A** master multitasker, huh? Well, hate to break it to you, but science has some bad news: only 2.5% of people can actually pull it off.[22] The rest of us? Well, we're just doing multiple things badly at the same time. In fact, multitaskers take 50% longer and make up to 50% more errors.[23] Talk about a recipe for disaster.

Here's the good news, though: you can train your brain to focus like a laser instead of a disco ball. By training your attention on the present moment, you develop the mental clarity to actually get things done. As James Clear, author of *Atomic Habits*, notes, "You do not rise to the level of your goals. You fall to the level of your systems."[24] Think about that. You don't just miraculously turn it on when the "S" hits the "F." You need a proven system. Mindfulness is the entry point to *that* system—the "elevate your mental game" one.

This 'systems' approach works big and small—employee to employer. Just ask Aetna. After rolling out a mindfulness program, employees gained an extra hour of productivity per week.[25] That's like finding a crisp $100 bill in your coat pocket. And the return on investment? A mouthwatering 11-to-1 ratio.[26] Not bad for a little mental spring cleaning. Of course, it's still an insurance company, so they probably found a way to bill you for that 'extra' hour.

The science gets even more compelling. A 2021 study published in *Frontiers in Psychology* found that mindfulness training improved both attention and working memory capacity.[27] In corporate terms, it's like upgrading both your mental hardware and software at once. You're not just working harder; you're working smarter. That usually translates to things you like: more praise, more promotions, and more paper, Big Dog!

Here's the thing: when you're fully present, you process information like a high-powered blender—smooth, efficient, and without chunks of distraction gunking up the works. You notice subtle flavors that others miss in conversations, catch the early signs of projects going stale, and maintain your cool when everyone else is losing theirs.

Plus, there's an extra bonus! Mindfulness isn't just about focusing better, it's about choosing what deserves your focus in the first place. It's like being the executive chef who knows exactly which dishes need immediate attention and which can simmer a while longer. That's what separates the pros from the amateurs.

Stress Less

2 **IF STRESS WERE** a food critic's rating, most corporate professionals would be getting five stars. But unlike a James Beard Award, chronic stress doesn't come with accolades—just a recipe for burnout served with a side of ulcers and an overwhelming urge to quit your job to open a fish taco stand in Belize.

But before we pack our bags, let's talk about an alternative—reducing stress. You've trained your focus like a laser beam, but what good is precision if your whole system is overheating? Stress isn't just an inconvenience—it's the workplace equivalent of turning the burner on high and forgetting about it. Things are going to boil over.

Mindfulness, however, is the simmer button on your stove—the thing that keeps you from burning out while still cooking up results. It doesn't eliminate stress, but it changes your response to it, turning reactive chaos into measured control.

Want proof? Try this: Before your next big meeting, use 4-7-8 breathing—inhale for four seconds, hold for seven, and exhale for eight—to reset your nervous system. Feeling tense? Drop your shoulders, unclench your jaw, and relax your hands, because stress lives in your body, not just your mind. Overwhelmed? Close unnecessary browser tabs—too many tabs, too many thoughts. And if your schedule feels like a never-ending sprint, take a three-minute buffer between meetings to breathe, stretch, or step outside. Small resets like these keep stress from stacking up like dirty dishes.

At the enterprise level, the results are pretty clear. Major companies like Google, General Mills, and Target have all invested in mindfulness.[28] Intel's *Awake@Intel* program reported a 20% reduction in stress, a 30% boost in well-being, and improvements in creativity, focus, and relationships.[29] That all impacts the bottom line—clarity equals better decisions, sharper performance, and teams that thrive instead of just survive. And in a world that rewards speed, mindfulness is the competitive edge that ensures you're not just moving fast—you're moving smart.

"Attention is the basis of all higher cognitive

and emotional abilities..."

— Chade-Meng Tan

Unilever: Cultivating Global Well-being[30]

The Challenge: Transform a traditional consumer goods company into a leader in employee well-being across diverse global operations.

The Approach: Under CEO Paul Polman's leadership (2009–2018), Unilever launched comprehensive well-being initiatives, including the "Thrive" program in 2016, to support holistic employee health. These programs provided access to counseling services, mindfulness-based stress reduction courses, life coaching, financial well-being resources, and resilience training, all tailored to local cultures and needs.

The Result:

- In 2022, Unilever signed the Mental Health at Work Commitment to prioritize employee well-being.
- By 2023, over 2,000 line managers and 1,000 employees were trained in psychological safety, promoting openness and support.
- 89% of employees believe Unilever cares for their well-being, according to the 2023 UniVoice survey.

The Take-Home Recipe:

- Make well-being a business priority for all roles.
- Adapt programs to local needs and cultures.
- Commit through training and open conversations.

As leadership expert Brené Brown emphasizes, when we're mindful, we "maintain a moment-by-moment awareness of our thoughts, feelings, and surroundings."[31] That awareness keeps stress from hijacking your reactions. It helps you answer the snarky email with professionalism instead of sarcasm, tackle a high-pressure project with clarity instead of question marks, and—most importantly—refrain from rage-quitting after Julie's 5:15 p.m. mandatory "quick sync" that could've been an email. (Damn you, Julie!)

So, the next time stress threatens to turn you into a human pressure cooker, remember: mindfulness is your cool-down setting. It's what keeps you from boiling over, makes you sharper under pressure, and ensures that—no matter what's on the menu—you're the one running the kitchen, not the other way around.

Breakthrough Brew

3 WE'VE SHARPENED OUR focus and turned down the heat on stress. Now, let's talk about the sweetest part of mindfulness: creativity. In the corporate world, innovation is like the perfect recipe—everyone wants it, few can create it, and some wonder if it's just kitchen mythology. But what if the ingredients for breakthrough thinking have been in your mental pantry all along, tucked behind your task lists and calendar reminders?

Mindfulness, it turns out, acts like a booster for creative thinking. A *Frontiers in Psychology* study found that mindfulness practices significantly enhance divergent thinking—the kind of thinking that leads to fresh ideas and inventive solutions.[32] It's like giving your brain permission to color outside the lines (and didn't that always feel a bit naughty).

Google's "Search Inside Yourself" program highlights how mindfulness fuels innovation and keeps them on tech's cutting edge.[33] Chade-Meng Tan, the program's co-creator, explains that meditation is essentially attention training, and attention is the fundamental building block of all cognitive functions. He encapsulates this sentiment neatly with this classic one-liner: "Attention is the basis of all higher cognitive and emotional abilities."[34] Essentially, mindfulness helps you tune into what truly matters—an essential skill not just for innovation, but for clear, effective communication. After all, great ideas don't just need to exist—they need to be articulated, shared, and acted upon.

That said, mindfulness isn't just about cooking up ideas—it's about knowing which ones to serve. It helps you prioritize. And in a world of potluck meetings filled with half-baked proposals, that shit is cri-tic-al! Mindfulness also sharpens your intuition (you know, that thing you're always bragging about?), helping you distinguish ideas that need more marinating from those ready to plate.

Think of mindfulness as culinary school for your mind. With practice, you'll gain the focus to spot promising combinations, the patience to let ideas develop, and the wisdom to know when they're fully cooked. Bonus: you'll truly earn that reputation for sharp instincts instead of just talking about it.

Your next breakthrough might already be simmering—you just need the clarity to serve it at the right time.

FIVE TASTE-TEST RECIPES

Mindfulness isn't one-size-fits-all—it's a menu to explore. Try one approach, adapt another, or mix and match until you find what works for you. These ideas are here to help you cultivate focus, your way.

1 **The Morning Amuse-Bouche:** Begin each workday with 60 seconds of focused breathing. It's like a shot of espresso for your mind. Set a timer, close your eyes, and focus on your breath. If your mind drifts to your inbox or that looming report, gently guide it back to your breath.

2 **The "Pomodoro Mindfulness Technique":** Work in focused 25-minute bursts, then take a mindful 5-minute reset to recharge. Use the break to check in with your body—scan for tension, then consciously relax those areas.

3 **The Bite of Appreciation:** Transform lunch from fast food to fine dining. Instead of inhaling your sandwich while scrolling through emails, eat like a food critic—savor the textures, flavors, and aromas. Your turkey on rye deserves better than being an afterthought between Zoom calls.

4 **The Mindful Meeting:** Kick off meetings with a minute of silence or breathing to refocus and align the team. It helps everyone transition and focus. Plus, it's a great way to wait for that ever-tardy coworker. (I'm lookin' at you, Charles!)

5 **The Tech Timeout:** Create 'no-phone zones' to recharge. Start and end your day distraction-free for 30 minutes. Give your brain a break from the constant ping of notifications—think of it as a daily mental reset. If possible, book-end your day like this!

LAST CALL

Mindfulness isn't about meditation apps or Zen retreats—it's about staying clear-headed in a chaotic workplace. Like a chef maintaining pristine *mise en place* during the dinner rush, effective professionals understand that focus and presence must be maintained, even amid disruption.

In this chapter, you've learned how mindfulness enhances professional performance through three key elements: *Focus Fortune*, which revealed how attention training creates measurable productivity gains; *Stress Less*, which showed how mindful practices reduce workplace pressure and improve decision-making; and *Breakthrough Brew*, which demonstrated how mental clarity leads to innovation and creative problem-solving. You've discovered that consistent mindfulness practice doesn't just reduce stress—it creates measurable improvements in leadership, effective communication, and organizational adaptability.

Sharpening your mental knife skills takes time—mindfulness isn't instant ramen; it's mastering French cuisine. The key is consistency, not perfection. The good news? You don't need special equipment or a meditation pod. You already have everything you need.

Your mind is your kitchen—show up ready to practice.

CEREBRAL SOUS VIDE

✓ What triggers disrupt my focus most, and how can I respond more mindfully?
✓ What does my best—focused, confident, in-control—feel like? And how can I train myself to stay there or return to it when it matters most?
✓ What small change in my communication could make me more present with others?

THE SELF-SERVE STATION

Need a clearer picture of how mindfulness can help you rise above the workplace whirlwind? These five reads will show you how staying present transforms stress into focus, distractions into clarity, and chaos into calm—just like a seasoned pro.

- *Radical Acceptance* by Tara Brach (2019) – Brach, a clinical psychologist and meditation teacher, offers a comforting yet profound take on self-compassion and mindfulness. It's like warm soup for the soul, teaching you to accept and embrace every experience.

- *The Power of Unwavering Focus* by Dandapani (2022) – A former monk (finally!) turned entrepreneur serves a hearty course on cultivating focus, breaking down ancient practices into simple, digestible exercises that bring mindfulness to the modern-day table.

- *The Comfort Book* by Matt Haig (2021) – Warning: These bite-sized mindfulness techniques woven through personal anecdotes might make you rethink everything you assumed about mental clarity. Perfect for readers seeking a fresh, relatable take.

- *How to Relax* by Thich Nhat Hanh (2016, reprint in 2021) – Though small, this book is packed with truth nuggets and powerful mindfulness practices from the late Zen Master. Each page is a mindful snack—easy to digest yet deeply nourishing for the mind.

- *10% Happier* by Dan Harris (2014) – From panic attack on live TV to mindfulness advocate, ABC news anchor Harris offers a skeptic's guide to meditation. His journey proves that even the most stressed-out professionals can find their zen. If you are seriously doubting mindfulness still, seriously read this book!

A SWEET & SAVORY SHOUT-OUT

A special nod goes to Jon Kabat-Zinn, who brought mindfulness to the Western table. In 1979, this molecular biologist had the audacity to suggest that ancient Buddhist practices could be served up to modern minds hungry for peace. His creation? Mindfulness-Based Stress Reduction (MBSR), a technique that's been adopted by hospitals, schools, and corporations worldwide.

Like a skilled restaurateur introducing a new cuisine to skeptical diners, Kabat-Zinn made mindfulness palatable to scientific and corporate tastes. His book *Wherever You Go, There You Are* (1994) remains the equivalent of Julia Child's *Mastering the Art of French Cooking* for the mindfulness world—a classic that transforms the exotic into the accessible.

But Kabat-Zinn wasn't content just writing cookbooks for your mental kitchen. He's been the head chef of mindfulness research, helping to plate up the scientific evidence for its benefits. His work has inspired generations to bring mindfulness everywhere, from classroom cafeterias to corporate boardrooms. And his influence didn't just make mindfulness accessible—it transformed it into a cultural phenomenon, blending ancient wisdom with modern rigor in ways few had imagined. His work showed that mindfulness isn't a retreat from life's pressures, but a powerful method for engaging with them more fully.

So, the next time you take a mindful breath during a hectic workday, raise your mental glass to Jon Kabat-Zinn. Without him, mindfulness might still be seen as an esoteric practice for monks and mystics— rather than an essential ingredient for professional success.

In his own words, "You can't stop the waves, but you can learn to surf." Or at least not worry about wiping out when the pressure rises.

10 QUICK BITES

- Only 2.5% of people can truly multitask effectively—the rest take 50% longer and make 50% more errors when attempting multiple tasks simultaneously.

- Intel's Awake@Intel program reported a 20% reduction in stress and a 30% boost in well-being, along with improvements in creativity, focus, and relationships.

- Aetna's mindfulness program led to healthcare cost savings of approximately $2,000 per employee, plus employees gained an extra hour of productivity per week.

- An eight-week mindfulness program resulted in a 32% decrease in stress, 30% decrease in anxiety, and 29% decrease in depression among participants.

- Mindfulness significantly enhances divergent thinking—the type of creative thinking that leads to fresh ideas and inventive solutions.

- Companies like Google, General Mills, and Target report benefits like improved creativity, focus, and workplace relationships from mindfulness programs.

- Mindfulness helps you process information more effectively, notice subtle details others miss in conversations, and maintain composure when others lose theirs.

- Using tech-free times and mindful transitions between tasks sustains focus, reducing the cognitive overload common in digital-heavy workplaces.

- Mindfulness training improves both attention and working memory capacity—like upgrading your mental hardware and software simultaneously.

- Mindfulness acts like a "simmer button" for stress.

Common Obstacle:

"My mind races during meditation."

Quick Fix:

Use the "Note and Return" technique

Long-term Solution:

Start with guided meditations, then gradually increase duration

---

Common Obstacle:

"I deal with constant interruptions."

Quick Fix:

Set status to "Focus Time" for 25-minute blocks

Long-term Solution:

Establish team protocols for urgent vs. non-urgent matters

Common Obstacle:

"I can't find quiet space."

Quick Fix:

Use noise-canceling headphones

Long-term Solution:

Work with HR to designate quiet zones, like Amtrak!

Notes

GROWTH MINDSET

APPETIZER

Ever notice how some people bounce back from
setbacks while others stay stuck in the soup? Been
there, done that! It's time for a growth mindset,
where "I can't" gets transformed into "I'm figuring
it out!" (And maybe even "I crushed it!")

MAIN COURSE

Mind Muscles: Unlock your hidden potential
(It's in there, trust me!)
Failure's (Yummy) Flavor: Making mistakes look
good on your resume
Growth Spice: Turn criticism into your career's super juice

DESSERT

The "Yet" Revolution: Your personal
playbook of possibilities
Mind-Gym Mornings: Where small
wins become big victories
Failure Friday: Sometimes falling flat leads to flying high

PAIRS WELL WITH

A fresh perspective on challenges
That feedback you've been avoiding
Your favorite success story
(that started with a face-plant)

CHAPTER 3

Growth Mindset—The Ultimate Leavening Agent

I'S ANOTHER "BIG Idea Friday." Your boss walks in and announces, "We need someone to lead the new AI initiative." Your first thought? *I barely scraped by in that one coding class back in college.* Your second? *Maybe Sarah should do it—she's naturally good with tech.* And just like that, you've fallen into the biggest workplace trap of all: believing the self-sabotaging stories we tell ourselves.

Greetings! You've just entered the wild world of self-talk, where your internal dialogue has more influence on your career than your LinkedIn recommendations and business school degree combined. It's that little voice that whispers "I can't" when opportunity knocks, or mumbles "I'm not ready" when promotion season rolls around. It's the one whispering that this chapter isn't for you (even though it definitely is).

Fortunately, there is a time-tested antidote to this negative self-talk. It's called a Growth Mindset. And it's pretty frickin' awesome.

Psychologist Carol Dweck, in *Mindset: The New Psychology of Success*, explains that a growth mindset is the foundation for unlocking potential.[35] Boiled down? It's about understanding that abilities aren't fixed traits—they can be developed through effort, learning, and resilience. Matthew Syed, in

You Are Awesome, echoes this, showing how people with a growth mindset see challenges not as tests of inherent ability but as opportunities to expand their capabilities.[36]

Think of a growth mindset like a rising agent—transforming the flatbread of fixed thinking into the brioche of boundless potential. And one of the key ingredients in that brioche? The stories we tell ourselves.

As Julia Galef writes in *The Scout Mindset*, reframing self-doubt with curiosity and truth-seeking helps turn fear into fuel.[37] The kind of fuel that launches careers, reinvents skill sets, and propels you toward the opportunities you once thought were out of reach. And this isn't just about personal breakthroughs—it scales.

The proof is in the pudding—or in this case, the data. A 2018 study published in *Harvard Business Review* found that employees in companies promoting a growth mindset report 47% higher trust in leadership and 34% greater commitment to their organizations.[38] Like a well-proofed dough, these organizations rise above their competitors, fostering a growth-oriented and innovative culture that outperforms their peers in terms of revenue growth and employee engagement.[39] Shawn Achor's *The Happiness Advantage* reinforces this idea, demonstrating how positive psychology and mindset shifts can significantly enhance workplace engagement, collaboration, and overall performance.[40]

I've seen this transformation firsthand. Back in 2010, I was handed what felt like an impossible task: build a 25-person, continent-wide startup inside a well-established Fortune 1000 company. I had never formally led a team before, let alone a geographically dispersed one. I had to build the program, hire the team, train everyone, and deliver results in under three months. The only thing louder than my new boss's constant check-ins was my initial fixed mindset screaming, "You're a fraud. You'll never pull this off!"

Lucky for me, an MBA classmate gifted me *Mindset: The New Psychology of Success* by Carol Dweck (yes, the same badass book I mentioned earlier). That Memorial Day weekend, while my family enjoyed the sun, I sat with that book and realized I had a choice: control my inner dialogue, or let it control me. I chose the former, and instead of marinating in self-doubt, I reframed the challenge like learning to cook: start with the basics (hire great sellers), expect some crispy edges (not everyone will be a perfect fit), and gradually refine the process until I had a high-performing team.

The result? An incredible three-year run that saw nearly 8x revenue growth, a program that continued for over a decade, and a treasure trove of great friendships and memories. And perhaps more importantly, I proved to myself that capabilities—even ones I didn't know I had—could be developed through dedicated discipline and practice.

If I've learned one thing in my career, it's this: success isn't about getting it perfect the first time. It's about shifting your self-talk from "I can't do this" to "I'm figuring it out." It's about having the courage to keep cooking, learning from each burnt batch, and believing that with the right mindset and enough practice, you can create something extraordinary.

So let's play a little game I like to call "Spot the Success Blocker." Trust me, it's way more fun than the "Block Every Opportunity" game your inner critic loves to play.

Imagine two versions of you walking into the same high-stakes meeting.

The first version operates from a fixed mindset. The moment you step into the room, your internal monologue starts plating up a disaster: *"I'm not good at public speaking,"* it insists, serving up a side of sweaty palms. *"That's just how I am,"* it adds, dressed with missed opportunities. And just for good measure, it sprinkles in some self-defeat with *"I'll never understand tech."* By the time the meeting ends, you're full—of doubt, frustration, and regret.

Now, let's switch up the menu. The second version of you walks in with a growth mindset. *"I'm working on my presentation skills,"* you remind yourself, marinating in possibility. *"I'm discovering new approaches,"* you think, slow-cooked in curiosity. And when faced with a tech-heavy discussion, instead of shutting down, you tell yourself, *"I'm learning one tool at a time,"* seasoned with patience. Same meeting, same environment—completely different outcome.

One leaves you with career heartburn. The other? A feast of opportunities. Which plate are you serving yourself?

In this chapter, we'll help you get that plating right! You'll learn how *Mind Muscles* can turn challenges into opportunities, how *Failure's (Yummy) Flavor* can transform setbacks into stepping stones, and how *Growth Spice* can make your professional journey feel less like a food critic's nightmare and more like a master chef in training. Because the stories you tell yourself aren't just garnish—they're the main ingredient that determines whether you'll stick to the safe, bland recipes of the past or dare to create something extraordinary.

Time to transform your mental menu from fast food fixes to five-star potential. Let's plate up our three main courses and transform that inner critic into your personal sous chef.

THREE MAIN DISHES

Mind Muscles

1 **FORGET EVERYTHING YOU** thought you knew about intelligence and talent. Your brain isn't a fixed system, locked in place since the day you first mastered an Excel formula. You *can* be a better conversationalist, you *aren't* doomed to always wake up late, and you can *actually* be decent at math. Well, maybe not the math part, but everything else? Absolutely yes!

Instead of thinking of the brain as fixed, think of it as a dynamic, ever-adapting network—one that strengthens and expands with every challenge it encounters. Just like endurance builds in an athlete or skill refines in a chef, your cognitive abilities grow through effort, learning, and persistence. This applies at work, in a hobby, or any pursuit you take on.

Neuroscience confirms it: the way we talk to ourselves about our abilities physically reshapes our brains. Talk about powerful communication! Each positive internal dialogue is like adding a new recipe to your mental cookbook. Neural imaging studies show that people with a growth mindset display increased brain activity when processing errors, suggesting they're more attentive to mistakes and better at learning from them.[41] It's a process called neuroplasticity, and it continues throughout our lives—turns out you can teach an old dog new tricks. Every time you tackle a new project, learn a new software, or even attempt to decipher your colleague's cryptic email, you're literally reshaping your brain.

And this isn't just feel-good psychobabble. When we change our internal dialogue from "I can't" to "I'm learning," we transform not just our mindset, but our actual capabilities. Research from Stanford University demonstrated that students who believed intelligence is malleable exhibited an upward trajectory in math grades over two years, compared to a flat trajectory among peers with fixed mindset beliefs.[42] All it took was belief! In the corporate world, that's like upgrading from an office park food truck to a Michelin-starred kitchen.

So, the next time you're faced with a daunting task or a steep learning curve, remember: you're not just doing your job. You're giving your brain a workout. Small shifts in self-talk create big shifts in ability, so embrace the challenge, push through the discomfort, and watch your mental muscles grow. Train that internal voice to be less Gordon Ramsay on a bad day and more Mary Berry on her best.

Failure's (Yummy) Flavor

2 **IN THE LAND** of Growth Mindset, failure isn't the career-ending, shame-inducing monster we've been conditioned to fear. It's more like that brutally honest friend who tells you when you've got spinach in your teeth—uncomfortable in the moment, but invaluable in the long run.

You can't bake great bread if you're afraid of a few flops. Each batch teaches you something. Adjust the heat, tweak the ingredients, and before you know it, you're on your way to a perfect rise.

Just as we learned to communicate gratitude and practice mindful interactions with others, we need to change how we communicate with ourselves about failure. The stories we tell ourselves about failure become our internal narrative. By rewriting these stories from "disaster" to "development," we don't just shift our mindset—we transform how we approach challenges.

In the corporate world, this mindset shift is the unlock for sustained innovation. The internal dialogue around failure shapes everything from team dynamics to breakthrough inventions. Google has made failure a key ingredient of success with its "postmortem" practice, where teams analyze mistakes to fuel future innovation.[43] This culture of learning from mistakes has led to some of their most successful products, including Gmail, which started as a failed attempt at something entirely different. (And definitely isn't just e-mail but with a "G.")

Another great example: the social media consultancy NixonMcInnes hosts "Church of Fail," where employees openly share mistakes and lessons learned—reinforcing a growth mindset. This practice has helped create a culture where employees are not afraid to take risks, fostering innovation, increased resilience, and collaborative problem-solving within the team.[44] Mmm, preach!

Embracing failure means changing the conversation from "I messed up" to "I'm cooking something up." Did your presentation bomb? Excellent—you've just gathered crucial feedback about your recipe for success. Did your project go off the rails? Wonderful—you've just completed a master class in what

"No quote here—just a reminder that you're doing great!"

— Best Guy Ever

Siemens: Engineering a Growth Mindset[45]

The Challenge: Foster a culture of continuous learning and innovation across a global workforce to adapt to rapid industry changes.

The Approach: Siemens implemented initiatives like the Intrapreneurs Bootcamp, empowering employees to develop innovative solutions and embrace a growth mindset. The company also prioritized re-skilling and lifelong learning, encouraging employees to adopt a growth mindset and continuously update their skills.

The Result:

- Enhanced employee engagement and collaboration through empowerment and growth mindset initiatives.
- Increased innovation, with employees developing new skills to keep pace with industry changes.
- Recognition as a top employer for talent development, reflecting a culture that supports continuous learning and growth.

The Take-Home Recipe:

- Empower employees to own innovation.
- Prioritize continuous learning and re-skilling.
- Embed growth mindset at every level.

to adjust next time. Did you set the break room microwave on fire trying to heat up a pot pie in its metal dish? Not great, but hey—you're still learning.

Remember, every master chef has burned more dishes than you've had hot dinners. The difference is, they used those culinary catastrophes as unique seasoning in their recipe for success. So go ahead—let that first batch of bread fall flat. Just make sure you're taking notes on the rise and fall of it all. That way you can start making some real *bread*!

Growth Spice

3 **IF FAILURE IS** the foundation of success, then feedback is the spice cabinet—the essential ingredient that elevates the ordinary into the extraordinary. In a growth mindset, feedback isn't a bitter pill to swallow; it's valuable data that enhances your potential. In other words: You want the feedback. You crave the feedback. You *need* the feedback!

Just as we've learned to mindfully process our experiences and cultivate gratitude, we need to develop a refined approach to feedback. It's quality control for your performance—every bit of input helps you adjust and improve. Research shows that when individuals are praised for their effort rather than their intelligence, they choose more challenging tasks and persist longer through obstacles.[46]

And the more specific the feedback, the better. Telling someone "You're smart" might feel good in the moment, but it sets a fragile expectation—what happens when they struggle? Contrast that with feedback like, "Your argument was well-structured, and your use of data made it even stronger." The first reinforces identity, while the second reinforces process. When people know exactly what contributed to their success, they're more likely to build on it, take risks, and push their abilities further. But waiting for feedback to appear isn't enough—you have to go after it. (And yeah, I'm talking to you—duh!)

In the professional world, this means *actively* seeking out feedback, even when it makes you want to trade your laptop for a banana stand in Newport Beach. (There's always money in the banana stand!) It means seeing your annual review not as an ordeal, but as a masterclass in refining your approach. Ask specific questions: "What's one thing I could improve in my presentations? How can I make my ideas clearer?" The more targeted your ask, the more actionable the response. And when you treat feedback as fuel for growth rather than judgment, you stop fearing it—and start using it.

Microsoft has revolutionized feedback with "growth dialogues"—conversations centered on learning and development rather than just performance metrics.[47] These conversations blend recognition of current achievements with opportunities for future growth. The result? Their employee engagement scores have risen consistently year over year.

But here's the key insight: feedback isn't just about receiving—it's about how you process and communicate it. Internally, it shapes your mindset, turning setbacks into stepping stones. Externally, it refines how you collaborate, present ideas, and lead.

The next time someone offers feedback, resist the urge to run. Pause, absorb, and respond with intention. Use it to sharpen both your internal dialogue and external impact. Your future self will thank you—probably with a bigger slice of the success pie.

FIVE TASTE-TEST RECIPES

A growth mindset is about experimentation, not perfection. These recipes are flexible—try what works, refine what doesn't, and revisit when needed. It's not about speed; it's about steady, intentional progress.

1. **The "Yet" Revolution:** Catch yourself saying "I can't do this"? Add "yet." This simple reframing transforms limitations into temporary challenges, reminding you that with effort and time, any skill can be developed.

2. **The Failure Recap:** Once a week, share a learning moment with your team, focusing on lessons learned and actionable improvements. Make vulnerability a strength—it's a key to real growth.

3. **The Skill-Stretching Challenge:** Pick one skill quarterly, set a measurable goal, and track progress with a growth partner. Set specific, achievable goals and track your progress. Embrace the learning process and invite a colleague to join your growth journey.

4. **The Feedback Forum:** Transform feedback into an action plan. Create a structured space where team members can share constructive input and celebrate progress. Make feedback a regular, positive part of your culture.

5. **The Mind-Gym Mornings:** Start or end each day with 10 minutes of intentional learning—read an industry article, watch a short development video, or practice a new skill. Set the tone for growth before your day even begins.

LAST CALL

Deploying a growth mindset isn't about positive thinking platitudes—it's about approaching challenges as ingredients for development. Like a chef who views each failed dish as data for improvement, effective professionals understand that setbacks are stepping stones to mastery.

In this chapter, you've learned how a growth mindset transforms professional development through three core elements: *Mind Muscles*, which showed how neural plasticity enables continuous improvement; *Failure's Flavor*, which revealed how setbacks become opportunities for learning; and *Growth Spice*, which demonstrated how feedback accelerates development. You've discovered that embracing a growth mindset doesn't just feel empowering—it creates measurable improvements in resilience, innovation, and career advancement.

As you develop your professional recipe box, remember your mind, like your kitchen, is equipped for continuous improvement. Keep tasting, testing, and refining your approach. Success isn't about having every ingredient—it's about mastering the ones you have.

And your best dishes? They're still ahead.

CEREBRAL SOUS VIDE

✓ How can I reframe a recent failure as a valuable learning opportunity?

✓ Who inspires me with their growth mindset, and what can I learn from them?

✓ How can I view feedback as a tool for improvement, not as criticism?

THE SELF-SERVE STATION

Not sure if a growth mindset really works? Perfect. These resources show how curiosity and persistence turn setbacks into stepping stones for success:

- *Mindset: The Updated Edition* by Carol S. Dweck (2023) – The definitive guide from the researcher who started it all. Dweck's updated classic brings fresh research and practical applications that transform how we think about potential in today's workplace. So good I'm about to call it out again on the next page!

- *Think Again: The Power of Knowing What You Don't Know* by Adam Grant (2021) – What's better than being right? Being bold enough to change your mind. Grant masterfully shows why intellectual humility might be your greatest professional asset.

- *The Extended Mind: The Power of Thinking Outside the Brain* by Annie Murphy Paul (2021) – Forget everything you thought you knew about thinking. This revolutionary look at how our environment shapes our cognition will transform how you approach learning and growth.

- *Harvard Business Review* article: "A Growth Mindset Doesn't Mean Endless Positivity" by David Brendel and Ryan Stelzer (2023) – A clear-eyed look at applying growth mindset principles without falling into toxic positivity. Practical insights for keeping it real while keeping growth at the forefront.

- *Smarter Tomorrow: How 15 Minutes of Neurohacking a Day Can Help You Work Better, Think Faster, and Get More Done* by Elizabeth R. Ricker (2021) – Watch out—side effects of reading this book may include questioning everything you thought you knew about your potential. Ricker's practical guide to cognitive enhancement is grounded in science, not hype.

A SWEET & SAVORY SHOUT-OUT

Dr. Carol S. Dweck didn't just study mindset—she turned it into a recipe for success, shaping academic and professional thinking for decades.

Her groundbreaking work on growth versus fixed mindsets has reshaped our understanding of learning, resilience, and human potential. Dr. Dweck's research shows that seeing abilities as developable rather than fixed leads to greater adaptability, openness to feedback, and resilience in the face of challenges. Simply put, how we view our potential directly impacts what we achieve.

Her impact spans far beyond psychology's borders. In education, her insights have inspired schools worldwide to praise students for effort over innate talent, helping young minds see challenges as stepping stones rather than stumbling blocks. This approach has fostered learning environments where students eagerly take on difficult subjects, bounce back from setbacks, and value the process of learning as much as the outcome.

In the corporate world, companies like Microsoft, General Mills, and Google have adopted growth mindset practices to encourage cultures of innovation and adaptability, where employees are empowered to learn from failure rather than fear it. Dr. Dweck's influence has reshaped how organizations define success, foster creativity, and develop leaders—creating more dynamic, resilient workplaces.

Dr. Dweck's research reminds us that our potential isn't predetermined by our initial capabilities, but by our willingness to learn and grow. The next time you push through a challenge or learn from a mistake, tip your mental hat to Dr. Dweck. Without her research, many of us might still be stuck in a fixed mindset, missing out on the resilience and success that come with growth.

In Dweck's words, "Becoming is better than being." Now that is some dope "mic-drop" shit right there!

10 QUICK BITES

- A growth mindset transforms challenges into opportunities, fostering 47% higher trust and 34% greater commitment in companies that embrace it.

- Embracing a growth mindset shifts internal dialogue from "I can't do this" to "I'm figuring it out," literally reshaping the brain through neuroplasticity.

- Neuroscience shows that positive self-talk rewires the brain, helping growth-minded individuals learn more effectively from mistakes.

- Students with growth mindset beliefs showed upward trajectory in math grades over two years, while fixed mindset peers remained flat.

- Growth-minded cultures view failure as a learning tool; Google's "post-mortems" turn setbacks into insights and building resilience.

- Praising effort over talent encourages employees to take on tougher tasks, persist through challenges, and build adaptability.

- In a growth mindset, feedback is a tool for improvement—more like refining a recipe than simple criticism.

- Waiting for feedback isn't enough—you have to go after it. Actively seeking specific, actionable feedback helps refine your skills and accelerates growth.

- Mindset shapes self-talk—reframing setbacks as learning moments turns inner criticism into constructive coaching.

- A growth mindset builds resilience in workplace challenges, seeing each task as an opportunity to expand skills and potential.

PREP CARD

Common Obstacle:

"Feedback triggers a defensive response."

Quick Fix:

Use the "24-hour rule" before responding–aka, don't respond for a day

Long-term:

Create a feedback collection system

Common Obstacle:

"Fear of failure prevents risk-taking."

Quick Fix:

Start with low-stakes experiments

Long-term:

Build a "learning from failure" portfolio and tolerance

Common Obstacle:

"Feedback feels like criticism rather than opportunity."

Quick Fix:

Respond to every piece of feedback with "This could help me improve (insert growth area here)"

Long-term:

Maintain a weekly "Growth Journal" tracking feedback

DO HARD BETTER

APPETIZER

Is your to-do list starting to look like a horror movie script? Time for a rewrite! This is the art of handling the heat! We're about to turn your workplace pressure cooker into your personal power station. No more getting burned. Time to master the heat, harness the pressure, and turn every challenge into fuel for your success.

MAIN COURSE

Embrace the Suck: Why the tough stuff is
actually your ticket to the top
Bite-Sized Battles: Break big scary goals into bite-sized wins
Heat Management: Your survival guide to thriving
under pressure (without melting!)

DESSERT

The Pre-Launch Checklist: Your high-stakes success checklist
The Pressure Protocol: Because steady hands steer the ship
The Recovery Rhythm: Master the work-to-
rest recipe that keeps you cooking

PAIRS WELL WITH

That impossible deadline you're staring down
Your emergency snack drawer
A reminder that diamonds are just coal
that handled pressure like a boss

CHAPTER 4:

Do Hard Better—The Searing Technique

T'S T-MINUS 15 minutes to your career-making presentation. Your laptop just blue-screened. Your rockstar teammate is stuck in traffic. And your boss just casually dropped three C-suite execs into the invite. *This shit is too hard*, you think. You want to call in sick. Fake a terrible bout of diarrhea. Only problem? You actually have diarrhea.

As Coolio once said, "If you can't take the heat, get yo' ass out of the kitchen." But here's the thing—the kitchen isn't optional. You're here now, and the heat is on. There's no getting around it—this is hard. So what's the solution?

Time to Do Hard Better.

No, this isn't another resilience speech that makes you want to throw your stress ball at the motivational poster on your wall. This is about turning "Oh Shit" moments into "Oh Shift" moments. Here's the reality: these moments aren't the exception in today's workplace—they're just called Tuesday. (And sometimes Wednesday. And definitely Monday.)

If you read Chapter 3, you might be asking: how is "Do Hard Better" different from "Growth Mindset"? Good question! (Seriously, you're on a roll with these. A+ for participation!)

While both concepts embrace challenge and development, they operate on different levels. Growth Mindset is the foundational belief that your abilities can be developed. It's like accepting that you *can* learn to cook despite having never done it or just having burned toast yesterday morning.

Doing Hard Better takes that mindset and turns it into an active strategy. It's not just about believing you can handle challenges—it's about actively seeking them out and applying specific techniques to tackle them. It's the difference between believing you can learn to become a chef and deliberately choosing to work in the busiest kitchen you can find to accelerate your development.

To do this, you need a system. Whether you're juggling client demands, racing deadlines, or trying to remember which version of that document is actually the "FINAL_Final_v3_REALLY_FINAL.doc," the heat is always on. And just when you think you've mastered the temperature of your professional kitchen, someone cranks the burner up to inferno. As James Clear explains in *Atomic Habits*, success isn't about one-time heroic efforts—it's about building systems that make hard things manageable.[48]

This isn't new news. You've been there before and have seen what happens when you Do Hard Better. You stop viewing challenges as roadblocks and start viewing them as your competitive advantage. It's not about making things easier, because things never get easier. But you get stronger. Each challenge, each setback, each failure becomes another rep in your professional growth. The trick isn't making the load lighter—it's learning to lift heavier with better form.

Think of building resilience like building spice tolerance—what once set your mouth on fire now barely registers as heat. The same goes for handling workplace challenges: what felt overwhelming yesterday is routine today. But make no mistake—it takes effort. Every promotion brings new pressures, every project delivers unexpected twists, and every boss comes with their own quirks. These aren't obstacles in your career—they *are* your career.

The key? Learning to manage the heat so you don't burn out before the main course.

Science supports this: success under pressure isn't about innate talent—it's about systematic approaches and deliberate practice. A 2022 study published in *Frontiers in Psychology* found that challenge stressors—work-related demands perceived as opportunities for growth—positively influence innovation performance, whereas hindrance stressors have a negative effect.[49] This finding dovetails perfectly with McKinsey's research showing that organizations with systematic pressure-handling approaches perform like well-oiled machines, not one-hit-wonders.[50] The cherry on top? *Harvard Business Review's* analysis reveals that the secret sauce isn't natural grace under pressure—it's having a tested recipe for handling heat.[51] (That's like literally what we're talking about here. So glad *HBR* agrees!)

In 2021, I earned my Ph.D. in Doing Hard Better during the "Supply Chain Apocalypse." Major customers heading for the exits? Check. Multiple team members peacing out in the same week? Double check. Vendors playing supply chain Jenga with our deliveries? Triple check.

"NOT SURE THIS IS WHAT THEY MEANT BY HAVING AN EXIT STRATEGY."

For a while, it felt like we were drowning. But after one particularly brutal call—where a longtime partner flat-out told us they were considering walking—we knew something had to change. (His name was Chris. Inside joke, but seriously... Chris?)

Instead of ducking the challenge, we turned it into our training ground. We broke down the crisis into manageable pieces, prioritized the most critical deliveries, established clear communication protocols, and most importantly, maintained our composure under fire. The result? Not only did we retain the account, but we emerged with a stronger relationship and a proven crisis management playbook. (Turns out Chris was pretty useful, too.)

In this chapter, we'll explore three techniques to Do Hard Better. First, we'll explore how to *Embrace the Suck*—learning to transform that "Oh shit, my laptop's dead" panic into "Challenge accepted." From there, we'll dive into strategic decomposition with *Bite-sized Battles*—breaking down that high-stakes presentation into manageable chunks, even when everything's going sideways. Finally, we'll master *Heat Management* by building systems and processes that ensure you can deliver even when your team's stuck in traffic and the C-suite is watching.

We're not trying to eliminate pressure. We're turning it into your superpower, so that next time your laptop dies (and there will be a next time), you'll know exactly how to cook under pressure.

THREE MAIN DISHES

Embrace the Suck

1 LET'S FACE IT—SOME things at work just suck harder than a Dyson in a dust storm. That big presentation requiring your third consecutive midnight dance with PowerPoint? Suck. That project you were "volun-told" to lead (because apparently saying "no" is *so* 2019)? Major suck. That monthly report that's about as well-read as your company's privacy policy? Supreme suck with a cherry on top.

Here's the thing about those 2 a.m. LinkedIn-updating moments: They're actually your career's catalysts for greatness. Each challenge, each obstacle is building your professional superpowers in ways that your comfort zone never could. Think of it like this: every career-defining breakthrough started as someone's "Embrace the Suck" moment. That promotion you're eyeing? It'll go to the person who can handle the heat when everything's on fire. That dream role you're after? They're looking for someone who's proven they can turn chaos into clarity. Your future self will thank you for every impossible deadline you crushed, every difficult conversation you navigated, and every crisis you turned into an opportunity.

Want to see this in action? Meet Jocko Willink, the Navy SEAL who turned "good" into the most powerful plot twist in leadership.[52] When everything goes sideways, Willink drops this mental judo move: "Good." Missed that deadline? "Good"—time to upgrade your project management game. Key player quit? "Good"—opportunity to build a stronger team. Accidentally replied-all to the entire company with a meme meant for your work bestie? "Good"—now leadership knows you have *range*. It's not toxic positivity. It's strategic optimism on steroids.

This plays out at the corporate level, too. In 2009, Toyota was facing the corporate equivalent of a five-alarm fire: 3.8 million vehicles recalled, stock doing a swan dive (down 20%), and $2 billion in sales up in smoke. Their initial response stunk, but by embracing the suck, they transformed their quality control into the industry gold standard.[53]

And Toyota isn't alone in the "embrace the suck" hall of fame. Take Netflix's 2011 Qwikster fiasco—a masterclass in embracing the suck if there ever was one. After hemorrhaging 800,000 subscribers and watching their stock perform an Olympic-worthy dive from $298 to $77, CEO Reed Hastings didn't hide from the disaster—he ran straight toward it: "I messed up." Instead of corporate damage control, they used their face-plant as a blueprint for handling failure.[54]

They didn't just embrace the suck—they learned from it, grew from it, and came out stronger.

So, the next time work serves you a shit sandwich with a side of chaos, take a deliberate pause. Spend two minutes identifying the skill this challenge will strengthen, mapping how it aligns with your career goals, and choosing one concrete action you can take right now. This isn't about becoming a corporate masochist—it's about recognizing that the path *through* the mess is the path *up* the ladder.

Every difficult task is another rep in your professional resilience workout. The question isn't whether things will get hard—that's guaranteed. The question is: are you ready to transform today's challenge into tomorrow's breakthrough?

Bite-Sized Battles

2 YOU'VE JUST BEEN handed The Project™. You know the one—it's got more moving parts than a Rube Goldberg machine and a deadline that makes "ASAP" look leisurely. Your palms start their own personal rain dance, your brain goes into blue-screen mode, and yes, your gut decides now's the perfect time for an impromptu drum solo straight out of a Slayer concert. No judgment—we've all conducted that symphony of stress. But there is hope. Here's where strategic decomposition becomes your career's best friend.

Breaking down complex challenges isn't just about organization—it's about working with your brain's natural operating system. Turns out, our brains can only process about four chunks of information at a time.[55] It's like trying to juggle—three balls is challenging but manageable; add a fourth or a fifth, and suddenly you're picking up balls and your dignity off the floor.

And the data dorks (not the juggling nerds) agree: projects that are broken down into smaller chunks, often referred to as iterative or agile approaches, are generally considered more effective than cramming a lot of information

"We all wait in life for things to get easier. It will never get easier. What happens is you handle hard better . . . So make yourself a person that handles hard well."

— Kara Lawson

DARPA: Where Impossible is the First Draft[56]

The Challenge: Rapidly develop groundbreaking technologies to maintain U.S. military superiority.

The Approach: Established in 1958, DARPA (Defense Advanced Research Projects Agency) exemplifies an organization's mastery of tackling seemingly impossible challenges through systematic innovation and calculated risk-taking. It operates with a high tolerance for risk and failure, fostering innovation through limited tenure for project managers and autonomy from traditional bureaucracy.

The Result:

- Pioneered ARPANET, the precursor to the internet, in 1969.
- Developed stealth technology, leading to the first successful flight of the "Have Blue" prototype in 1977.
- Advanced mRNA vaccine technology, contributing to rapid COVID-19 vaccine development.

The Take-Home Recipe:

- Big breakthroughs require bold risks.
- Embrace failure as a tool for growth.
- Hard challenges demand focused, agile teams.

or work into a single large effort.[57] Think of it as turning your elephant-sized project into bite-sized elephant canapés. You know—the whole one bite at a time thing.

Want to see this in action at the enterprise level? Let's time-travel to IBM in the early '90s. Facing a staggering $15 billion loss, CEO Lou Gerstner didn't try to boil the ocean. Instead, he broke this corporate Titanic-meets-iceberg scenario into focused chunks: stop the bleeding, streamline operations, shift to services, and rebuild culture.[58] Just like your big projects, he took it piece by piece. The scale might be different, and even the epoch, but the principle is the same—for everything from transforming a Fortune 500 company to tackling your own first major project, success comes from tackling the right problems, in the right order, without losing your head in the process.

The proof is in the productivity pudding: teams that adopt this bite-sized approach see significantly better results. According to the Project Management Institute, high-performing organizations using these methods meet goals 65% more often and waste 28 times less money than their low-performing peers.[59] And when it comes to large-scale change, McKinsey research shows that success hinges on breaking complex transformations into clearly defined, sequenced initiatives—essentially a corporate form of chunking. Companies that take this structured approach are up to three times more likely to achieve their transformation goals.[60]

The math made sense for Lou, even 30+ years ago. And it still makes sense today—breaking things down works because it aligns with how our incredibly powerful yet selectively lazy brains function.

So, the next time work hands you an impossible project, resist the urge to panic-scroll job listings. Instead, map out all the components visually, ruthlessly prioritize the most critical elements, and break them into bite-sized, time-bound targets. Hold short recurring check-ins focused solely on those priorities. And remember this simple mantra: What Would Lou Do?

Heat Management

3 BY NOW, YOU'VE embraced the suck and mastered breaking down challenges. But handling pressure isn't just about grit—it's about systems. High performers don't just survive pressure; they build repeatable, scalable strategies to turn it into fuel.

Every high performer (hint: that's you) needs a heat management system. Not vague stress management tips, but real, structured responses that keep you in control. Think of it like a professional fire extinguisher—you hope you won't need it, but when the metaphorical popcorn starts burning, you'll be glad it's there.

Psychologists call this a "pressure protocol"—a structured approach to handling high-stress situations. Research shared in the National Library of Medicine highlights that structured stress management interventions—such as mental rehearsal, breathing techniques, and performance routines—have been shown to enhance adaptability and resilience under pressure in military and high-stress professional settings.[61] Instead of juggling multiple boiling pots, they follow a plan and kick butt because of it.

And it's not just about handling personal pressure—teams function better when leadership is distributed. Harvard's Heidi K. Gardner found that shared decision-making and cross-disciplinary collaboration foster deeper trust, higher engagement, and improved overall performance in complex professional environments.[62] And since those attributes tend to lead to better performance and lower stress, organizations that promote shared leadership structures experience greater efficiency and better crisis response. And aren't you always dealing with a crisis these days?

So, what does a great heat management system include? Funny you should ask. I happen to have the answer right here:

1. **Clear Triggers ➜ Pre-Heat (Preparation)**
   Recognizing early warning signs allows you to activate your pressure protocol before stress escalates. Triggers can be external (looming deadlines, high-stakes meetings) or internal (rising frustration, racing thoughts). For example, if tight deadlines typically cause last-minute panic, a clear trigger could be receiving a complex assignment. Your

Pre-Heat response? Mapping out key milestones before the stress compounds.

2. **Specific Responses ➔ Mid-Heat (Execution)**

   When pressure hits, pre-planned responses prevent spiraling. Your approach should match the intensity of the situation. Example: If a high-pressure presentation spikes your adrenaline, your Mid-Heat response might be a 4-7-8 breathing reset (inhale for four seconds, hold for seven, exhale for eight). If decision fatigue slows you down, use a decision-making framework like Eisenhower's Matrix to prioritize immediate action.

3. **Feedback Loops ➔ Post-Heat (Recovery)**

   After high-pressure moments, reflection ensures continuous improvement. Without this step, you risk repeating mistakes or carrying unnecessary stress forward. For example, after a tough negotiation, your Post-Heat recovery could be a 10-minute post-mortem (What worked? What needs adjusting?). This prevents reactive habits from becoming ingrained.

By aligning triggers with Pre-Heat, responses with Mid-Heat, and feedback loops with Post-Heat, you create a repeatable, scalable system for handling pressure. Instead of reacting impulsively, you stay in control, leading to stronger decision-making, clearer communication, and sustained high performance. Not to mention a new way to blow the socks off your work peers!

FIVE TASTE-TEST RECIPES

To Do Hard Better takes practice and experimentation. Heck, it's not even easy to say! But these starting-point recipes can help—use one, adapt another, or keep them in mind for the future. The goal is progress, not perfection. (Unless you're my mom. Then it has to be perfect!)

1   **The Pre-Launch Checklist:** Before any major challenge, take 10 minutes to map your mission: list required components, identify failure points, and establish success metrics. Smart preparation prevents poor performance.

2   **The Pressure Protocol:** Develop a stress playbook: 60-second pauses, clarifying questions, and a trusted advisor to consult. Practice on small challenges so you're ready when big ones hit.

3   **The Recovery Rhythm:** Follow the 52/17 rule—a research-backed method (on ultradian rhythm) where 52 minutes of focused work is followed by 17 minutes of real recovery. These breaks aren't luxuries—they're necessities for sustained peak performance. (Don't spend that extra minute all in one place.)

4   **The Communication Cascade:** Create templates for updates and emergency plans to keep communication seamless under pressure. Know who needs what information and when. Clear protocols prevent chaos when the heat rises.

5   **The Post-Service Review:** Review wins and lessons after challenges. What worked? What didn't? What changes next time? Document these insights, because they're your blueprint for future success.

LAST CALL

Doing Hard Better isn't about grinding it out—it's about tackling workplace challenges strategically. Like a chef mastering high-heat techniques without getting burned, top professionals know that intensity requires both skill and system.

In this chapter, you've learned how to master difficulty through three essential elements: *Embrace the Suck*, which revealed how accepting challenges leads to breakthrough performance; *Bite-Sized Battles*, which demonstrated how breaking down complex problems makes progress more manageable; and *Heat Management*, which demonstrated how systematic approaches turn pressure into productivity. You've discovered that Doing Hard Better requires creating sustainable systems for handling workplace intensity.

When you master these techniques, the benefits ripple far beyond your own career. Your ability to embrace challenges inspires teammates to step up their game. Your breakdown methods become team protocols, transforming overwhelming projects into manageable victories. Your heat management system becomes part of your organization's DNA, creating a culture where pressure doesn't break people, but builds stronger teams.

Look at you! All rizzed up with that heat management glow, embracing the suck, and ready to win those bite-sized battles.

CEREBRAL SOUS VIDE

✓ What's my personal plan for managing recurring stressful situations?

✓ Who do I admire for their resilience, and what can I learn from their approach?

✓ What process change could help me handle future crises more smoothly?

THE SELF-SERVE STATION

Ready to lean into the tough stuff—or at least dip a toe in? These resources will teach you how to tackle pressure, build resilience, and turn challenges into opportunities:

- *Extreme Ownership* by Jocko Willink and Leif Babin (2017) – Ever wonder how Navy SEALs handle pressure while the rest of us stress about printer jams? This isn't just another "tough guy" manifesto—it's your battlefield-tested playbook for turning chaos into victory. Side effects may include extreme accountability and sudden urges to wake up at 4 a.m.

- *The Making of a Manager* by Julie Zhuo (2019) – Think managing people is like herding cats? Zhuo's been there, done that, and wrote the manual you wish you'd had before accepting that promotion. Perfect for anyone who's ever felt like they're playing corporate dress-up in the big chair.

- *Stress-Proof* by Mithu Storoni (2019) – Finally! A book about stress that won't stress you out more. Storoni breaks down the brain science without making your brain hurt, offering practical strategies that work better than that stress ball you've squeezed into oblivion.

- *Peak: Secrets from the New Science of Expertise* by Anders Ericsson and Robert Pool (2016) – The science behind why some people thrive under pressure while others crack like an egg in a microwave. Spoiler: it's not about natural talent. It's about smart practice. Consider this your roadmap to turning difficulty into your personal playground.

- *Better Under Pressure: How Great Leaders Bring Out the Best in Themselves and Others* by Justin Menkes (2011) – Think pressure is the enemy? Menkes' research with top CEOs reveals why some leaders shine when the heat is on. Part playbook, part wake-up call, this is your guide to turning pressure from a pain point into a power move.

A SWEET & SAVORY SHOUT-OUT

Kara Lawson is an absolute badass. When the former WNBA star isn't coaching Duke University's women's basketball team, she's teaching the art of doing hard better—one game at a time.

Lawson's mantra, "Handle hard better," (yes, I am totally sampling hard on this one) has become a rallying cry for her team and a philosophy that extends far beyond the basketball court. She challenges her players to embrace difficult tasks, push through discomfort, and continuously improve their skills—even when it's tough, especially when it's tough.

But Lawson doesn't just talk the talk. As the first woman to coach a Japanese professional men's team and one of the few female coaches in men's professional basketball, she's lived the principle of tackling hard challenges head-on. Her journey from player to coach to trailblazer is a testament to the power of embracing difficulty as a path to growth.

What makes Lawson's approach special is her ability to make "hard" feel like an essential ingredient rather than an unwanted addition. She treats challenges like a chef treats high-heat cooking—not as something to avoid, but as a technique for unlocking the best flavors. In her words, "We all wait in life for things to get easier. It will never get easier. What happens is you handle hard better ... So make yourself a person that handles hard well." It's like she's telling her team: the higher the heat, the better the result.

When facing your own high-pressure moments, channel your inner Coach Lawson. Treat each challenge like she would—not as a burden to endure, but as an essential step in creating something exceptional.

In the spirit of Lawson's kitchen-tested wisdom, here's to Doing Hard Better—whether you're on the court, in the boardroom, or yes, even in the kitchen. Thanks, Coach Lawson, for proving that victory isn't about dodging challenges—it's about mastering them.

10 QUICK BITES

- A 2022 study found that challenge stressors—work-related demands perceived as opportunities for growth—positively influence innovation performance.

- McKinsey research shows that organizations with systematic pressure-handling approaches perform like well-oiled machines, not one-hit-wonders.

- The Project Management Institute found that teams using bite-sized approaches meet goals 65% more often and waste 28 times less money.

- Research confirms that our brains can only process about 4 chunks of information at a time, making strategic decomposition essential.

- Projects broken down into iterative or agile approaches are generally considered more effective than cramming work into single large efforts.

- National Library of Medicine research shows structured stress management interventions enhance adaptability and resilience under pressure.

- Toyota's 2009 crisis response to 3.8 million vehicle recalls transformed their quality control into the industry gold standard.

- Netflix's Qwikster fiasco saw CEO Reed Hastings embrace failure openly: "I messed up"—using the disaster as a blueprint for handling failure.

- IBM's Lou Gerstner tackled a $15 billion loss by breaking the crisis into focused chunks: stop bleeding, streamline, shift to services, rebuild culture.

- McKinsey shows companies using structured breakdown approaches are up to three times more likely to achieve their transformation goals.

Prep Card

Common Obstacle:

"Too many urgent priorities."

Quick Fix:

Pick your "Core Four" items that truly move the needle

Long-term:

Create weekly priority mapping sessions with clear delegation paths

---

Common Obstacle:

"My team becomes overwhelmed during crises."

Quick Fix:

Institute 10-minute morning/afternoon status huddles

Long-term:

Build and test response playbooks for common crisis scenarios

---

Common Obstacle:

"Communication breaks down under pressure."

Quick Fix:

Create three key message templates: updates, escalations, and action items

Long-term:

Regular crisis simulation training and practice protocols

MOMENTUM MIRAGE

APPETIZER

Feel like you're stuck in career traffic while everyone
else is zooming by? Plot twist: you're actually in
your preparation montage! It's plateau conquering
time—where tomorrow's overnight successes
are quietly doing their homework today.

MAIN COURSE

Hidden Heat: Why "nothing's happening"
usually means everything's happening
Compound Power: Turn tiny habits
into your success springboard
Brilliant Boredom: Why watching paint
dry might be your cheat code

DESSERT

Narrative Reframe: Five ways to rewrite your plateau blues
The 1% Challenge: Your 'barely trying'
guide to massive change
The Growth Gazette: Spot success hiding in plain sight

PAIRS WELL WITH

That voice telling you to quit
Your growing collection of half-finished projects
A long-term vision that both thrills and terrifies you

CHAPTER 5

Momentum Mirage—The Slow-Cook Method

S IX MONTHS INTO your digital transformation project, you've followed every best practice, hit every milestone, and led your team through countless late nights. Yet, the needle hasn't moved. The metrics are flat, adoption is crawling, and your team's starting to whisper about moving on to "more promising initiatives." Then comes that dreaded moment when you hear from the steering committee: "Maybe we should reallocate these resources elsewhere." Your stomach drops. Are you about to abandon a potential breakthrough—right before it takes off?

Sadly, this is where most transformation efforts fail. It could be a workplace transformation, the battle to turn love handles into a six-pack, or that guitar in the corner collecting dust instead of applause. Honestly, I've had all three at once! We've all seen it before: good work gets abandoned, promising initiatives fizzle out, careers stagnate, and New Year's resolutions plunge in the mid-January abyss.

You may think to yourself (because you've pragmatically and courteously read Chapters 1 through 4): I've built the foundation (Gratitude), maintained my focus (Mindfulness), embraced the challenge (Growth Mindset), and handled the heat (Do Hard Better). But where are the results?

Well, my friend, enjoy the view. This is the Momentum Mirage—that deceptive, seemingly endless horizon where progress remains invisible... until, suddenly, the landscape shifts. This isn't a failure. It's a launchpad disguised as a roadblock, and recognizing it might be the key to reaching your next peak.

Now, this isn't just another "push through the pain" manifesto. There will be frustrating days, draining meetings, and moments when quitting feels like the only option, but the stories we tell ourselves during tough moments often determine whether we persist or give up just before the breakthrough. Like that complex sauce that needs time to reduce and develop its flavors, real transformation rarely happens overnight. Don't get me wrong—the challenge is real. But just as any chef will tell you, you can't rush the process. The magic happens in those seemingly quiet moments when nothing appears to be changing.

And mastering difficulty isn't optional anymore. According to the *World Economic Forum's Future of Jobs Report* in 2020, 50% of all employees will require significant re-skilling by 2025 due to technological advancements. That same report predicts 85 million jobs will disappear—while 97 million new ones take their place.[63] And if you haven't noticed, by the time you are reading this book, it's already 2025 or later. So giddy-up!

Put simply: we're all going to hit roadblocks, and we need to know how to navigate them. You can't microwave your way to mastery on this one, like say accounting or finance or lawyering. You know, the simple stuff.

Great organizations understand this, too. When Amazon Web Services (AWS) launched in 2006, it didn't immediately revolutionize the tech landscape. For years, many questioned its relevance to Amazon's core business. Today, AWS generates over $90 billion annually.[64] That initial struggle wasn't failure. It was incubation.

Let me be vulnerable for a second. For two years, this book lived in the margins—between global team calls, family dinners, and those precious, quiet weekend hours. Progress felt glacial, and more than once, I considered moving on to my other true passion: writing corporate buzzword haikus. (Funny how those two things ultimately converge at the end of this chapter.)

Serendipitously, I stumbled across James Clear's Plateau of Latent Potential sketch in *Atomic Habits*. Instantly, it clicked. Slower progress wasn't no progress. I had a solid manuscript framework, mountains of research, and a clearer vision than I'd had on day one. Sure, my 'one-week-per-chapter' plan was hilariously optimistic. But two years without a finished book wasn't failure—it was necessary development. I re-tooled my expectations, took a moment to honor the work and energy that I had invested, put down my haiku journal, and got back to writing this book. And now, thanks to James Clear, you are blessed enough to be reading this absolute plateau-crushing work of art. As such, if you have any complaints, please contact James Clear directly. This is all on him.

Grasping the concept of this plateau transforms the very experience of work itself. It turns the daily grind into a meaningful journey, setbacks into expected parts of the process, and perseverance into a skill that compounds over time. As Angela Duckworth, author of *Grit*, puts it, "Our potential is one thing. What we do with it is quite another."[65]

In this chapter, we'll tap into your potential by exploring three essential elements. First, *Hidden Heat* explains why progress happens beneath the surface—just like water undergoes invisible changes before suddenly freezing. Next, *Compound Power* shows how small actions lead to seismic results, similar to how minute adjustments in seasoning can transform a dish. Finally, *Brilliant Boredom* teaches us to embrace the apparent stagnation that often precedes breakthrough, much like the quiet fermentation period that gives sourdough its distinctive character.

Think of these concepts as your kitchen fundamentals—like mastering knife skills or understanding flavor profiles. While they might seem basic at first glance, they're the foundation upon which every breakthrough is built. Like perfecting a complex sauce reduction, the path through these slow-burn stretches requires patience, precision, and most importantly, faith in the process.

Whether you're gunning for that promotion, leading a team through a tough project, or writing a pretty awesome business book about effective communication, understanding the Momentum Mirage isn't just helpful—it's fundamental.

Because what feels like treading water is often the deep work that fuels your next leap. Progress isn't always visible, but it's always happening. Stay the course, and when the breakthrough comes, the view will be worth the climb.

And now, for your reading pleasure, my other love... the corporate buzzword haiku:

Synergies unlock,
Low-hanging fruit gets circled—
Let's take this offline.

P.S. This was a joke. Haikus are not my other love. I'm actually more of a limerick guy.

THREE MAIN DISHES

Hidden Heat

1 **PICTURE AN ICE** cube on a table. The room is 25°F. You start warming it—26°F, 27°F, 28°F... nothing. 29°F, 30°F, 31°F... still solid. Then, at 32°F, something magical happens—the ice melts into water. This is the perfect metaphor for the Momentum Mirage. All that energy you're pouring in? It's not wasted. It's accumulating, preparing for a dramatic phase shift that will seem to happen "overnight."

Chemistry and neuroscience align on this one. Research published in *Neuron* shows that when learning new skills, our brains undergo significant structural changes—even during periods of apparent stagnation.[66] New neural pathways form, existing ones strengthen, and beneath the surface, performance primes itself for a breakthrough.

A study in *The Journal of Neuroscience* reinforces this concept: when adults practiced juggling (Yes, that's a thing—I looked it up.) over a three-month period, their brains showed no immediate structural changes. But with continued effort, MRI scans revealed an increase in gray matter in key regions responsible for motor and visual coordination.[67] This means that even when progress seems invisible, change is happening at the neurological level—your brain is physically rewiring itself in preparation for a breakthrough. Right now, your brain is literally forming new pathways, and you didn't even know it. (You're welcome!)

The same hidden progress that fuels personal breakthroughs also drives business success. Just as individuals experience the Mometum Mirage—practicing a skill with no visible improvement—companies often spend years refining their product, tweaking their strategy, and pushing forward with little to show for it. But beneath the surface, momentum is building.

Airbnb spent 1,000 days in what co-founder Brian Chesky called the "trough of sorrow"—flat bookings, skeptical investors, and no visible progress. But behind the scenes, they refined their product, built relationships, and laid the groundwork for explosive growth.[68] When their moment came, they transformed from a struggling startup into a global hospitality giant.

Slack followed a similar path. Initially a gaming company called Tiny Speck, their online game *Glitch* failed to gain traction and was shut down. But in the process, they built an internal communication tool that proved far more valuable. By pivoting to focus on it, they created Slack, redefining workplace messaging and collaboration.[69]

Both companies seemed stuck, but beneath the surface, momentum was building. When the breakthrough finally arrived, it looked sudden—but it had been years in the making.

So, the next time you're slogging through an enterprise-wide company project with no apparent progress, or just practicing a personal skill with no visible improvement, remember the ice cube. Just because you can't see the change doesn't mean it's not happening. Keep applying heat. A phase shift is coming. And while you're waiting for that dramatic transformation, there's another powerful force at work—the compound effect of small, consistent improvements.

Let's explore how these tiny gains accumulate into seismic results.

Compound Power

2 **IN THE WORLD** of finance, compound interest is hailed as the eighth wonder of the world. A mere 1% improvement, compounded daily for a year, doesn't add up to 365% growth—it skyrockets to 3,778%! This principle isn't just for your bank account; it's a powerful lens through which to view your efforts during the Momentum Mirage.

The concept is beautifully simple: small actions compound invisibly until reaching a tipping point that yields seismic results. This is where Gratitude, Mindfulness, Growth Mindset, and Doing Hard Better converge into a strategy for navigating those slow, silent stretches where progress hides. Whether you've read those chapters or jumped straight to this one, these principles stack powerfully.

Take gratitude—seemingly insignificant in the moment, but transformative over time. A landmark study in the *Journal of Personality and Social Psychology* found that participants who kept regular gratitude journals experienced significantly greater life satisfaction and positive mood compared to those who focused on daily hassles—demonstrating how compounding a simple habit

"Great things come from hard work and perseverance. No excuses."

— Kobe Bryant

Peloton: Pedaling Through the Plateau[70]

The Challenge: Establish a premium at-home fitness brand amid market skepticism.

The Approach: Founded in 2012, Peloton invested $50 million in studios and proprietary technology to create an ecosystem of high-end bikes, live-streamed classes, and community engagement. They embraced the Plateau of Latent Potential, focusing on long-term progress despite slow early traction and skepticism about their $2,245 bikes. By building a foundation of loyal customers and refining their product, Peloton positioned itself for a major breakthrough. In 2023 under new CEO Barry McCarthy, Peloton's

focusing on digital subscriptions and partnerships (like with Amazon)— proving that even after a steep climb, there's always another hill to conquer!

The Result:

- $2.7B in revenue by 2024
- Revenue surged 172% year-over-year to $1.8B during the COVID-19 pandemic in 2020.
- Became a leader in the home fitness market with millions of subscribers and a global brand presence.

The Take-Home Recipe:

- Progress builds quietly on the plateau.
- Invest now; the breakthrough will come.
- The plateau is a step, not the end.

can profoundly shift our well-being.[71] The real kicker? The benefits kept growing months after the study ended, showing up as increased resilience and stronger relationships.

The key to harnessing this effect is breaking big goals into micro-tasks and letting small wins build momentum. This is known as The Compound Effect method, a concept popularized by Darren Hardy. Instead of tackling an overwhelming project all at once, chip away at it daily with tiny, manageable steps.[72] Take writing a book—rather than waiting for the perfect, distraction-free weekend to draft an entire chapter, write a single sentence today, a paragraph tomorrow, and a page the next day. (This would have been particularly useful to me two years ago. Thanks for nothing, Darren!)

Toyota revolutionized manufacturing with this same idea through their Kaizen philosophy of continuous improvement.[73] Tiny optimizations, nearly invisible alone, transformed their entire production system and, eventually, the auto industry itself.

James Clear puts a nice bow on this idea: "Success is the product of daily habits—not once-in-a-lifetime transformations."[74] In other words, it's about showing up every day, making those 1% improvements, even when progress feels stalled.

This works everywhere: ten push-ups today, eleven tomorrow. Five minutes of deep work before checking your phone. One page of reading before bed. These micro-habits quietly reshape your identity in ways that compound into massive change.

So, embrace 1% better every day. Your daily mindfulness practice, your efforts to cultivate a growth mindset, your willingness to do hard things better—they're all compounding, quietly setting you up for exponential growth. What feels like a flatline is actually the runway for your breakthrough.

Now that we understand how small actions compound, let's explore perhaps the most counterintuitive advantage of this quiet phase: the productive power of being bored.

Brilliant Boredom

3 **THEY SAY A** watched pot never boils. (After four chapters of cooking metaphors, I'm legally required to include this idiom somewhere.) But here's the truth: the more you obsess over progress, the longer it takes to show up. The Momentum Mirage, with its lack of visible progress, can feel mind-numbingly boring. But therein lies its hidden superpower.

Neuroscientific research has shown that boredom, far from being a waste of time, actually stimulates creativity and problem-solving. A study published in the *Academy of Management Discoveries* found that individuals who experienced boredom performed better in creative tasks compared to those who did not.[75] Researchers suggest that when our brains are deprived of external stimulation, they default to deeper thinking and problem-solving. This is why moments of boredom—like long showers or waiting in line—often lead to unexpected bursts of insight.

This momentum mirage isn't just theoretical. Let's revisit Slack for a second. It emerged from the ashes of a failed gaming company during a period when the founders were, in their own words, "boring ourselves to death."[76]

This stretch of seeming failure and boredom became the fertile ground for a multi-billion dollar idea.

And the principle extends beyond business. Kobe Bryant's legendary "4 A.M. Club" had him shooting 800 baskets every morning before regular practice. It wasn't exciting. It wasn't innovative. But as Kobe put it, "Great things come from hard work and perseverance. No excuses." Marathon runners log the same training routes day after day, building endurance through repetition. Not sexy, but required.

The implications are clear: The ability to persist through boredom—to continue showing up when the work feels monotonous—is itself a skill that separates high achievers from the rest.[77] And what's more, this paradox intersects beautifully with the practice of mindfulness. By staying present and engaged even during the seemingly uneventful growth lulls, you train your mind to notice subtle changes and opportunities that others might miss.[78]

So next time you hit a stall in momentum, resist the urge to crank up the heat or throw in the towel. Instead, trust the process and lean in. That phase isn't a waiting room for success—it's your test kitchen, where your next big idea is quietly simmering.

Embrace it. Let it marinate.

FIVE TASTE-TEST RECIPES

Those still moments are often precursors to breakthroughs. These ideas are here to help you navigate and power-up stagnant moments. Try a recipe or two, modify them as needed, and uncover the hidden flavors of progress waiting just beneath the surface.

1. **The Narrative Reframe:** When hitting a plateau, ask: "What's the story I'm telling myself?" Then reframe it five different ways. This communication-focused exercise helps you identify limiting narratives and create empowering alternatives.

2. **The 1% Challenge:** Focus on improving by just 1% each day. Whether it's adding a new skill, refining an existing one, or extending your comfort zone slightly longer, small changes, consistently applied, yield remarkable results. Remember: these will be tiny daily changes!

3. **The Accountability Alliance:** Form a small "momentum mirage support team" of 2-3 peers. Meet weekly using the TAG format: Tell your story (5 mins), Ask for specific feedback (5 mins), Get to it, a.k.a. turn insight into action (5 mins).

4. **The Growth Gazette:** Keep a structured breakthrough journal using the "SIR" method: Situation (what happened), Internal Dialogue (what you told yourself), Reframe (how you'll view it differently).

5. **The Experiment Sprint:** Stop overthinking and start testing. Instead of just brainstorming new perspectives, pick one experiment and act on it today. Set a five-minute timer, generate three small, low-risk experiments, and immediately commit to one. Shift, test, adapt—momentum comes from action, not analysis paralysis.

LAST CALL

Progress isn't always visible—like a stock reducing to its essence, the most powerful transformations happen beneath the surface. The Momentum Mirage operates the same way: a period of apparent stagnation where effort accumulates before a breakthrough. Just as a great chef trusts the chemistry of slow cooking, top professionals know that breakthroughs require patient development.

In this chapter, you've learned how to navigate through these quiet stretches three critical elements: *Hidden Heat,* which revealed how progress continues beneath apparent stagnation; *Compound Power,* which showed how small actions accumulate into significant results; and *Brilliant Boredom,* which demonstrated how apparent stillness often precedes breakthrough. You've seen that these slow phases aren't obstacles—they're vital stages of invisible growth. (Unlike, say, my waistline, which is sadly very visible.)

As you simmer in your own development, remember that every reduction requires patience. Trust the process. Your flavors are concentrating, even when you can't see the change.

CEREBRAL SOUS VIDE

- ✓ What unseen progress might be brewing in my current "stuck" phase?
- ✓ How did patience during a plateau contribute to my last breakthrough?
- ✓ What story can I tell myself to find meaning in this plateau?

THE SELF-SERVE STATION

Stuck in neutral and wondering if growth is even possible? These resources will help you uncover hidden progress, reimagine the mirage, and ignite the next phase of your journey:

- *Tiny Habits: The Small Changes That Change Everything* by BJ Fogg (2019) – Think big changes require massive motivation? Stanford's habit guru proves that tiny is mighty. Fogg's science-backed approach shows why those "go big or go home" transformations usually send you straight home. A must-read for anyone who's ever ditched a New Year's resolution by January 3rd (so... everyone).

- *The Compound Effect* by Darren Hardy (2020) – Warning: This book will make you rethink everything you know about progress. Hardy's practical framework reveals why tiny actions, repeated consistently, lead to breakthrough moments.

- *The Long Game* by Dorie Clark (2021) – Tired of overnight success stories? Clark reveals why the most meaningful achievements come from embracing the slow burn. Perfect for anyone feeling stuck in the "valley of disappointment."

- *Grit* by Angela Duckworth (2016) – Duckworth's research on persistence will have you looking at your plateau periods like a detective examining clues rather than a prisoner marking time.

- *The Plateau Effect: Getting From Stuck to Success* by Bob Sullivan and Hugh Thompson (2021) – Finally, someone explains why feeling stuck might be your best sign of impending breakthrough. It offers science-backed insights and strategies for identifying why we get stuck and, more importantly, how to break through those periods of stagnation to achieve new levels of success and happiness.

A SWEET & SAVORY SHOUT-OUT

Let's talk about James Clear—the guy who turned "I'll do it tomorrow" into "I'm doing it right now, and tomorrow, and the next day." His book *Atomic Habits* cracked the code on the Plateau of Latent Potential. His work bridges the gap between rigorous research and real-world application, translating complex behavioral science into actionable strategies. What's particularly remarkable is how he manages to make habit-formation feel less like a chore and more like a fascinating experiment in human potential.

Clear created a framework for understanding how progress really works, often invisibly and non-linearly. Suddenly, people and organizations everywhere realized they weren't failing—they were just in the phase before the breakthrough.

Think he's done? Not even close! He continues to explore and expand our understanding of habit formation, behavioral change, and continuous improvement. He turns brain-bending science into "Oh, now I get it!" insights, making complex ideas accessible to everyone—from CEOs to students.

The magic of Clear? He's like that friend who points out the constellation you've been staring at but couldn't quite see. He helps us spot the power of tiny gains, why your morning routine matters more than your New Year's resolutions, and the transformative potential of consistency. In his words, "You do not rise to the level of your goals. You fall to the level of your systems."

Through his writing, speaking engagements, and popular 3-2-1 newsletter, Clear continues to champion the power of small habits and incremental progress. His message resonates because it's both profound and practical: meaningful change doesn't require dramatic action, just consistent attention.

So here's to you, James Clear. Thanks for proving that extraordinary results come from tiny, consistent actions—and for making it okay to celebrate the microscopic wins that add up to massive change. Also, I really dig your barber.

10 QUICK BITES

- Research shows that during quiet growth phases, our brains rewire themselves, creating new neural pathways even when progress feels invisible.

- The World Economic Forum predicts 50% of employees will need significant re-skilling by 2025, making navigating slow-growth stretches a crucial skill.

- A mere 1% improvement compounded daily yields 3,778% growth over a year—the math behind why slow-build periods matter.

- Studies show that individuals who experienced boredom performed better in creative tasks, making still stretches prime time for innovation.

- Airbnb's "trough of sorrow" lasted 1,000 days before their breakthrough, proof that stalled seasons often come right before success.

- The Compound Effect method, popularized by Darren Hardy, suggests tackling an overwhelming project by chipping away at it daily with tiny steps.

- Toyota's Kaizen philosophy proves tiny improvements, though invisible day-to-day, compound into revolutionary results.

- Slack emerged from a "boring ourselves to death" slow phase to become a multi-billion dollar platform.

- The ice cube effect demonstrates why progress happens invisibly before dramatic breakthrough.

- A gratitude study found participants experienced significantly greater life satisfaction, with benefits continuing to grow months after the study ended.

Common Obstacle:

"My team feels overwhelmed by large projects."

Quick Fix:

Choose one "1% improvement" task that can be done today. Celebrate the small wins!

Long-term:

Use the Compound Effect method to break projects into micro-tasks

---

Common Obstacle:

"Frustration rises during plateaus of no visible progress."

Quick Fix:

Document one small win each day, no matter how minor it seems

Long-term:

Create weekly milestone maps with measurable checkpoints

Common Obstacle:

"We lose momentum during challenging phases."

Quick Fix:

Partner with a colleague to share daily progress, even if it's minimal

Long-term:

Design a "Plateau Playbook" with actions like tracking habits

TWO

The Cooking Line—How You Communicate With Others

WELCOME TO THE interpersonal side of our professional kitchen!

After mastering our internal ingredients, it's time to focus on how we blend with others. And if you thought getting your inner kitchen in order was challenging, just wait until you're orchestrating an entire staff of passionate Type-A chefs with competing recipes and clashing Outlook calendars. We're shifting from solo prep work to conducting a full culinary symphony—where success hinges not just on individual skill, but on how well we harmonize the flavors of personality and perspective that make up any workplace team.

Just as we learned to stock our mental pantry with gratitude, mindfulness, and a growth mindset, we now turn to the indispensable skills that transform workplace interactions from chaotic to choreographed. In this second section, we'll explore five essential dynamics that turn workplace chaos into collaboration:

6. **Humor—Adding the Right Spice**: Learn how appropriate levity transforms workplace dynamics and builds genuine connections. We'll explore why humor, when properly seasoned, is a powerful tool for trust and tension relief. Because if you can't laugh at work, how else will Linda from Legal remember there's life beyond litigation? #iheartalliteration

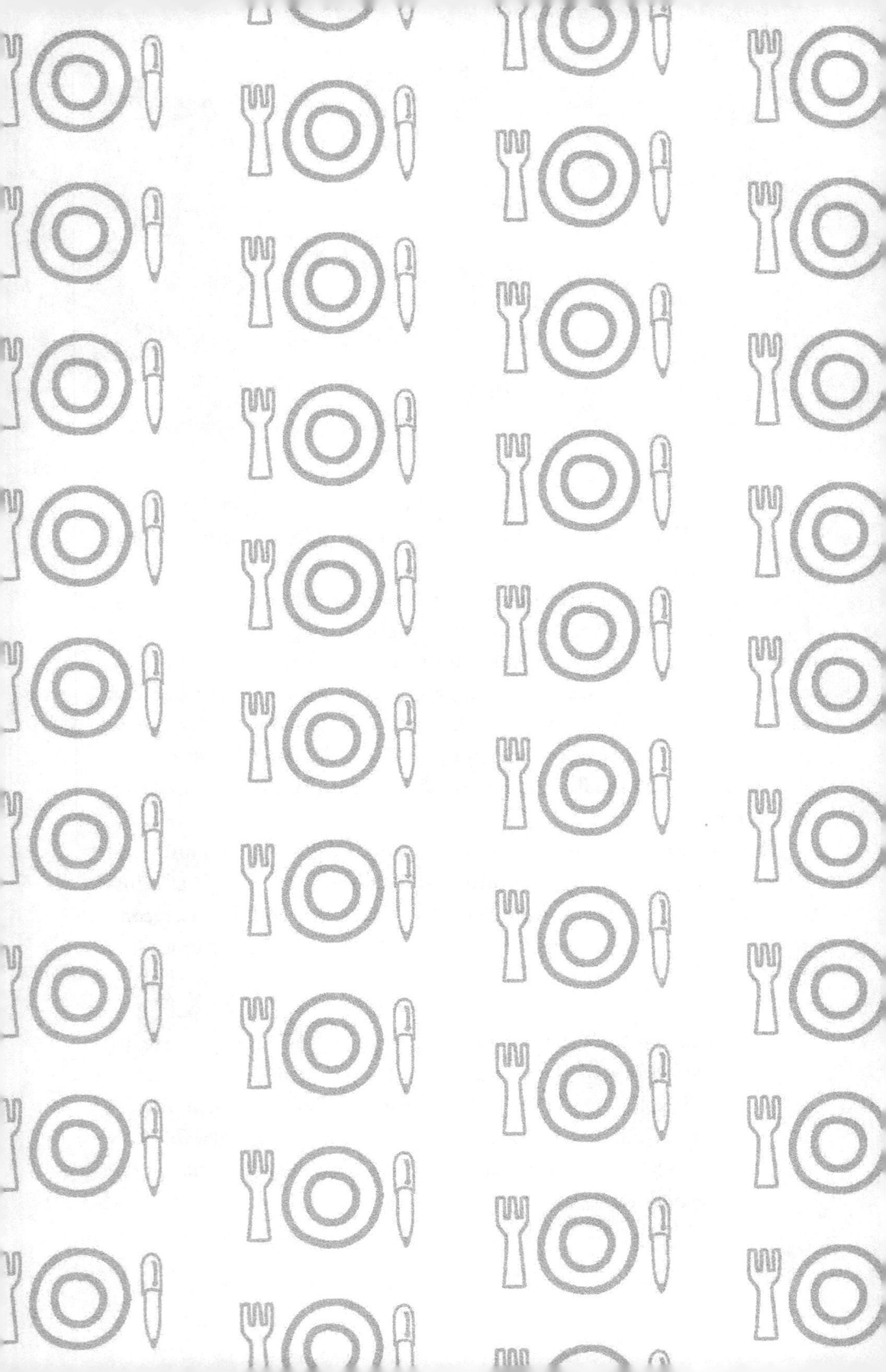

7. **Humility—The Master's Mindset**: Discover why true confidence comes from acknowledging what we don't know. In other words, how to be confident without being a jerk. (It's possible, I promise.)

8. **Listening—The Taste Test**: Beyond just hearing words, real listening means sampling subtle flavors and understanding unspoken ingredients. Master the art of truly absorbing what others share. P.S. Please don't fact-check any of this with my wife.

9. **Energy Management—The Kitchen Flow**: Time management is out, and energy management is in. Learn to maintain sustainable performance by understanding your natural rhythms and peak productivity periods.

10. **Psychological Safety—The Perfect Simmer**: Create an environment where innovation thrives and people feel safe to experiment. Like controlling kitchen temperature, psychological safety requires careful calibration.

Now, you might be thinking, "Wait a minute, I thought I was done with all this self-improvement jazz from Section I!" Wrong! Personal growth and interpersonal skills are two sides of the same shiny corporate coin. Think of it this way: Section One was about tuning your instrument; Section Two is about playing well in the orchestra—even if some colleagues are clearly playing kazoos.

These dynamics work together, creating an atmosphere where teams don't just survive—they thrive. When combined effectively, they transform workplace interactions from stressful to seamless.

Think about it: What good is a brilliant recipe if you can't share it? How valuable is your expertise if you can't collaborate? And let's be real—how far will you climb the corporate ladder if you're leaving behind a trail of burnt bridges and overcooked relationships?

So, ready to upgrade your kitchen dynamics? Let's dive in and discover how these ingredients combine to create something truly extraordinary. By the end of this section, you'll be leading with the wisdom of a master chef, the precision of a pastry artist, and the listening skills of . . . well, someone who's actually good at listening (we're still working on that one ourselves).

Let's do this thang!

HUMOR

APPETIZER
Feel like your presentations are met with stone-cold silence? Wonder why some leaders seem to have an effortless knack for connection while others feel stuck in robotic professionalism? Yup, samesies! Let's see how the right joke at the right time isn't just entertainment; it's a strategic edge.

MAIN COURSE
Laughter's Logic: Use humor to make your messages memorable and your presentations engaging
Bridge & Bond: Build stronger connections and break barriers with shared laughter
Pressure Release: Ease pressure, reduce stress, and refocus your team with well-timed humor

DESSERT
The Absurdity Audit: Find the humor in workplace chaos
The Pun It to Win It Challenge: Exactly what it sounds like
The "Oops, I Did It Again" Moment: Turn missteps into moments of connection

PAIRS WELL WITH
That tense quarterly meeting you've been dreading
A team that could use a morale boost
Presentations in need of a personality upgrade

CHAPTER 6

Humor—Adding the Right Spice

T HE EXECUTIVE LEADERSHIP team has just settled down, and the quarterly numbers splash across the screen like a Jackson Pollock painting done entirely in red ink. The silence is so thick you could stack bricks on top of it. That's when your CFO looks up from his iPad and deadpans: "Well, folks, on the bright side, our burn rate isn't nearly as bad as my golf handicap." Suddenly, the room transforms—shoulders unlock, breath returns, and solving this quarter's dumpster fire feels . . . possible. That's not just luck—that's strategic humor doing its job.

Here's the real power play: in an era where AI can write your emails and automation can run your meetings, humor remains your uniquely human superpower. It's the difference between being a walking LinkedIn profile and an actual person people want to work with. While ChatGPT masters formulas, it still can't nail the timing of a perfectly placed "That's what she said." (Source: Michael Scott. P.S. Usually not work-appropriate.)

Have you ever wondered why that one colleague with mediocre spreadsheet skills keeps getting promoted? They've cracked what I call the Engagement Equation:

(Technical Skills × Communication) + Strategic Humor = Influence^2

The math might be questionable, but the principle isn't—your ability to connect often outweighs your ability to compute. Understanding humor at work is like trying to explain why a cat video goes viral—the moment you start analyzing it, it loses its magic. And let's be honest: most of us think we're either destined for Netflix stand-up specials or completely hopeless at making people laugh, even though both are probably wrong (actually, I can pretty much guarantee the first one is wrong).

Think of humor like a well-timed pause in a presentation—you don't need to be a master of improv to use it effectively, but you do need to know when to deploy it.

Let me tell you about Doug Conant, former CEO of Campbell's Soup and the person who taught me that gravitas and humor aren't opposites—they're dance partners. I met Doug through the Higher Ambition Learning Institute, where he was my mentor. Picture this: a CEO who turned around a Fortune 500 company, wrote best-sellers, survived a near-fatal car accident—and still managed to make every leadership lesson feel intimate, enjoyable, and memorable. Through his masterful use of well-timed wit and self-deprecation, he demonstrated how humor could make even the most serious leadership messages resonate and stick.

I learned many things over a year-long journey of self-discovery with Doug, but one of my biggest takeaways was that Doug's power wasn't in his titles, his wealth, or his intellect—it was in his humanity. And his humor brought that to life in every interaction we shared.

Doug's example isn't just a one-time success story—the data reads like a love letter to laughter. A comprehensive meta-analysis spanning 49 studies shows that strategic humor acts like a performance-enhancing drug for your career.[79] We're talking higher work performance, increased job satisfaction, and improved team cohesion.

A 2019 *Society for Human Resource Management* article highlights that humor in the workplace isn't just a mood booster—it's a strategic tool that can enhance employee engagement, reduce stress, and improve performance. In a climate where only 30% of employees report being engaged at work and businesses lose billions annually due to stress and disengagement, laughter is more than just a reprieve. Research cited in the article, including insights from a Wharton study, shows that humor promotes creativity, strengthens analytical thinking, and helps employees become better problem-solvers. It also fosters trust, lowers workplace tension, and boosts overall job satisfaction—critical ingredients for thriving, resilient teams.[80]

The World Economic Forum's research confirms that humor boosts collaboration and prevents burnout.[81] And a 2023 study in *Healthcare* found that humor helps reduce perceived stress, especially when paired with avoidance-based coping strategies. Rather than simply distracting, humor acts as a stabilizing force—supporting emotional well-being and buffering against psychological strain in challenging situations.[82] Turns out you can be both funny and functional.

As Leslie Blodgett, former CEO of bareMinerals, puts it: "People want authenticity. If you're not a joke teller, don't practice joke telling. Practice being yourself."[83] This isn't about becoming the office equivalent of a TikTok sensation or collecting dad jokes like they're cryptocurrency. It's about wielding humor like a precision instrument, not a sledgehammer.

In this chapter, we'll explore three essential techniques for strategic humor—the same ones that transformed our opening's grim quarterly update into a catalyst for change. First, we'll master *Laughter's Logic,* where we'll turn dry data into memorable messages that stick long after the meeting ends. Then, we'll dive into *Bridge & Bond,* creating authentic relationships across hierarchical levels that turn colleagues into collaborators. Finally, we'll tackle *Pressure Release* and learn how to defuse high-pressure situations without diminishing their importance.

We're not trying to eliminate seriousness—we're adding a powerful tool to make it more effective. Because next time you're staring down a room full of executives (and there will be a next time), you'll know exactly how to shift the energy from panic to possibility. Like any essential ingredient, timing and measurement matter. Too little falls flat, too much overwhelms, but get it just right, and everyone wants seconds.

So, ready to master strategic humor? Unlike Michael Scott, you won't need seven seasons to get that promotion.

THREE MAIN DISHES

Laughter's Logic

1 IN THE COMPLEX landscape of professional communication, humor emerges as an unexpected but neurologically powerful tool. Humor isn't just about getting laughs—it's a catalyst for memory, connection, and trust. Its effectiveness is deeply rooted in neuroscience.

Beyond its surface appeal, humor serves as a bridge that connects people across roles, departments, and even hierarchies. It breaks down barriers and encourages open dialogue, creating psychological safety and shared understanding. Research indicates that humor can lead to better workplace relationships because laughter induces the release of oxytocin—the "bonding hormone" that deepens trust.[84]

But that's not all—laughter also releases endorphins, the brain's natural mood boosters. These biochemical shifts don't just make people feel good; they reduce stress, increase resilience, and improve overall workplace performance.[85] When teams share well-placed moments of levity, they develop stronger bonds, collaborate more effectively, and communicate with greater authenticity.[86] You want all of those things!

Humor doesn't just help us connect—it helps us cope. In high-pressure environments, where stress silently undercuts productivity, humor acts as a cognitive reset. By triggering dopamine, humor enhances problem-solving and creativity, helping teams navigate challenges with greater agility.[87]

Like any powerful tool, humor requires strategic timing and an understanding of context. The goal isn't to make light of serious issues, but to create a shared experience of "we're all in this together." Used well, humor doesn't dilute your message—it amplifies it, making complex ideas more memorable and strengthening relationships at the same time.

Understanding the science of humor is one thing. Using it to influence, inspire, and lead is another. Laughter isn't just a bonding tool; in the right hands, it's a leadership superpower. Let's explore how humor doesn't just connect people—it elevates them.

Bridge & Bond

2 **BEYOND ITS ROLE** in individual interactions, humor functions as a deliberate tool for organizational effectiveness. Leaders who use humor strategically make their messages more memorable, their presentations more impactful, and their leadership more relatable. Memorable. Impactful. Relatable. Not a bad line-up!

Studies show that humor in the workplace isn't just a morale booster—it's a performance driver. Another Wharton study found that laughter promotes creativity and sharper analytical thinking.[88] When woven into company culture, humor enhances focus, builds morale, and fosters enthusiasm for shared goals.

The organizational impact of humor extends beyond immediate interactions. One of humor's greatest strengths is its ability to flatten hierarchies. Leaders who use humor effectively appear more confident and competent, making them more relatable and approachable.

Research from Stanford Graduate School of Business underscores that humor isn't just an optional leadership trait—it's a competitive advantage. Teams with humor-driven leadership report higher collaboration, trust, and risk-taking.[89]

Humor also closes the gap between leadership expectations and employee needs, unlocking organizational potential. Teams operating in humor-positive cultures tend to show higher engagement, more innovation, and greater resilience.[90] Employees in these environments contribute more ideas and approach challenges with higher levels of optimism.

But humor can be a double-edged sword. Strategic use of humor requires leaders to read the room. Leaders must be mindful of how and when they employ humor to ensure it fosters inclusivity and positivity. Misapplied humor—whether off-color, mistimed, or exclusionary—can alienate rather than unify. So, like, don't do that.

In essence, humor multiplies workplace effectiveness. Teams that laugh together perform better together, as shared humor builds trust, enhances collaboration, and reinforces culture. Even Presidents stand by it. Dwight Eisenhower once said, "A sense of humor is part of the art of leadership, of getting along with people, of getting things done."[91] And he wouldn't even make the Top 40 list of funny U.S. Presidents!

"A sense of humor is part of the art of leadership, of getting along with people, of getting things done."

— Dwight D. Eisenhower

The Motley Fool: Investing in Humor[92]

The Challenge: Transform the traditionally staid financial advisory industry into an engaging, approachable, and educational experience for investors.

The Approach: Founded in 1993 by brothers David and Tom Gardner, The Motley Fool has embedded humor into its company culture and public communications. Their core value, "Fun: Revel in your work," encourages employees to infuse enjoyment into their daily tasks, fostering a workplace where humor and productivity coexist. This emphasis on fun extends to their content, where they use witty commentary and entertaining insights to demystify complex financial concepts, making investing accessible and engaging for a broad audience.

The Result:

- A dedicated community of millions of investors who appreciate the unique blend of humor and financial advice.
- Recognition as a company that values employee satisfaction and a positive workplace culture.
- A distinctive brand identity in the financial industry, setting them apart from competitors.

The Take-Home Recipe:

- Make humor part of your culture.
- Use humor to simplify and amplify your message.
- Fun and professionalism aren't opposites—they're partners.

Humor doesn't just help us connect—it helps us survive. Work can be stressful, overwhelming, and at times, utterly ridiculous. But the right joke at the right moment? That's not just comic relief—it's a lifeline. Let's talk about how humor isn't just a leadership tool, but a personal stress hack.

Pressure Release

3 **IN THE PRESSURE** cooker of corporate life, where deadlines loom like storm clouds and "inbox zero" is as mythical as a self-aware influencer, humor can be your pressure release valve. It's like popping bubble wrap or watching a kid try wasabi for the first time—oddly satisfying, stress-relieving, and a little addictive.

But humor isn't just a feel-good trick; it has measurable effects on our bodies and minds. We learned earlier that laughter produces a chemical cocktail purposely designed to reduce stress. The boosting of dopamine, oxytocin, and endorphins also reduces cortisol—the body's primary stress hormone.[93]

This biochemical shift enhances mood, motivation, and overall well-being, making challenges seem more manageable.

Research indicates that individuals with a sense of humor report less stress and anxiety, even when facing the same work-related challenges as their peers.[94] It doesn't erase the challenges, but it reshapes how we experience them, acting as a mental buffer that prevents stress from becoming overwhelming. Humor provides psychological distance, allowing us to reframe setbacks as temporary or even absurd, rather than insurmountable.

Need more proof? A study published in the *National Library of Medicine* found that employees who engaged in humor-based activities experienced meaningful reductions in stress and improvements in overall job satisfaction.[95]

The research suggests that humor isn't just a coping tool—it's a performance enhancer. When laughter becomes part of workplace culture, employees build stronger emotional resilience, communicate more effectively, and navigate high-pressure situations with greater ease.

Incorporating humor into your workday is like adding the perfect seasoning to a complex dish. It doesn't change the fundamental ingredients, but it enhances the flavors, making the experience more enjoyable and the outcome more palatable.

So, sprinkle in some laughter, savor the moments, and watch as the daily grind becomes a gourmet experience.

FIVE TASTE-TEST RECIPES

Time to put the "fun" back in "fundamental." (Sorry. Really, really sorry.) These recipes offer simple ways to bring levity into your work. Experiment, adapt, or let them inspire your unique approach to leadership any way you want.

1. **The Absurdity Audit:** Each week, identify one absurd workplace moment and find a way to reframe it positively in team meetings. Turning frustrations into humor creates shared moments of connection and builds resilience.

2. **The Pun it to Win it Challenge:** Give internal projects engaging, lighthearted names. Try 'Operation: Ctrl+Alt+Elite' for an IT upgrade or 'Mission: Impossible—Deadline Protocol' for a tight turnaround. This strengthens team identity and creates shared reference points.

3. **The Lighten Up Lightning Round:** Start meetings with a 60-second round of lighthearted stories to build connection. Lead by example, sharing your own story first. This creates psychological safety and transitions teams into productive collaboration.

4. **The Meme-orable Wall:** Create a "Meme-orable Wall"—a digital board or physical cork board where team members can post work-appropriate memes about projects, industry quirks, or workplace humor. It's today's version of a water cooler chat and an easy way to build connection.

5. **The "Oops, I Did It Again" Moment:** End each week with a quick, lighthearted share of a small mistake and what was learned. Example: "I replied-all instead of BCC'ing—now the whole company knows my lunch order." Normalizing failure with humor builds resilience and keeps perfection from killing progress.

LAST CALL

Strategic humor isn't about cracking jokes all day (although if you have any good ones, please let me know!). It's about using levity to build trust and ease tension. Like a chef who knows when to lighten a heavy dish, effective leaders understand that appropriate humor creates approachability without sacrificing authority.

In this chapter, you've learned how humor enhances leadership through three key elements: *Laughter's Logic* establishes humor as a neurological and psychological tool; *Bridge & Bond* moves from individual benefits to how humor strengthens teams and leadership; and *Pressure Release* zooms in on humor's role in stress relief and resilience. You've discovered that appropriate humor isn't just entertaining—it creates measurable improvements in team dynamics, innovation, and organizational culture.

As you season your leadership style with humor, your humility toolkit— from transparent error-processing to strategic feedback-gathering—becomes a catalyst for organizational excellence. A workplace without humor is like a meal without salt: technically functional, but missing the magic.

CEREBRAL SOUS VIDE

✓ How can I use humor to ease tension and build stronger connections?
✓ When did shared laughter last strengthen my team, and how can I create more moments like that?
✓ What one adjustment in my humor style could make me more approachable?

THE SELF-SERVE STATION

Who said work has to be all business? These reads will show you how humor can drive creativity, build connection, and make work way more enjoyable (for everyone):

Humor, Seriously: Why Humor Is a Secret Weapon in Business and Life by Jennifer Aaker and Naomi Bagdonas (2021) – Two Stanford professors walk into a boardroom . . . and prove that humor isn't just for comedians. Packed with research, case studies, and strategies that'll make you rethink everything you thought you knew about workplace levity.

Humor That Works: The Missing Skill for Success and Happiness at Work by Andrew Tarvin (2019) – Humor isn't just fun—it's functional. Tarvin delivers real-world strategies to boost effectiveness, engagement, and workplace culture, proving that a little laughter can lead to serious results.

The Humor Code: A Global Search for What Makes Things Funny by Peter McGraw and Joel Warner (2014) – Ever wonder why some jokes land while others crash harder than a reply-all email fail? This global investigation into humor's mechanics offers insights that'll transform your communication game. Perfect for anyone who's ever wondered why we laugh and how to use that knowledge strategically.

Yes, And: Lessons from The Second City by Kelly Leonard and Tom Yorton (2015) – Second City's masterclass in turning improv principles into business gold. Less about becoming a comedian, more about becoming an agile communicator who can handle any corporate curveball with grace and wit.

The Humor Habit: Rewire Your Brain to Stress Less, Laugh More, and Achieve More by Paul Osincup (2024) – Humor isn't just a talent—it's a habit. Osincup breaks down how to train your brain for levity, offering practical strategies to boost resilience, productivity, and workplace culture—one well-timed laugh at a time.

A SWEET & SAVORY SHOUT-OUT

Dr. Rod A. Martin changed the game in workplace humor research. I mean, this guy was destined for comedy with a name like Dr. Rod, am I right? His groundbreaking 'Humor Styles Questionnaire' reshaped how we understand humor's impact on team dynamics.

His seminal book *The Psychology of Humor: An Integrative Approach in Work, Life, and Clinical Practice* became the definitive text on how humor shapes our professional and personal interactions. Martin systematically demonstrated how different types of humor either enhance or undermine workplace relationships, team cohesion, and individual well-being. The affiliative and self-enhancing styles, in particular, show significant positive correlations with psychological well-being and social relationship satisfaction.

What sets Martin apart is his ability to translate complex psychological concepts into practical insights. His research identifies how humor serves multiple functions in the workplace: building relationships, reducing stress, enhancing creativity, and creating psychological safety. He demonstrated that humor is more than making people laugh—it's a sophisticated social tool that can transform workplace dynamics.

Martin's work revealed that individuals who effectively use positive humor styles (affiliative and self-enhancing) report higher levels of self-esteem, greater relationship satisfaction, and improved emotional well-being. His studies also uncovered how negative humor styles (aggressive and self-defeating) can damage team dynamics and workplace relationships. Reminder: don't do these!

Perhaps most importantly, Martin's research established humor as a measurable, learnable skill rather than just an innate trait. His work shows that people can develop more effective humor styles through awareness and practice, leading to better interpersonal outcomes.

Thanks, Dr. Rod! Sometimes the best way to achieve serious results is to take ourselves a little less seriously.

10 QUICK BITES

- Strategic humor isn't about constant jokes—it's about using levity to shift energy, build trust, and ease tension.

- In a world where AI can automate almost everything, humor remains a uniquely human superpower.

- Your ability to connect with people determines your influence. Humor makes you memorable, not just competent.

- Humor and gravitas aren't opposites—leaders like Doug Conant prove they work together to create memorable leadership.

- A comprehensive meta-analysis spanning 49 studies shows that strategic humor boosts work performance, job satisfaction, and team cohesion.

- Humor flattens hierarchies, making leaders more relatable—Stanford research shows teams with humor-driven leadership report higher collaboration, trust, and risk-taking.

- Laughter releases oxytocin (bonding hormone), endorphins (mood boosters), and dopamine while reducing cortisol—literally enhancing creativity, problem-solving, and physical health.

- Authenticity is key—as bareMinerals' former CEO Leslie Blodgett says: "If you're not a joke teller, don't practice joke telling. Practice being yourself."

- Like seasoning in a dish, humor requires balance—too little is bland, too much overwhelms, but just right transforms the experience.

- Master humor in leadership, and you won't just make work more enjoyable—you'll make it more effective.

Common Obstacle:
"Humor feels forced or inauthentic."

Quick Fix:
Start with self-deprecating observations about universal experiences

Long-term:
Build a collection of genuine stories from your own work journey

---

Common Obstacle:
"Our team is resistant to lighthearted moments."

Quick Fix:
Begin meetings with a brief share of the week's most absurd challenge

Long-term:
Create structured opportunities for connection through shared experience

---

Common Obstacle:
"I'm worried that my humor won't land."

Quick Fix:
Start small—use light observational humor about shared experiences

Long-term:
Pay attention to what gets genuine smiles and refine your approach

HUMILITY

APPETIZER

Tired of leaders who never admit mistakes? Wondering why some executives inspire deep loyalty while others just demand it? We'll humbly explore humility—because strength isn't about having all the answers, but about asking the right questions.

MAIN COURSE

Mirror, Mirror: Master authentic
self-awareness for stronger leadership
Trust Currency: Build credibility through genuine humility
The Curiosity's Edge: Transform listening
into your leadership superpower

DESSERT

The "I Don't Know" Challenge: Master the art
of turning uncertainty into collaboration
The Credit Catapult: Amplify others' achievements
The Feedback Fishing Expedition: Transform
critique into concrete opportunities for growth

PAIRS WELL WITH

Teams thirsting for authentic leadership
Your collection of well-earned mistakes
Anyone who thinks vulnerability is weakness
(prepare to be surprised)

CHAPTER 7

Humility—The Master's Mindset

THE QUARTERLY ALL-HANDS meeting is in full swing. You're confidently walking through next year's strategy when the new hire, Ashley, raises her hand. "I think there might be a flaw in those market projections," she says, voice slightly shaking. The room holds its breath, waiting to see if you'll serve up the corporate equivalent of "Do you know who I am?" Instead, you pause, smile, and say, "Tell me more."

That single moment of genuine humility just reinforced or transformed your company culture more effectively than a year's worth of team-building exercises.

Let's be honest—humility rarely gets the spotlight in a world obsessed with swagger. In a culture where 'Fake it 'til you make it' is a mantra, confidence is often mistaken for competence, and humility can feel as welcome as a food critic at a family barbecue. But here's the thing: while confidence might open the door, it's humility that keeps people in the room. And like any master chef knows, the most powerful ingredients often work their magic in the background, enhancing every other element of the dish without overwhelming it.

Humility isn't a sign of weakness—it's a key ingredient that separates good leaders from great ones, meaningful connections from superficial networking, and sustainable success from flash-in-the-pan achievements. And contrary to popular belief, it's the foundation of genuine confidence, not its opposite.

Let's drop some knowledge, shall we? A study published in the *Journal of Management* found that humble leaders foster tighter teams, higher engagement, and more creative problem-solving.[96]

In other words, humility could be the difference between being the boss everyone avoids and the leader people would run through a wall for (though please don't test that literally).

What sounds nice in theory—and feels even better in practice—actually translates directly to business results. A qualitative study published in the *Academy of Management Journal* by Owens and Hekman (2012) highlights that humble leadership behaviors can foster organizational growth and team effectiveness. These findings have been referenced by the University of Washington Foster School of Business, which further reported that companies led by humble CEOs tend to achieve superior performance outcomes, including higher returns on assets and increased market share in niche sectors.[97]

That's right—those "aw, shucks" moments might just be padding your company's bank account.

Even more compelling, in a world where change is the only constant and "disruption" is less a buzzword and more a way of life, humility is your ticket to staying relevant. According to an *American Journal of Health Promotion* paper, humble leaders are more likely to be open to new ideas and continuous learning—essential traits required in our rapidly evolving business landscape.[98] Think of humility as your self-updating OS, constantly integrating new perspectives and adapting to change.

Like many lessons in this book, I learned this one the hard way. A few years ago, I was leading a program rollout with a group of sales executives. I had run dozens of these before and walked in confident—borderline cocky—about how the session would unfold. My approach was structured, my slides polished, and I was sure I had thought through every possible challenge.

Then, halfway through, a regional director raised her hand. "I don't think this applies to our market at all," she said. My instinct? Push back—I had the data, after all! But something in her tone made me pause. Instead of launching into a defense, I took a breath and said, "Tell me more."

She described specific customer behaviors in her region that challenged my assumptions. Then, others chimed in with their own insights. What I had designed as a top-down rollout was quickly turning into a real-time strategy session. So, instead of doubling down on my framework, I pivoted. I started asking better questions, incorporating their feedback, and by the end of the session, we had co-created a revised approach that actually worked for them.

That moment changed how I lead. I realized humility isn't about underselling yourself—it's about being open enough to course-correct in real-time. And as I learned that day, sometimes the strongest leadership move isn't defending your expertise. It's knowing when to listen.

As it turns out, the most innovative companies already understand this. Ed Catmull, co-founder of Pixar, built humility into the company's DNA. In *Creativity, Inc.*, he explains how fostering a culture of openness to feedback was crucial to Pixar's success. Their "Braintrust" meetings—where even junior employees critique projects—have helped create some of the most beloved (and profitable) animated films ever. As Catmull puts it, "If there are people in your organization who feel they're not free to suggest ideas, you lose."[99]

And that principle applies far beyond animation. It's a cornerstone of great leadership.

In this chapter, we'll explore three essential elements of humility that can transform your communication and leadership. First, we'll dive into *Mirror, Mirror*, discovering how authentic self-awareness creates the foundation for genuine connection and growth. Then, we'll explore *Trust Currency*, revealing why humility might be your fastest route to building lasting credibility. Finally, we'll examine *Curiosity's Edge*, exploring how humility turns listening into a superpower that drives innovation and creates an environment where meaningful dialogue flourishes.

Remember that new hire, Ashley, who spoke up at the all-hands? Six months later, her insight helped the company pivot to capture an emerging market opportunity worth millions. More importantly, her example inspired others to speak up, turning quarterly meetings from monologues into genuine dialogues. That's the power of humility in action. It doesn't just improve your communication; it transforms the entire conversational menu.

So, let's set ego aside and explore how humility, when properly applied, might be your most powerful leadership ingredient. After all, in a world overflowing with self-proclaimed "thought leaders" and "influencers," the most influential words you can say might be: "I could be wrong. What do you think?"

THREE MAIN DISHES

Mirror, Mirror

JUST AS A chef needs a clean mirror to check their presentation before service, authentic self-awareness reflects who we truly are—strengths, weaknesses, and blind spots included. According to research by Owens and Hekman published in *The Academy of Management Journal*, humility enables leaders to recognize both their capabilities and limitations, leading to more informed decisions and better results.[100]

When you communicate with genuine humility, you create space for honest self-reflection. As Argandoña's research in the *Journal of Business Ethics* demonstrates, humble leaders remain more receptive to feedback, allowing them to identify and address blind spots.[101] Does this sound like your boss? Or, honestly... you?

This isn't about self-deprecation or humblebragging—it's about self-honesty. Nielsen, Marrone, and Slay's conceptual research in the *Journal of Leadership & Organizational Studies* underscores humility as a core component of socialized charismatic leadership, influencing how leaders view themselves and engage with others.[102]

Building on this foundation, a recent empirical study published in *Frontiers in Psychology* demonstrates that humble leaders with high emotional intelligence are better equipped to mitigate employee conflict and foster stronger, more collaborative team relationships.[103]

This synthesis of conceptual and empirical insights shows how humility, when paired with emotional intelligence, enhances leadership effectiveness and team cohesion. It's like having a well-calibrated sense of your own impact: not too bland (underselling yourself), and not too overpowering (masking insecurity with bravado).

The practical implications are clear: When you communicate with genuine humility, you demonstrate both confidence and vulnerability. This balanced approach creates an environment where others feel safe to be equally authentic. For organizations, it fosters a culture where self-reflection leads to more thoughtful decisions and stronger team culture.

Take Ray Dalio, founder of Bridgewater Associates. He built his company's culture around "radical transparency," where everyone—himself included—is expected to acknowledge mistakes and knowledge gaps. This practice isn't just about openness; it's about humility. In *Principles*, Dalio writes, "Successful people are those who can go above themselves to see things objectively and manage those things to shape change."[104] That kind of self-awareness—grounded in the humility to admit what you don't know—is what helped Bridgewater become one of the most influential firms in its industry.

True humility isn't thinking less of yourself—it's thinking about yourself less. When you get the seasoning right, humility transforms from a seemingly soft skill into your secret sauce for sustainable success.

However, this is just the start to what makes humility work. Self-awareness alone isn't enough. You can know your strengths and weaknesses inside and out, but if your team doesn't trust you, none of it matters. That's where humility turns from an internal advantage into an external superpower—building credibility, connection, and influence.

Trust Currency

2 **IN A BUSINESS** world seasoned with skepticism, humility might not seem like a credibility booster. But research proves otherwise: a recent study in *Behavioral Sciences* found that humble leaders are not only perceived as more approachable, but also foster greater team harmony and collaboration. When paired with emotional intelligence, humility helps reduce conflict and strengthens team dynamics—key ingredients for higher engagement and morale.[105]

Consider the simple act of saying "I don't know" or "I made a mistake." These moments of vulnerability aren't signs of weakness—they're demonstrations of strength that build authentic connections. Amy Edmondson's research at Harvard Business School reveals that leaders who openly acknowledge errors and actively seek input create environments of psychological safety where innovation thrives.[106] When you communicate with genuine humility, people don't just hear you—they believe in you.

This trust-building effect extends throughout organizations. A meta-analysis published in the *Journal of Organizational Behavior* demonstrates that humble

"If there are people in your organization who feel they're not free to suggest ideas, you lose."

— Ed Catmull

Patagonia: The Power of Corporate Humility[107]

The Challenge: Build a sustainable business while openly acknowledging the inherent environmental impact of manufacturing and selling consumer goods.

The Approach: Under Yvon Chouinard's leadership, Patagonia embraced radical transparency about their environmental shortcomings while actively working to minimize them. Their "Don't Buy This Jacket" campaign on Black Friday 2011 openly discouraged excessive consumption of their own products. In 2022, Chouinard transferred ownership of the $3 billion company to a trust and nonprofit dedicated to fighting climate change, demonstrating unprecedented corporate humility.

The Result:

- Following the 2011 "Don't Buy This Jacket" campaign, Patagonia saw a 30% increase in sales, proving consumer support for its environmental stance.
- The campaign strengthened customer loyalty by reinforcing Patagonia's reputation as a sustainable and ethical brand.
- By 2022, the company grew to $3 billion in revenue while maintaining premium margins, showing that profitability and purpose can coexist.

The Take-Home Recipe:

- Own your flaws—they're your best teachers.
- Let your mission trump your ego.
- Turn weaknesses into opportunities.

leadership helps bridge hierarchical gaps, strengthening bonds across all levels and reducing communication barriers.[108] When leaders practice humility, information flows more freely, and collaboration becomes natural rather than forced.

Just look at Alan Mulally's leadership at Ford during the 2008 financial crisis. When he took over as CEO, Ford's culture discouraged admitting problems. There was no trust. Alan Mulally changed this by introducing a simple yet powerful practice: in executive meetings, he celebrated leaders who reported challenges rather than hiding them. In one notable instance, when an executive admitted to a major production issue, Mulally applauded—literally. This gesture marked a turning point, fostering a culture of trust and transparency that helped Ford become the only major U.S. automaker to avoid bankruptcy during the financial crisis.[109]

You can't mandate trust—it must be earned through consistent demonstrations of humble, authentic leadership. When you get this essential ingredient right, everything else in your organizational recipe becomes more effective, from innovation to execution. The trust multiplier effect isn't just about being liked—it's about building the credibility that turns good leaders into transformative ones.

Trust lays the foundation. But humility isn't just about trust—it's also about curiosity.

Curiosity's Edge

3 **LIKE A MASTER** chef who tastes each component before combining them, humble leaders understand that true wisdom comes from perpetual curiosity. Research published in the *Harvard Business Review* by Francesca Gino demonstrates that curious, humble leaders are more likely to actively listen to their teams,[110] creating an environment where every voice adds flavor to the final result. (And a nice prelude to Chapter 8!)

When leaders approach conversations with humility, they transform standard interactions into opportunities for discovery. According to insight published in the *Journal of Applied Psychology*, teams led by humble leaders report significantly higher levels of psychological safety and knowledge sharing.[111] It's as if humility acts as a natural tenderizer, breaking down the tough barriers that often prevent open communication.

The organizational impact is substantial. Research in *Organization Science* reveals that humble leadership fosters a culture of curiosity and continuous learning, directly contributing to innovation and team performance.[112] Microsoft's Satya Nadella exemplifies this approach. After taking over as CEO in 2014, he shifted the company's culture from "know-it-alls" to "learn-it-alls."[113] This humble approach helped transform Microsoft's market value from $300 billion to over $2 trillion, proving that curiosity and humility can fuel unprecedented growth.

In a world increasingly dominated by artificial intelligence and automated responses, this human capacity for humble curiosity might just be our most valuable asset. Humility amplifies curiosity, and curiosity fuels innovation. After all, you can't google your way to genuine understanding—that requires the kind of deep listening that only humility can inspire. Just ask our political leaders!

FIVE TASTE-TEST RECIPES

Humility isn't just a nice trait—it's a leadership cheat code. Try one of these ideas, stack them like a winning poker hand, or keep them holstered for the perfect mic-drop moment when humility turns a challenge into a breakthrough.

1 **The "I Don't Know" Challenge:** For one week, acknowledge uncertainty at least once per day. When you don't know something, say it directly—then follow with 'I'll find out' or 'What do you think?' Turn knowledge gaps into opportunities for collaboration.

2 **The Credit Catapult:** In team meetings, highlight the unsung heroes. Skip the generic praise—pinpoint exactly how someone's contribution moved the project forward or made an impact.

3 **The Reverse Mentoring Program:** Have a junior colleague teach you something new—whether it's emerging technology, market insights, or evolving methodologies. Position yourself explicitly as the learner rather than the expert.

4 **The Failure Fess-Up:** Share recent mistakes with your team, focusing on lessons and improvements. Frame the conversation around specific changes implemented, creating space for others to view errors as growth opportunities.

5 **The Feedback Fishing Expedition:** Actively seek improvement-focused feedback across organizational levels. Rather than asking for general input, request specific insights about particular projects or behaviors. Demonstrate genuine appreciation for candid responses, especially in growth areas.

LAST CALL

Humility isn't about diminishing your accomplishments—it's about making space for collective excellence. Like a chef who understands that every ingredient plays a crucial role, effective leaders recognize that success comes from orchestrating talent rather than hogging the spotlight. True humility amplifies rather than diminishes leadership impact.

In this chapter, you've learned how humility strengthens leadership through three vital elements: *Mirror Mirror*, which revealed how self-awareness enhances decision-making; *Trust Currency*, which showed how vulnerability builds authentic connections; and *Curiosity's Edge*, which demonstrated how humble inquiry drives innovation. You've discovered that leadership humility isn't just admirable—it creates measurable improvements in team psychological safety, organizational learning, and sustainable success.

As you develop your leadership recipe, remember that the best chefs let their dishes speak for themselves. Your influence grows when you focus on elevating others. The kitchen thrives when every cook has room to contribute their best. And if all else fails, just confidently say, "That was intentional," and move on.

CEREBRAL SOUS VIDE

- ✓ What's one way I can give visible credit to someone else this week?
- ✓ How would embracing "I don't know" improve my credibility in tough situations?
- ✓ How do I show that I value learning from my team, and how can I do this more often?

THE SELF-SERVE STATION

Does humility sound like taking a backseat? Far from it. These resources show how leading with humility builds trust, inspires loyalty, and takes teams to the next level while keeping you in the pole position:

Leaders Eat Last: Why Some Teams Pull Together and Others Don't by Simon Sinek (2014) – Think leadership is about office dimensions and convenient parking spots? Sinek flips the script by showing why true leaders are more interested in filling their team's plates than their own. A wake-up call for anyone who thinks the best view is from the top of the ladder.

Humble Leadership by Edgar H. Schein and Peter A. Schein (2018) – Being an all-knowing boss is so 2004. This game-changing book proves it. The Scheins show how humble leadership creates the psychological safety that drives innovation. It's your complete guide to turning vulnerability into organizational velocity.

Daring Greatly by Brené Brown (2012) – Want to know why some leaders inspire unprecedented loyalty while others just inspire updated resumes? Brown's research reveals how embracing vulnerability—humility's close cousin—transforms both leadership and organizational culture. Learn how showing up as authentically human becomes a superpower.

Ego Is the Enemy by Ryan Holiday (2016) – Think success requires an oversized ego? Holiday's masterful blend of ancient wisdom and modern case studies reveals how the world's most effective leaders succeed through continuous learning rather than self-promotion. Warning: may cause unexpected outbreaks of genuine collaboration.

WorkLife podcast by Adam Grant – When a renowned organizational psychologist dives deep into how intellectual humility drives innovation, you listen. Grant's evidence-based exploration of humble leadership will transform how you think about power, influence, and organizational success.

A SWEET & SAVORY SHOUT-OUT

A heartfelt tribute to Jim Collins, whose groundbreaking research redefined our understanding of leadership excellence. His work, especially the concept of "Level 5 Leadership" introduced in *Good to Great*, revolutionized how we view the relationship between humility and business success.

Collins and his research team spent five years studying 1,435 Fortune 500 companies, ultimately identifying 11 that made the leap from good to great. Their surprising discovery? The leaders driving these transformations weren't charismatic celebrities, but humble, determined individuals who combined personal humility with unwavering professional will.

What sets Collins apart is his dedication to letting data challenge conventional wisdom. His research revealed that companies led by humble, Level 5 leaders outperformed the market by seven times over 15 years compared to their more egotistical counterparts. This finding fundamentally challenged the myth of the larger-than-life CEO.

Collins' "window and mirror" concept nails humble leadership: great leaders look out the window to credit others, and in the mirror to own their mistakes. His research shattered the myth that humility is a weakness and showed it for what it is—the foundation of lasting success.

The impact of Collins' work continues to ripple through boardrooms and beyond, reminding us that transformative leadership isn't about commanding the spotlight, but about creating the conditions for others to shine. In a world obsessed with personal branding and self-promotion, Collins showed us something profound: true greatness isn't achieved through ego, but through its absence.

You go, JC!

10 QUICK BITES

- While confidence might open the door, humility keeps people in the room and serves as the foundation for genuine success.

- A study in the *Journal of Management* found that humble leaders foster tighter teams, higher engagement, and more creative problem-solving.

- Companies led by humble CEOs tend to achieve superior performance outcomes, including higher returns on assets and increased market share in niche sectors.

- Humble leaders are more likely to be open to new ideas and continuous learning—essential traits in our rapidly evolving business landscape.

- Humility enables leaders to recognize both their capabilities and limitations, leading to more informed decisions and better results.

- Harvard research reveals that leaders who openly acknowledge errors and actively seek input create environments of psychological safety where innovation thrives.

- A meta-analysis in the *Journal of Organizational Behavior* demonstrates that humble leadership helps bridge hierarchical gaps, strengthening bonds across all levels.

- *Harvard Business Review* research shows curious, humble leaders are more likely to actively listen to their teams.

- Teams led by humble leaders report significantly higher levels of psychological safety and knowledge sharing.

- Research reveals that humble leadership fosters a culture of curiosity and continuous learning, directly contributing to innovation and team performance.

Common Obstacle:

"I'm afraid of appearing weak as a leader."

Quick Fix:

Start by openly acknowledging one area where you need help

Long-term:

Create regular forums where vulnerability is modeled and celebrated

---

Common Obstacle:

"I struggle to balance confidence with humility."

Quick Fix:

Replace "I know" statements with "I think" or "What are your thoughts?"

Long-term:

Build reflection practices that examine both successes and failures

---

Common Obstacle:

"My team is hesitant to speak up with feedback."

Quick Fix:

Actively celebrate the next person who challenges your thinking

Long-term:

Establish structured feedback processes that normalize constructive criticism

LISTENING

APPETIZER

In a world of constant chatter, true listening has become our... Wait! Did you hear that? Well you will after this discourse on listening. Better leadership starts not with talking, but with tuning in, and transforming your listening from background noise to game-changing insight.

MAIN COURSE

The Listening Brain: Discover how brains sync for genuine understanding
Leveled Up: Master the four levels of listening ninja-hood
Resonance Recipe: Build a culture where listening creates breakthrough results

DESSERT

The Three Dimensions Practice: Note the words, emotions, and unspoken desires
The Echo & Enhance Technique: Reflect back and dig deeper
The Clear Focus Challenge: Eliminate distractions for five full minutes

PAIRS WELL WITH

Marathon meetings with zero progress
Leaders who mistake volume for value
Your tendency to finish other people's...

CHAPTER 8

Listening—The Taste Test

YOU KNOW WHAT we all hear all the time but never actually feel? "I hear you." Three simple words that we toss around like spare change, yet rarely spend. In an age where everyone's talking, posting, streaming, and broadcasting, the art of truly listening has become as rare as a Real Housewife with her original jawline.

Here's a sobering thought: we spend 70-80% of our workday communicating, with nearly half of that time spent 'listening'—but research shows we retain only 25% of what we hear.[114]

That means most of our conversations are just noise, meetings turn into game-of-telephone disasters, and critical details slip through the cracks before we even hit "mute." We think we're listening, but in reality, we're just waiting for our turn to talk.

Let me take you back to two moments that transformed my understanding of listening. The first was in 2003, walking into my first improv class at Second City in New York. I arrived armed with what I thought was comedy gold—a mental archive of pre-planned jokes and witty responses. My instructor, Kevin Scott (still one of the funniest humans I've ever met), watched me crash and burn through my first scene. His feedback? "Coming to the stage with a preconceived notion of what to say is the fastest way to kill a scene—and a guarantee you won't be funny." The lesson was clear: real comedy, like real connection, comes from listening and responding authentically, not from waiting to deliver your prepared material.

The second wake-up call came a year later, in 2004, from my sales mentor Dan (let's call him that because that's his name). After watching me deliver what I thought was a masterful pitch to a potential client, he hit me with an unforgettable truth bomb: "After a great sales call, you don't come back with a sore throat. You come back with sore ears."

Both lessons hit the same nerve. I was so focused on what I wanted to say that I wasn't really listening. In improv, this meant missed opportunities for genuine comedy. In sales, it meant missed opportunities to understand what customers actually needed. The solution in both cases? Shut up and listen. Not the passive, waiting-for-your-turn-to-talk kind of listening, but the active, fully engaged kind that makes connections come alive.

Research confirms that effective listening drives organizational success. A 2016 study by Zenger and Folkman found that leaders who listen well are perceived as more effective, leading to higher engagement and increased innovation.[115] Gallup reports that organizations with high employee engagement experience significant increases in productivity and profitability.[116] Furthermore, organizations that actively engage with employee feedback tend to experience lower turnover.[117]

Marriott International proves this principle at scale. Through its *Serve 360* initiative, the company prioritized employee well-being and structured listening into its culture. This approach helped Marriott secure a spot on Fortune's "100 Best Companies to Work For" list for 25 consecutive years. By implementing ongoing feedback systems and regular engagement check-ins, the company created a culture where every voice had the opportunity to be heard. Their efforts helped Marriott solidify their reputation as a leader in employee engagement and organizational resilience.[118]

In this chapter, we'll build off the success companies like Marriott have had and explore three transformative dimensions of listening that can revolutionize your communication. First, in *The Listening Brain*, we'll examine how neurological research reveals the science behind truly engaged listening. Next, in *Leveled Up*, we'll unlock the four distinct levels that separate casual hearing from deep understanding. Finally, in *Resonance Recipes*, we'll investigate how to create environments where authentic listening resonates throughout an organization and amplifies every voice.

My fellow Second City "alum" (who sadly never quite reached my level of obscurity) Tina Fey shared a memorable line in *Bossypants*: "I have a great gynecologist who is as gifted at listening as she is at rectal exams."[119] Oddly enough, there's a sharp insight buried in the punchline: great listening is a skill, and often an underappreciated one. In business—just like in improv—it's not just about hearing words. It's about being fully present, tuning into tone, body language, and all those unspoken signals that elevate a good decision into a great one.

So—ready to level up your listening? (And yes, I get the irony—you're listening with your eyes. Unless this is the audiobook, in which case, I assume they got Jon Hamm to narrate. It's gotta be Hamm, right? That voice could sell ice to a penguin.)

THREE MAIN DISHES

The Listening Brain

1 **WHEN TWO PEOPLE** truly connect through conversation, something remarkable happens in their brains. It's not just metaphorical when we say we're "on the same wavelength"—neuroimaging reveals that during moments of deep listening, our neural patterns actually synchronize with those of the speaker in what scientists call "neural coupling."[120] This isn't just fascinating neuroscience; it's the biological foundation of genuine understanding.

Think about the last time you truly felt heard. That deep connection? It wasn't just in your head. Well, actually, it was, but in a much more literal way than you'd expect. When we engage in deep listening, multiple regions of our brain fire up simultaneously, creating a complex symphony of neural activity that enhances both comprehension and empathy.[121] This biological boost to understanding is what transforms casual conversation into meaningful connection.

But here's where it gets even more compelling for professionals: managers that demonstrate strong listening skills foster what researchers describe as a "person-oriented" or "considerate" leadership style. This kind of attentive listening not only enhances how leaders are perceived—it also positively influences team dynamics, improving both productivity and collaborative problem-solving.[122] In effect, active listening helps create a shared cognitive space that supports innovation and effective communication.

The biological impact goes even deeper. During these moments of genuine listening and connection, our brains release oxytocin—often called the "trust hormone"—which strengthens social bonds and catalyzes collaboration.[123] This isn't just team building; it's brain chemistry at work.

The implications for workplace relationships are profound. When we understand that listening isn't just a soft skill but a neurological event, we can approach it with the same precision we'd use in following a complex recipe. Every moment of genuine attention becomes an opportunity to literally sync minds with our colleagues, creating the neural foundations for trust, innovation, and collective success. And let's be honest— who doesn't love a good neural connection?

Understanding the neuroscience of listening is fascinating. But knowing how to put it into practice is what separates good communicators from great leaders. Now this is getting juicy!

2 CASUAL LISTENING IS like fast food—it fills a gap, but you're missing out on a real meal. When you start climbing the listening ladder, you're moving from toaster strudel to crème brûlée. Let's break down the four essential "courses" of listening that transform workplace conversations from bland exchanges into rich experiences that nourish innovation and understanding.

Level 1: The Drive-Thru Listener—In many professional environments, communication often lacks depth, with exchanges focusing more on efficiency than engagement.[124] This creates a fast-food culture of communication where speed trumps substance. We've all done it—half-listening while mentally drafting an email or deciding what's for lunch. This is the workplace equivalent of eating a burger while driving. You're getting the calories, but you're missing the meal. (And spilling ketchup on your blouse.)

Level 2: The Casual Café Listener—Here's where you start actually sitting down for the meal. You're present, making eye contact, maybe even nodding along. But like a distracted diner checking their phone between bites, you're still mostly focused on formulating your response rather than truly understanding what's being shared.[125] It's better than drive-thru listening, but you're still missing the subtle flavors of true understanding.

Level 3: The Bistro Listener—Now we're cooking! At this level, you're not just hearing words—you're picking up on tone, body language, and unspoken cues, the ingredients that give communication its real zest. Like a skilled chef tasting every component of a dish, you're actively processing both verbal and non-verbal signals, which is essential for reducing workplace miscommunication. Leaders who excel in active listening are perceived as more effective by their teams, fostering better communication and collaboration, and those who cultivate strong listening habits often find it easier to build trust and lead through change.[126]

"Most people do not listen with the intent to understand; they listen with the intent to reply."

— Stephen Covey

Lincoln Financial: The Power of Being Heard[127]

The Challenge: Enhance employee engagement and satisfaction within a large financial services organization.

The Approach: Lincoln Financial implemented a comprehensive employee listening strategy that spans the entire employee lifecycle. This includes regular company-wide engagement surveys covering aspects such as leadership, benefits, career growth, and well-being. Additionally, they conduct monthly pulse surveys, host input sessions, and facilitate both formal and informal forums between employees and senior leadership. This multidimensional approach ensures that employee voices are heard and acted upon.

The Result:

- Regular engagement surveys and feedback mechanisms have increased employee engagement, fostering a more motivated and committed workforce.
- Consistent feedback loops between employees and senior leadership have enhanced trust and transparency across the organization.
- Cultivated a responsive culture, contributing to long-term organizational resilience and success.

The Take-Home Recipe:

- Make listening a ritual, not an event.
- Build trust through open doors and open minds.
- Transform feedback into visible change.

Level 4: The Master Chef Listener — This is where listening becomes an art form. Like a master chef who understands not just the ingredients they use but how they interact, you're tuning into the complete experience—words, emotions, context, and implications. Organizations that prioritize this level of listening report higher engagement and better problem-solving outcomes[128], as great listeners create an environment where innovation and understanding thrive. Listening transcends skill and becomes instinct. (Cue the choir of angels singing.)

While understanding and working to progress through these listening levels is crucial, the next challenge lies in creating environments where deep listening becomes part of the organizational DNA.

Resonance Recipes

3 IN HIS CLASSIC work, *The 7 Habits of Highly Effective People*, Stephen Covey observed something profound about human conversation: "Most people do not listen with the intent to understand; they listen with the intent to reply."[129] This insight reveals our fundamental challenge: creating environments where true listening becomes the norm, not the exception. Like a master chef who knows great cuisine depends on both ingredients and atmosphere, leaders must cultivate organizational cultures where deep listening can flourish.

This shows up best in high-performing teams who exhibit what scientists call "conversational turn-taking."[130] Think of it as passing dishes around a shared table, ensuring everyone gets a chance to both serve and be served. At its core, this is about listening—not just waiting for your turn to talk, but actively creating space for others to contribute. When this balance is achieved, teams develop rhythms of speaking and listening that build trust, encourage participation, and transform group dynamics.

There's good evidence to support this, too. Psychological safety thrives when people feel heard, not just spoken to. When organizations prioritize this, teams solve problems faster and innovate more.[131] Google's *Project Aristotle* found this was the defining trait of high-performing teams—not just raw intelligence, but the ability to create an environment where every voice matters.[132]

Harvard's Amy Edmondson calls these workplaces "innovation incubators," where people feel safe to speak up, challenge ideas, and take risks without fear of embarrassment or punishment.[133] But you can't really speak up if no one is listening. You know what the old adage says: if an employee voices a concern in an open office, but everyone's wearing noise-canceling headphones, does it make an impact?

Even office design plays a role. Bernstein and Turban found that open offices designed to foster collaboration often do the opposite, creating more distractions and worse communication.[134] Smart organizations create dedicated spaces for focused listening. And the impact is clear: organizations that prioritize strong listening cultures experience higher employee engagement and improved productivity.

Creating a listening-rich culture isn't just about policy—it's about practice. Organizations must continually refine their listening practices through regular feedback systems, structured listening sessions, and leaders who model deep listening in every interaction. When these elements come together, organizations create environments where listening becomes instinctive and innovation thrives—or at least where people stop pretending to take notes while actually reordering their pet supplies.

FIVE TASTE-TEST RECIPES

Listening. It's an art, a science, and honestly, one of the hardest skills to master (I get it—you have important things to say!). These recipes offer tools to deepen your listening skills and be heard, too. Explore them one at a time, mix them up, or create your own variation.

1 **The Three Dimensions Practice:** After each meaningful conversation, note three things: main takeaways, emotional undercurrents, and unstated desires. This practice sharpens your ability to read between the lines, turning casual exchanges into deeper connections.

2 **The Echo & Enhance Technique:** Before responding, reflect back what you've heard in your own words. "What I'm understanding from what you've shared is..." Follow up with a thoughtful "how" or "when" question to dig deeper—this small step can turn a good conversation into a great one.

3 **The Build & Bridge Session:** Run meetings with two golden rules: build on others' ideas before sharing your own, and use "Yes, and..." to keep ideas flowing. Watch how your team transforms from isolated thinking to rich collaboration.

4 **The Deep Dive Dialogue:** Schedule one deep conversation per week with a colleague you'd like to understand better. Create space for real connection and unexpected insights. These conversations often serve up the most unexpected and valuable ideas.

5 **The Clear Focus Challenge:** During important conversations, eliminate all distractions—no phone, no email, no multitasking. Like cleansing your palate between courses, this reset helps you fully appreciate what's being served. Start with five minutes of complete attention and build from there.

LAST CALL

Active listening isn't about polite nodding—it's about detecting the subtle flavors in every conversation. Like a chef with a refined palate who can identify every spice in a dish, effective communicators know that true listening requires full engagement. Every conversation holds layers of meaning waiting to be uncovered. Mmm… just gobble them up!

In this chapter, you've learned how listening transforms communication through three essential elements: *The Listening Brain*, which explored how neural synchronization enhances understanding; *Leveled Up*, which showed how different depths of listening serve different purposes; and *Resonance Recipe*, which demonstrated how deep listening creates breakthrough insights. You've discovered that masterful listening is more than courteous—it creates measurable improvements in team alignment, problem-solving, and organizational intelligence.

As you refine your listening skills, remember that every conversation deserves your full attention. Your understanding deepens when you listen with intention rather than waiting to speak. True communication happens in the spaces between words. (And yes, we managed to get through this summary without a single "lettuce listen" pun… until now.)

CEREBRAL SOUS VIDE

✓ How often do I listen fully versus planning my next response?
✓ How well do I notice tone and body language in conversations?
✓ When did I last feel deeply engaged while listening, and what made it possible?

THE SELF-SERVE STATION

Can't hear what I'm saying? These resources will help you master the art of deep listening, transforming your conversations and unlocking stronger connections with your team:

Just Listen: Discover the Secret to Getting Through to Absolutely Anyone by Mark Goulston (2015) – Ever wonder why some leaders inspire unprecedented trust while others just inspire eye rolls? Goulston's deep dive into listening psychology reveals how genuine attention can become a leadership superpower.

You're Not Listening: What You're Missing and Why It Matters by Kate Murphy (2020) – Being a constant broadcaster is fine if you're an actual broadcaster. Murphy's fascinating exploration proves why turning down your mental noise might be the key to turning up your impact.

Crucial Conversations: Tools for Talking When Stakes Are High by Patterson, Grenny, McMillan, Switzler (2021) – Master the art of dialogue when it matters most. This practical guide shows how to transform high-stakes discussions from potential disasters into breakthrough moments of understanding.

Listen Like You Mean It: Reclaiming the Lost Art of True Connection by Ximena Vengoechea (2021) – A former tech executive reveals the hidden power of authentic listening. Through real-world examples and actionable techniques, learn to move beyond passive hearing to genuine understanding.

"What Great Listeners Actually Do" by Jack Zenger and Joseph Folkman (2016) – This groundbreaking *Harvard Business Review* article shatters common myths about listening. Based on research with over 3,000 participants, discover the surprising behaviors that separate good listeners from great ones.

A SWEET & SAVORY SHOUT-OUT

A standing ovation for Tina Fey, whose improv wisdom has shown us that active listening isn't just for the stage—it's a secret weapon in the boardroom, too. Fey's work, especially her book *Bossypants* and her time at Second City and Saturday Night Live, demonstrates how deep listening transforms the business world. (And while this was an easy fit, boy was it hard not to have her also headline the chapter on Humor, as well! This is one talented lady!)

Fey didn't just write a hilarious memoir. She provided a master-class in how genuine listening can transform communication and creativity in any setting. Her emphasis on being fully present and creating a supportive environment where every voice matters has applications far beyond comedy.

What sets Fey apart is her ability to blend humor with profound insights into authentic connection. She shows us that being a good listener isn't just about being polite—it's about creating an environment where understanding can flourish and every team member feels valued and heard.

Fey's approach to engagement and her emphasis on genuine presence over performance offer a powerful model for modern leadership. In her world, listening is about being present, not just about being quiet.

So, the next time you're in a conversation or trying to solve a tricky problem at work, channel your inner active listener. Listen intently, stay fully present, and don't be afraid to embrace silence in the pursuit of understanding.

In the spirit of genuine connection, let's raise our metaphorical glasses to listening with open ears and open minds—not just because it makes for great communication, but because it makes for great business too. Thanks, Tina, for showing us that in the world of business, sometimes the best way to get ahead is to stop talking and start listening. And maybe throw in a well-timed joke or two.

10 QUICK BITES

- During moments of deep listening, neural patterns actually synchronize between speaker and listener in what scientists call "neural coupling."

- While professionals spend nearly half their workday listening, research shows they retain only 25% of what they hear.

- Like moving from fast food to fine dining, effective listening progresses through four levels: Drive-Thru, Casual Café, Bistro, and Master Chef.

- A 2016 study found that leaders who listen well are perceived as more effective, leading to higher engagement and increased innovation.

- Psychological safety—confirmed by Google's Project Aristotle—was the defining trait of high-performing teams, not just raw intelligence.

- Open offices designed to foster collaboration often do the opposite, creating more distractions and worse communication.

- Organizations that prioritize listening cultures see measurable gains in employee engagement and productivity, as well as reduced turnover.

- During genuine listening and connection, brains release oxytocin— the "trust hormone"—which strengthens social bonds and catalyzes collaboration.

- High-performing teams practice "conversational turn-taking," ensuring every voice contributes to the collective dialogue.

- True listening requires presence and engagement, not just silence.

Common Obstacle:

"I find myself too busy planning responses to truly listen."

Quick Fix:

Count to three after each person speaks before responding

Long-term:

Practice improv exercises to build authentic response skills

Common Obstacle:

"My mind wanders during important conversations."

Quick Fix:

Take quick notes about body language and tone, not just words

Long-term:

Create dedicated "deep listening" spaces free from devices

Common Obstacle:

"I tend to dominate discussions out of enthusiasm."

Quick Fix:

Track your talk-time in your next three meetings

Long-term:

Build "listening rounds" into team meetings where each person gets uninterrupted time

ENERGY MANAGEMENT

APPETIZER

Why do some people breeze through the day while others feel like they're running on fumes by noon? The difference isn't willpower—it's energy management. Let's explore how to stop burning out and start fueling up in a way that keeps you steady, focused, and in control.

MAIN COURSE

Energy Triumphs: Discover why managing energy trumps managing time
Fuel Quadrant: Master the four dimensions of sustainable performance
Burnout Shield: Build a culture where strategic recovery creates breakthrough results

DESSERT

The Energy Tasting Menu: Check all four energy dimensions daily
The Seasonal Stock Rotation: Align tasks with your natural energy peaks
The "Yutori Plating" Technique: Create intentional white space for renewal

PAIRS WELL WITH

Back-to-back meetings with zero energy left
Teams running on fumes by 3 PM
Your overstuffed daily menu

CHAPTER 9

Energy Management— The Kitchen Flow

YOUR THIRD COFFEE of the day sits untouched as you stare at the presentation slides for a new product launch—reading the same bullet point for what feels like the millionth time. The words are doing that fun dance where they rearrange themselves into nonsense—probably revenge for skipping breakfast in favor of a 7 AM call with Singapore. You stand to head to the conference room, and whoa—the room decides to do a little spin, too. That's when you catch yourself deep in conversation with the office plant about Q4 projections. And the truly terrifying part? The plant's financial analysis is actually making more sense than your boss's.

Sadly, this is the world we have created. We have no one to blame but ourselves. Certainly not the Danes or the Fins. They get it. But us… we've mastered the art of cramming 25 hours of work into a 24-hour day, and we somehow forgot that humans aren't actually smartphones you can just plug in for a quick recharge when that day is done.

These numbers tell a story that might sound familiar. In a 2022 survey of 31,000 professionals across 31 countries, Microsoft found that over half acknowledged burnout as a growing problem, challenging the long-held belief that overwork is a badge of honor.[135] This burnout culture isn't just affecting our productivity—it's destroying our ability to connect and communicate effectively.

When your physical energy is depleted, your words slur and your body language screams "I'd rather be anywhere but here." Low emotional energy turns every minor piece of feedback into a potential drama series. Mental fatigue clouds your judgment like a chef who's lost their sense of taste, and without a sense of purpose and connection, your messages lack the authenticity that makes communication truly resonate. In our hyper-connected world, where every interaction is an opportunity to either build or burn bridges, running on fumes isn't just uncomfortable—it's professionally combustible.

The truth is, pushing harder isn't always the answer—it's usually just the fastest way to burn out. Just as a sushi master knows when to age the fish and when to serve it fresh, those who excel at managing their energy recognize the perfect balance between intense effort and necessary recuperation. A survey by The Energy Project and *Harvard Business Review* found that employees perform at their best when four core ingredients—physical, emotional, mental, and spiritual energy—are in sync.[136] You feeling in sync? (Don't answer that, Timberlake. And yes, I assume he bought a first edition run of this book—total fanboy.)

Unfortunately, most of us are not in sync. We're so focused on delivering results that we forget to recharge ourselves. Think of your professional energy like a well-stocked toolkit—you need more than just one tool to make magic happen. You've got your physical energy (your foundation), emotional energy (your resilience), mental energy (your focus), and spiritual energy (your purpose). When all four are ready to go, you're not just working—you're excelling. But if even one of these is out of whack... well, let's just say you're one step away from Chris Kirkpatrick's dreadlocks. Things are getting messy, and no one's quite sure why.

Enough of my boy band fetish—let me serve up a spicy dish of reality from my own leadership kitchen. During my first year leading global teams across Asia, I was obsessed with time management. My calendar looked like a doomsday prepper's daily schedule—surviving every minute, fortifying every hour, hoarding time like it was the last resource on Earth. My schedule was so airtight, even oxygen had to RSVP. Yet—between us friends—I honestly never felt productive. I was barely hanging on while pretending to have it all together.

The wake-up call came during a leadership meeting in our Tokyo office. I was running through my fourth consecutive presentation of the day, when I mixed up our quarterly revenue projections with last year's numbers... for Korea. Instead of owning the mistake, I caught myself blaming my back-to-back schedule. After the meeting, a seasoned team member pulled me aside and quietly asked, "In your pursuit of filling every minute, have you forgotten to fill yourself?" I was too exhausted to even make the obvious joke, but I had enough sense to at least ask him what he meant. He explained his culture's concept of "yutori"—the space between things that allows for renewal and growth.

Yutori hit me... hard. A master chef knows that you can't continuously reduce a sauce without occasionally adding fresh stock. But I was trying to concentrate my productivity while evaporating my vitality. I realized I had been treating my energy like an infinite resource when it was more like a seasonal well that needs regular replenishment.

I had to change. For the results I wanted. For my personal sanity. And for my team.

So I did. The spaces between meetings became my power stations. The gaps in my schedule, my recharge zones. I started going back to the gym and eating better (would have been hard to eat worse, in fairness), and I slowed down a bit. It became clear that it wasn't about surviving each minute—it was about having the energy to make every minute matter.

And look around. The stakes couldn't be higher... for all of us. Generally speaking, we make about 35,000 decisions every day—including about five that are really important![137] Each one of these decisions takes a little bite out of your energy reserves. It's no wonder we're all depleted by 3 PM! And just like you can't substitute rest with more caffeine, your brain can't make smart choices when it's running on fumes.

When decision fatigue kicks in, your judgment becomes questionable. Your decisions get increasingly erratic, and suddenly, replying-all to that company-wide email seems like a brilliant idea. Solving complex problems with a foggy mind might still technically be possible, but nobody's going to enjoy the results. And the impact goes beyond individual performance. One burnt-out manager can throw off the whole team, setting off a chain reaction. If one key player's energy tanks, the whole game can be lost.

In this chapter, we'll explore three game-saving approaches to energy management that transform how you work and lead. First, we'll dive into *Energy Triumphs*, discovering why energy mastery trumps time management for sustainable success. Then, we'll explore *Fuel Quadrant*, revealing how balancing four essential energy dimensions creates unstoppable momentum.

Finally, we'll examine *Burnout Shield*, uncovering how strategic energy protection doesn't just prevent burnout—it unleashes your full potential and helps you thrive in today's demanding workplace.

Treating your calendar like a sprint is a race you'll never win. It's time to stop running on fumes and start treating your energy like the VIP it is. Ready to upgrade from surviving to thriving? Let's do this—smarter, not harder.

THREE MAIN DISHES

Energy Triumphs

1 PICTURE TWO EXECUTIVES, Kylie and Jeff. Both brilliant, both ambitious, both working with the same 24 hours each day. Kylie's calendar looks like a game of Tetris on expert mode—every minute accounted for, every second optimized. Jeff's calendar has what he calls "energy buffers"—strategic spaces between meetings, time blocked for deep work, and yes, even lunch breaks that don't involve eating over his keyboard. Six months later, Kylie's burning through her third executive assistant while Jeff's team is delivering record results.

The difference? Kylie's playing a time management game she can't win, while Jeff is mastering the art of energy management.

As Jim Loehr and Tony Schwartz explain in their groundbreaking work *The Power of Full Engagement*, "Energy, not time, is the fundamental currency of high performance."[138] This principle is backed by the Forbes Human Resources Council, which found that while traditional time management focuses on cramming more tasks into limited hours, energy management recognizes that our capacity for high performance can be systematically expanded and renewed.[139] It's not about finding more burners on your stove—it's about mastering the ones you have.

Think of it this way: Google's famous 20% free time policy didn't create game-changing products because people found extra hours in the day. It worked because they let their people cook up ideas when their creative energy was sizzling, not when the calendar said it was "innovation o'clock." When you align work with your natural energy peaks, it's like having a perfectly seasoned cast iron pan—everything just works better.

The World Health Organization isn't just being dramatic when they classify burnout as an occupational phenomenon—it's a warning that many of us are overcooking ourselves, like that cauliflower you left in the oven while answering "just one more email."[140] Managing your energy levels means you can simmer when needed and bring the heat when it counts.

"Energy, not time, is the fundamental currency of high performance."

— Jim Loehr and Tony Schwartz

Johnson & Johnson: Energizing Employee Performance[141]

The Challenge: Enhance employee well-being and productivity within a global healthcare organization.

The Approach: Johnson & Johnson introduced the "Energy for Performance in Life" program, developed by the Johnson & Johnson Human Performance Institute. This program focuses on training employees to manage and expand their energy across four dimensions: body, emotions, mind, and spirit. It includes modules on physical health, emotional resilience, mental focus, and aligning personal values with work. The program is available to all employees worldwide, either as a webinar or in person.

The Result:

- Effective energy strategies significantly enhanced employee focus, efficiency, and overall productivity.
- Aligning work with personal values strengthened employee commitment, satisfaction, and sense of purpose.
- Holistic well-being initiatives fostered sustainable employee health, resilience, and long-term performance.

The Take-Home Recipe:

- Balance body, mind, and spirit.
- Make training accessible for all.
- Embed renewal into daily routines.

When you shift from time-hoarding to energy-flowing, you're not just changing your schedule—you're transforming your entire approach to work. It's like switching from a microwave to a slow cooker. Sure, it takes patience, but the results? *Chef's kiss!*

Fuel Quadrant

2 JUST AS A precision instrument requires multiple systems working in harmony, human excellence depends on the synchronized management of four distinct energy dimensions. This isn't just theory—it's the science of human performance in action.

Let's start with physical energy, our body's powerhouse. According to Upstartist's framework, physical energy forms the foundation upon which all other energy is built.[142] It begins with the basics: sleep, nutrition, movement, and recovery. Instead of reaching for a third coffee to push through the afternoon slump, a well-rested professional taps into sustainable energy—trading exhaustion for consistent, high-level performance. Something as simple as blocking off 30 minutes for a midday walk, drinking water before caffeine, or enforcing a no-screens-before-bed rule can turn depletion into renewal.

The emotional dimension adds another critical layer. Arootah's analysis shows that emotional energy doesn't just make you feel good—it makes you resilient.[143] A stressful meeting can derail your entire day, or you can reset with a quick walk, a deep breath, or a laugh with a colleague. The difference? Managing emotions before they hijack your productivity. Journaling a quick list of wins at the end of the day, swapping vent sessions for solution-focused conversations, or even watching a two-minute comedy clip can shift your emotional state and re-energize your mindset. (Maybe just re-read a chapter from this book—funny and informative!)

Next comes mental energy, our capacity for focus and deep work. In our always-on world, distractions kill momentum. Instead of battling endless Slack pings and email alerts, a high performer sets boundaries—turning off notifications, single-tasking, and completing in 90 minutes what would otherwise take all day. Starting the day with a "must-do" task before checking email, using the Pomodoro technique to stay locked in (that's 25 minutes of focused work, followed by a short break), or even setting a specific playlist for deep work can create the mental environment for sustained concentration. Again—smarter, not harder.

Finally, spiritual energy fuels long-term motivation. As outlined by Mindfulness with Kiran, this isn't about religion—it's about purpose.[144] When work feels like an endless to-do list, reconnecting with the bigger picture makes all the difference. Maybe it's the impact you create, the mentorship you provide, or the freedom it gives your family. Taking five minutes to reflect on why a task matters, volunteering for a cause tied to your values, or sharing success stories with your team can reignite your drive and make the daily grind feel meaningful again.

The magic happens when all four energy dimensions work in sync. Neglect one, and the others suffer. It's like driving with a flat tire. You might move forward, but it won't be smooth. But when you manage your energy holistically, you unlock what The Energy Project calls sustainable high performance[145]—showing up as your best self, day after day. And don't you—and your teams—deserve that?

Burnout Shield

3 IN TODAY'S HIGH-PRESSURE work environment, burnout isn't just a trendy term thrown around in water cooler conversations. The American Psychological Association has identified burnout as a serious condition that can significantly impair our cognitive functions—the very tools we rely on most for professional success.[146] This isn't just about feeling tired; it's about protecting your most valuable resource: you. After all, the best ability is availability. That doesn't mean just showing up in zombie-mode. It means fully present, dialed in, and ready to kick some ass.

And as we all know from Captain America, to really kick butt, you need a shield. Well, the shield-building process happens piece by piece, through daily habits and practices. According to research, the most effective burnout prevention strategy isn't a single grand gesture, but rather a series of intentional practices: taking regular breaks, cultivating emotional self-awareness, maintaining mental focus, and connecting with purpose-driven work.[147] Each of these elements strengthens our resilience against the mounting pressures of modern work life.

The shift from vulnerability to resilience doesn't happen overnight. The smart folks at Forbes tell us that preventing burnout requires a fundamental mindset change in how we view professional sustainability—moving away from the "sprint" mentality that glorifies constant hustle toward a "marathon" approach that prioritizes sustained energy management.[148] This shift isn't just about working differently; it's about thriving permanently.

Consider the difference between a sprinter and a marathoner. The sprinter explosively expends all their energy in a short burst, while the marathoner strategically manages their resources for the long haul. The APA's findings confirm that this marathon mindset—characterized by paced effort, strategic recovery, and sustained focus—isn't just preferable, but essential for cognitive function and professional longevity.[149]

When we build our burnout shield, we're not just protecting ourselves from exhaustion. We're creating the conditions for lasting success.

FIVE TASTE-TEST RECIPES

Think of your energy like a bank account—spend recklessly, and you'll be overdrawn fast. These strategies are like smart deposits, keeping you fueled for the long game. Choose what clicks, make adjustments, and build habits that pay dividends.

1. **The Energy Tasting Menu Ritual:** Take two minutes to taste-test your four essential ingredients: physical vitality, emotional temperature, mental clarity, and spiritual seasoning. This quick assessment lets you adjust before the day's service begins.

2. **The Seasonal Stock Rotation:** Map your peak freshness periods for one week—when you're sharp and when you're stale. Like a chef scheduling prep, align your most demanding dishes with your kitchen's prime hours.

3. **The Kitchen Reset:** Build in 10-minute breaks between meetings. Use these gaps for three deep breaths, a quick stretch, or a walk to refill your water. These resets prevent energy cross-contamination, while keeping your performance fresh.

4. **The Energy Buffet Strategy:** Create a three-course recovery menu: five-minute bites (desk stretches), 15-minute small plates (walking meetings), and 60-minute main courses (proper lunch breaks). When energy dips, order from your menu instead of downing another espresso.

5. **The "Yutori Plating" Technique:** Block 20% of each day as white space—intentional gaps between your main events. Like thoughtful plating that lets each element breathe, these buffers aren't empty calories—they're essential ingredients for sustainable performance. Start with one 30-minute buffer and build from there.

LAST CALL

Energy management isn't about pushing through exhaustion—it's about or-chestrating your personal and professional vitality with precision. Like a chef who knows when to turn the heat up and when to let things simmer, effective professionals understand that sustainable performance requires rhythmic in-tensity. Your energy, like your finest ingredients, must be carefully managed for maximum impact.

In this chapter, you've learned how energy management drives sustainable performance through three key elements: *Energy Triumphs*, which revealed how managing energy outperforms managing time; *Fuel Quadrant*, which showed how balancing physical, mental, emotional, and spiritual energy creates peak performance; and *Burnout Shield*, which demonstrated how strategic recovery prevents professional depletion. More importantly, you understand how to deploy it strategically, from the Japanese concept of yu-tori to science-backed evidence showing that burnout isn't just personal—it's professionally combustible.

As you calibrate your professional burners, remember that every kitchen needs recovery periods between services. Your performance improves when you respect your natural rhythms. Sustainable excellence comes from mastering the art of strategic renewal.

Now go take a walk and drink some water!

CEREBRAL SOUS VIDE

- ✓ When did I last feel energized at work, and how can I replicate that state?
- ✓ How can I treat breaks between meetings as opportunities to recharge?
- ✓ Where am I managing time well but neglecting my energy, and what's one fix?

THE SELF-SERVE STATION

Running on fumes and wondering if there's a better way? These resources will show you why managing your energy—not just your time—is the key to sustainable performance:

- *Do Epic Shit* by Ankur Warikoo (2021) – Warikoo delivers real talk for modern professionals: honest lessons on consistency, burnout, decision-making, and emotional resilience—all with humor and zero fluff. This is the pep talk-meets-playbook for anyone trying to succeed without losing their soul in the process.

- *Peak Performance: Elevate Your Game, Avoid Burnout, and Thrive with the New Science of Success* by Brad Stulberg and Steve Magness (2017) – Through fascinating case studies spanning athletes to artists, this deep dive reveals why sustainable excellence isn't about grinding harder—it's about oscillating between strategic stress and recovery.

- *Deep Work: Rules for Focused Success in a Distracted World* by Cal Newport (2016) – In our age of constant digital interruptions, Newport's blueprint for protecting your mental energy and accessing sustained concentration might be the most valuable skill you'll ever master.

- *The Power of Positive Leadership: How and Why Positive Leaders Transform Teams and Organizations and Change the World* by Jon Gordon (2017) – Success isn't just about talent or tactics—it's about energy. Gordon shows how great leaders fuel performance through optimism, resilience, and purpose. With real-world examples and actionable insights, he proves that a leader's mindset shapes culture, engagement, and results.

- *When: The Scientific Secrets of Perfect Timing* by Daniel Pink (2018) – Pink dives into the science of timing, revealing how our energy levels fluctuate throughout the day and how to align tasks with peak performance windows. Mastering when to work, rest, and recharge isn't just smart—it's a game changer for productivity and well-being.

A SWEET & SAVORY SHOUT-OUT

In a world obsessed with time management hacks and productivity apps, Tony Schwartz and Jim Loehr dared to ask a different question: What if we're managing the wrong resource? In their seminal book *The Power of Full Engagement*, they challenge a core belief of modern work culture: that working more hours automatically leads to better results.

Loehr, a renowned performance psychologist, brought decades of experience coaching elite athletes, while Schwartz expanded these principles into the corporate arena. Together, they offered something revolutionary: the science of energy management. Their research revealed that sustainable excellence doesn't come from relentless pushing, but from strategic oscillation between stress and recovery—a principle as true for Olympic athletes as it is for executives and knowledge workers.

Their work revealed a truth many of us sense but rarely articulate: our work days have natural rhythms, and fighting them is like swimming against the tide. Through collaborations with Fortune 500 companies, they showed that intentional recovery isn't a luxury—it's essential for peak performance. While time is finite, energy is renewable—if you know how to replenish it.

The most profound lesson? High performance isn't about constant output, but mastering your energy—knowing when to push, when to pause, when to sprint, and when to recover. Those "unproductive" moments—a walk between meetings, a real lunch break, or a genuine connection with colleagues—aren't distractions, but vital ingredients for sustainable success.

By challenging the "more is more" mentality, Schwartz and Loehr didn't just write about workplace transformation—they catalyzed it. Their legacy is not merely a new management theory, but a profound shift in how we view human performance.

Thank you, Tony and Jim, for showing us that in the pursuit of excellence, sometimes the bravest act is to pause.

10 QUICK BITES

- In a 2022 Microsoft survey of 31,000 professionals across 31 countries, over half acknowledged burnout as a growing problem.

- Research suggests we make approximately 35,000 decisions daily, each one taking a bite from our energy reserves.

- Employees perform best when four core ingredients—physical, emotional, mental, and spiritual energy—are in sync.

- Google's 20% free time policy shows innovation flourishes when aligned with natural energy peaks rather than forced time slots.

- The World Health Organization now classifies burnout as an occupational phenomenon, recognizing it as a serious workplace concern.

- Physical energy forms the foundation upon which all other energy is built, beginning with sleep, nutrition, movement, and recovery.

- Forbes Human Resources Council found that energy management expands capacity systematically, while traditional time management just crams more tasks into limited hours.

- Neglecting any of the four energy dimensions affects the others—like trying to drive with a flat tire.

- The American Psychological Association identifies burnout as a condition that significantly impairs cognitive functions—our primary professional tools.

- As Jim Loehr and Tony Schwartz explain in The Power of Full Engagement, "Energy, not time, is the fundamental currency of high performance."

PREP CARD

Common Obstacle:

"I find myself running on fumes by 3 p.m. daily."

Quick Fix:

Schedule your most demanding work before 2 p.m.

Long-term:

Map your natural energy peaks and valleys for a week, then redesign your schedule around them

Common Obstacle:

"Back-to-back meetings drain all my energy."

Quick Fix:

Block 10-minute recovery zones between meetings

Long-term:

Create an "energy buffet" menu of recharge activities: five-minute resets, 15-minute recharges, and 60-minute deep refreshes

Common Obstacle:

"I'm constantly feeling overwhelmed and scattered."

Quick Fix:

Start each day with a 2-minute energy check across all four dimensions

Long-term:

Build white space into your calendar using the yutori principle

PSYCHOLOGICAL SAFETY

APPETIZER

Some teams spark creativity effortlessly, while others smother ideas before they catch fire. Psychological safety is the difference—when people trust they can speak up without fear, innovation thrives. Let's explore how to create a culture where bold ideas aren't just welcomed, but expected.

MAIN COURSE

The Failure Celebration: Learn why embracing mistakes is the recipe for innovation
Whispers to Roars: Transform quiet insights into powerful team breakthroughs
Trust Bridges: Build trust that empowers candid conversations and collaboration

DESSERT

The "Oops" Board: Create a shared space to celebrate failures and turn missteps into lessons
The Devil's Advocate Rotation: Rotate a team member to challenge ideas and spark constructive debate
The "What If" Workshop: Fuel out-of-the-box thinking with sessions where there are no bad ideas—only possibilities

PAIRS WELL WITH

Teams trapped in endless "nice but nothing" meetings
Innovation stifled by a fear of failure
Fake grins, zero real talk

CHAPTER 10

Psychological Safety—
The Perfect Simmer

T'S 9:17 A.M. on a Tuesday, and you've just spotted a massive flaw in the product launch strategy your Director of Marketing is presenting. The kind of flaw that could turn next quarter's projections from champagne-popping to pain-drowning. Your heart races, palms sweat, and suddenly that morning's breakfast burrito feels like it's doing parkour in your stomach. You open your mouth to speak, then close it. The words are there, but they're trapped behind an invisible wall of *what ifs*.

What if I'm wrong? What if I look stupid? What if this gets me labeled as "not a team player"? What if this burrito makes a beeline for the nearest exit?!

Sound familiar? You're not alone in that silent struggle. In fact, right now, across thousands of conference rooms, brilliant insights are dying quiet deaths behind pressed lips and polite nods. Like an overcooked steak, these unspoken thoughts get tougher to swallow with each passing moment. The issue isn't just having something to say—it's feeling safe enough to say it.

Psychological safety is a hot topic, and plenty of frameworks attempt to break it down. You'll find acronyms like SAFE, VOICE, and FRICTION. But the one that stuck with me after it was introduced to me during a leadership workshop in New Orleans was **SAFETY**. This framework comes from the Brain Leadership Institute, and I first learned it from my then-colleague Heather, who absolutely crushed it. I'm just here trying not to mangle her brilliance too badly.

Here's what made her breakdown unforgettable and this framework so powerful:

- **Security** – Team members need to feel safe from retaliation, embarrassment, and losing their job.
- **Autonomy** – Employees perform best when they have ownership over their ideas and decisions.
- **Fairness** – A culture of psychological safety ensures that all voices are heard and valued equally.
- **Esteem** – Acknowledging contributions and making people feel respected fosters engagement.
- **Trust** – This takes on a slightly less obvious meaning; here it's about the need to belong to and protect our in-group.
- **You** – Psychological safety is personal. Every individual plays a role in creating and sustaining it.

This framework stuck with me because it wasn't just theory—it was a roadmap.

My team was stacked with talent, but something was missing. Meetings were polite but uninspired. Brainstorming sessions lacked real debate. And too often, the best ideas surfaced in hallway conversations—never in the room where decisions were made.

After some healthy skepticism (I'm a New Yorker, after all), this framework reshaped my leadership approach. When I looked at my team through this lens, I realized we were struggling with *Esteem* and *Security*. Too many people, especially junior team members, weren't sure their input mattered—or worse, feared that speaking up could backfire.

So, I started small. I began every meeting with *"There are no bad ideas here,"* and I backed it up by sharing my own messy, half-baked thoughts. We introduced round robins, ensuring everyone contributed at least one idea, no matter how out there it seemed. Most importantly, I made a point to publicly acknowledge when someone's criticism helped us dodge a mistake.

Over time, the shift was undeniable. No defensive posturing. No passive-aggressive email threads. Just sharper thinking, better collaboration, and ultimately a far stronger strategy.

And that's when I knew: psychological safety wasn't just a concept. It was an unlock.

Here's an even bigger insight: psychological safety isn't just about encouraging people to speak up—it's about rewiring how teams communicate. It shifts internal dialogue from *"better stay quiet"* to *"this is worth sharing."* It turns team dynamics from careful diplomacy into real dialogue. It transforms organizations from top-down directives into multi-directional conversations where the best ideas rise, no matter where they start.

And by the way, it wasn't just my team where this stuff worked. This pattern showed up everywhere. Charles Duhigg, reporting for *The New York Times*, found that the highest-performing teams weren't necessarily the smartest or most skilled—they were the ones where everyone felt safe to speak up, take risks, and be heard. The secret wasn't raw IQ, but a culture of psychological safety.[150] When people feel safe to speak up, collaboration deepens, trust strengthens, and innovation skyrockets.

At its core, this transformation depends on trust. Stephen Covey nails it in *The 7 Habits of Highly Effective People* when he writes, "Trust is the glue of life. It's the essential ingredient in effective communication. It's the foundational principle that holds all relationships."[151] Trust isn't something you can mandate or download like a software update. It's built moment by moment—through actions that prove people's voices matter, their insights are valued, and yes, even their mistakes are welcome.

In this chapter, we'll explore three key elements of psychological safety. First, *The Failure Celebration* reveals why embracing failure fuels innovation. Next, *Whispers to Roars* uncovers how amplifying quiet voices unlocks hidden potential. Finally, *Trust Bridges* shows how fostering connection turns silent observers into confident contributors. The goal isn't to create some utopian workplace where everyone agrees all the time—it's creating a culture where great ideas don't die in silence. Where problems get solved before they become disasters. Where real collaboration replaces performative participation.

After all, the most dangerous communication isn't the wrong answer—it's the unspoken one.

THREE MAIN DISHES

The Failure Celebration

1 MOST PROFESSIONAL KITCHENS have a *mistake bucket*—a place where imperfect dishes meet their quiet demise. But in truly innovative kitchens, those *mistakes* often become tomorrow's signature specials. Organizations could learn from this, yet most treat failure like food poisoning—something to be avoided at all costs.

And to be frank—it starts with leadership. If people don't feel safe failing, they don't take risks. And if they don't take risks, innovation stalls.

Tim Brown, IDEO's former CEO, emphasizes that creating an environment where failure is acceptable—expected, even—becomes the foundation for breakthrough innovation. At IDEO, teams are encouraged to fail early and often, leading to sharper solutions and stronger outcomes.[152] When a project falls short, team members don't whisper behind closed doors—they openly dissect what went wrong. This transparent dialogue creates a feedback loop where every failure feeds future success.

This is captured perfectly by Amy Edmondson in *The Fearless Organization*, defining psychological safety as "a belief that one will not be punished or humiliated for speaking up with ideas, questions, concerns, or mistakes."[153] And that mindset shift doesn't just change what we say—it changes how we say it. Instead of "I think something might be wrong," people learn to say, "I spotted a potential issue we should discuss." The language shifts from tentative to confident, from defensive to constructive. It's the type of open communication we not only crave—but need!

Now, think about your own workplace. Where do you see psychological safety at play in your own work? Do you hesitate before speaking up in meetings? Have you ever held back an idea because you weren't sure how it would land? And if you're leading a team, how often do people challenge the status quo in your presence? If the answer is "not often," ask yourself why. (P.S.—read the chapter on diplomacy before trying this out ;)

Google X operates under this exact principle—failure is not only encouraged, it's institutionalized. As Astro Teller explains, teams are urged to "run at the hardest parts of a problem first" and celebrate when projects prove unworkable.[154] Why? Because every "failure" produces critical insights that shape future success. When a project gets shut down, team members don't update their resumes—they update their understanding.

This approach doesn't just work at the company level—it transforms how employees think, too. And the research backs it up. A 2023 study found that implementing "Failure Awards"—recognition given to employees who take bold risks that don't succeed—increases risk-taking behaviors and reduces the tendency to keep investing in failing projects.[155] When organizations stop treating failure like a career-ending event and start seeing it as a learning opportunity, they unlock their team's full creative potential. Think of failure celebration as a new language. Where excuses once flourished, insights now bloom. Where silence once reigned, questions now flow.

This transformation isn't about lowering standards—it's about raising the quality of conversation. About what works, what doesn't, and most importantly, why.

Now, failure is one thing—but what about the ideas that never even get voiced?

Whispers to Roars

2 **RESEARCH CONSISTENTLY SHOWS** that organizations thrive when every voice has the opportunity to contribute. Yet too often, brilliant insights fade into silence or fail to be raised at all. The "voice amplifier" principle seeks to change this by creating an environment where everyone feels not just safe, but energized to speak up. It's about turning quiet ideas into powerful catalysts for innovation and growth.

Look at Netflix. Renowned for its culture of candor, Netflix embraces radical honesty through its Freedom and Responsibility culture, which encourages employees to give and receive direct, constructive feedback at all levels. Instead of relying on rigid hierarchies, Netflix fosters an open system where ideas flow freely. Patty McCord, Netflix's former Chief Talent Officer, emphasizes in *Powerful* that fostering a culture of honest communication and individual accountability is crucial for effective decision-making and innovation.[156] This goes beyond the theoretical. Daniel Goleman's research on emotional intelligence backs it up, showing that leaders who recognize and respond to

"Trust is the glue of life. It's the essential ingredient in effective communication. It's the foundational principle that holds all relationships."

— Stephen Covey

LEGO: Building Safety, Sparking Creativity[157]

The Challenge: Encourage employees to take creative risks and share unpolished ideas without fear of judgment in a competitive, innovation-driven environment.

The Approach: The LEGO Group has implemented a "Creative Play" workshop series for teams, emphasizing that no idea is too small or too wild. Using LEGO bricks, employees physically model and share ideas, fostering open communication and trust. Leaders also receive specialized training on active listening and how to respond to unconventional suggestions positively. This initiative is part of LEGO's broader strategy to embed psychological safety into its creative processes, ensuring every employee feels valued for their contributions.

The Result:

- Teams produced more groundbreaking and creative ideas during high-pressure design sprints.
- Employees openly shared unpolished concepts, fostering a culture of continuous innovation.
- Creative Play workshops enhanced collaboration and trust while strengthening teams.

The Take-Home Recipe:

- Brainstorms ignite bold innovation.
- Rough ideas are shared without fear.
- Diverse voices craft better solutions.

emotional cues foster environments where team members feel safe to share their perspectives.[158] When people feel truly heard, they don't just contribute more—they innovate more and turn whispers into roars.

Think of this as unlocking your organization's collective genius. As *Forbes* notes, when employees can share ideas without fear of humiliation, both individual and organizational creativity flourishes.[159] But this requires more than an open-door policy. It demands systems that actively gather, value, and act on input from all levels.

Leadership plays a critical role. A *McKinsey & Company* article highlights that consultative leadership behaviors—such as actively soliciting input from team members—directly enhance psychological safety and improve team performance.[160] This means leaders must move beyond passive encouragement and take deliberate action to ensure every voice matters.

The transformation begins with powerful questions that spark real dialogue, structured forums where ideas can flow freely, and consistent follow-through that shows every perspective is valued. When organizations succeed in amplifying all voices, they create a communication ecosystem where innovative solutions naturally emerge, and potential challenges are addressed before they become crises.

The result? Stronger teams. Faster innovation. More resilient organizations. All things you and your company should like a lot!

Amplifying voices is an absolute game-changer—but without trust, even the most open forums fall flat. That's why it's the final ingredient of psychological safety—it's the one that holds everything together.

We saved the best for last...

Trust Bridges

3 **AT ITS CORE,** psychological safety is built on trust—the foundation of authentic communication and smart risk-taking. Research shows that organizations excel when they create environments where vulnerability and openness are seen as strengths, not weaknesses.[161]

But trust isn't a one-time event—it's a repeated action. High-performing organizations implement systems that reinforce reliability, competence, and genuine care for team success.

Look at Zappos, renowned for its employee-first approach. At their All Hands meetings, employees at all levels voice concerns, share ideas, and engage in real discussions about strategy.[162] By stripping away bureaucracy, Zappos empowers employees to make bold decisions—fueling consistent innovation and market leadership.

Trust also requires vulnerability from leaders. Admitting when you don't have all the answers, seeking input, and openly learning from mistakes creates a two-way street where information flows freely and authentically. As Brené Brown reminds us, psychological safety starts with leaders who model openness, admit mistakes, and invite tough conversations.[163] When they do, teams respond by showing up fully, speaking up boldly, and solving problems creatively. Vulnerability isn't weakness—it's the foundation of innovation and trust.

The impact? In high-trust organizations, 43% of employees report trusting their leaders to act in their best interests, driving higher collaboration, engagement, and overall productivity.[164]

The challenge? Trust isn't built overnight. It's forged moment by moment when a leader genuinely listens to a concern, follows through on a promise, or credits a team member's contribution. These small acts compound on each other, shaping a culture where psychological safety thrives. When companies focus on follow-through, transparent communication, and actionable feedback, they don't just build trust—they unlock sustainable success.

Building trust isn't just about creating a more pleasant workplace—though it often does. It's a strategic imperative that transforms how teams collaborate, innovate, and communicate to achieve their best outcomes.

FIVE TASTE-TEST RECIPES

Psychological safety isn't built on wishful thinking—it's built on action. These ideas are meant to inspire, so try one, modify another, or revisit them when your team is ready to embrace bold, collaborative growth.

1. **The "Oops" Board:** Create a space—physical or digital—where team members can share mistakes and lessons learned. Think of it as a celebration of learning through failure. The best blunder of the month earns a quirky prize—golden facepalm statue, anyone?

2. **The Reverse Mentoring:** Pair junior team members with senior leaders, but flip the script—the juniors mentor the execs. This builds cross-level relationships, highlights fresh perspectives, and, as a bonus, watching the CEO try to decode Snapchat is priceless.

3. **The Devil's Advocate Rotation:** In meetings, assign someone to play the devil's advocate, challenging ideas and identifying potential flaws. Rotate this role to ensure everyone gets a turn. It normalizes constructive disagreement and shows that even the boss's ideas aren't sacred.

4. **The Vulnerability Jar:** Kick off meetings with a vulnerability jar—an anonymous space for sharing challenges, opening discussions, and finding collective solutions. It fosters a safe, judgment-free environment for support and problem-solving.

5. **The "What If" Workshop:** Host sessions where no idea is off-limits—seriously, none. Encourage out-of-the-box thinking. What sounds absurd today might become your billion-dollar breakthrough tomorrow.

LAST CALL

Psychological safety is all about fostering an environment where honest dialogue thrives. Like a kitchen where chefs feel confident to experiment with new techniques, effective teams succeed when members feel secure enough to take calculated risks. Innovation requires the freedom to fail forward.

In this chapter, you've learned how psychological safety transforms workplace dynamics through three crucial elements: *The Failure Celebration*, which revealed how embracing mistakes accelerates learning; *Whispers to Roars*, which showed how amplifying quiet voices strengthens team intelligence; and *Trust Bridges*, which demonstrated how psychological safety enables breakthrough collaboration. You've seen that psychological safety isn't about comfort—it's about growth. Teams that embrace it don't just get along better—they innovate faster, solve problems smarter, and build resilience that lasts.

As you shape your team's culture, remember: every great kitchen balances high standards with high support. When fear steps aside, potential steps up. True excellence happens when people feel safe enough to bring their whole selves to work—and bold enough to push the boundaries of what's possible.

CEREBRAL SOUS VIDE

- ✓ When have I hesitated to speak up, and what would make me feel safe to share next time?
- ✓ How can I create space for others to express their ideas and concerns more openly?
- ✓ What's one way I can model vulnerability to build trust within my team?

THE SELF-SERVE STATION

Think psychological safety is all fluff and no function? These reads will prove otherwise, showing how it powers innovation, builds trust, and fosters true collaboration under any conditions:

- *TouchPoints: Creating Powerful Leadership Connections in the Smallest of Moments* by Douglas Conant and Mette Norgaard (2011) – This book reveals how brief interactions can build trust, encourage openness, and create an environment where employees feel safe to share ideas. A practical guide for leaders embedding psychological safety into daily routines.

- *Smarter Faster Better: The Secrets of Being Productive in Life and Business* by Charles Duhigg (2016) – Duhigg explores the role of team norms, especially psychological safety, in driving high performance. Includes insights from Google's Project Aristotle, highlighting why trust and open communication are critical to success.

- *Dare to Lead: Brave Work. Tough Conversations. Whole Hearts.* by Brené Brown (2018) – Brown unpacks how vulnerability and courageous leadership foster trust and psychological safety. A must-read for leaders aiming to create an environment where team members feel safe to bring their full selves to work.

- *Trust Factor: The Science of Creating High-Performance Companies* by Paul J. Zak (2017) – Zak blends neuroscience and organizational behavior to show how building trust—an essential pillar of psychological safety—leads to higher engagement, innovation, and productivity.

- *The Culture Code: The Secrets of Highly Successful Groups* by Daniel Coyle (2018) – Coyle delves into the principles behind successful teams, with a focus on creating belonging, trust, and safety. Filled with real-world examples, this book provides actionable insights for building cohesive, high-performing groups.

A SWEET & SAVORY SHOUT-OUT

Harvard Business School professor Dr. Amy Edmondson didn't just coin the term psychological safety—she revolutionized the way we understand team dynamics and organizational success. Her groundbreaking research unveiled a game-changing truth: the highest-performing teams aren't those with the smartest people or the flashiest resources, but the ones where everyone feels safe to speak up, take risks, and admit mistakes without fear of humiliation.

What sets Edmondson apart is her unique ability to translate rigorous academic research into actionable insights for leaders. Through her work, she's shown that psychological safety isn't a soft skill or a "nice-to-have"; it's a strategic imperative that drives innovation, resilience, and sustainable success. Companies across industries, from healthcare to technology, have adopted her principles to create cultures of candor and collaboration.

Edmondson's framework is a masterclass in building trust and fostering a learning mindset. Her work reminds us that openness and vulnerability are the cornerstones of creativity and growth. By focusing on actionable strategies rather than abstract ideals, she has inspired organizations to measure and sustain psychological safety as a key performance metric. She challenges leaders to move beyond superficial fixes—urging them to create environments where every voice is valued and no idea is too bold to explore.

So, the next time you hesitate to speak up in a meeting, channel your inner Amy Edmondson. Remember, great ideas—and great teams—are born in environments where risk-taking feels less like a gamble and more like an invitation.

Here's to a trailblazer in proving that in today's fast-paced business world, the safest way to lead is to create a space where everyone feels empowered to contribute. Thanks for showing us that sometimes, the riskiest thing is staying silent. Her legacy isn't just a new way to think about teamwork—it's a blueprint for building workplaces that thrive on trust, authenticity, and courageous collaboration.

10 QUICK BITES

- Teams with psychological safety don't just get along better—they innovate faster, collaborate smarter, and solve problems more effectively.

- The SAFETY framework (Security, Autonomy, Fairness, Esteem, Trust, You) provides a roadmap for creating a culture where people can thrive.

- Fear of speaking up stifles progress—great ideas die in silence when teams lack the confidence to challenge the status quo.

- In high-trust organizations, 43% of employees report trusting their leaders to act in their best interests, driving higher collaboration and productivity.

- Google X institutionalizes failure celebration—teams are urged to "run at the hardest parts of a problem first" and celebrate when projects prove unworkable.

- Netflix's Freedom and Responsibility culture embraces radical honesty, encouraging employees to give direct, constructive feedback at all levels.

- McKinsey research shows that consultative leadership behaviors—such as actively soliciting input from team members—directly enhance psychological safety.

- As Brené Brown reminds us, psychological safety starts with leaders who model openness, admit mistakes, and invite tough conversations.

- Psychological safety isn't about comfort—it's about growth, enabling teams to take smart risks and push boundaries without fear of backlash.

- Charles Duhigg found that the highest-performing teams weren't the smartest—they were the ones where everyone felt safe to speak up and take risks.

PREP CARD

Common Obstacle:

"Silence dominates our team discussions."

Quick Fix:

Start meetings with a quick round-robin for input

Long-term:

Foster open dialogue by encouraging team members to respectfully question and refine each other's ideas

---

Common Obstacle:

"Fear of failure kills our creativity."

Quick Fix:

Highlight lessons learned from recent missteps in team updates

Long-term:

Celebrate bold risks with lighthearted awards or shoutouts

Common Obstacle:

"Trust feels surface-level, not real."

Quick Fix:

Open meetings by sharing a leader's recent mistake and its lesson

Long-term:

Create consistent opportunities for open, candid discussions across all levels

THREE

The Perfect Plating—How You Communicate With The World

ALRIGHT, YOU MAGNIFICENT corporate chameleon, it's time to step into the spotlight! We're in the home stretch—the grand finale of this business mastery journey: how we communicate with the world. We've honed our internal craft, mastered team dynamics, and now it's time to bring it all to the main dining room. After all, a restaurant with a perfect kitchen still needs to fill its tables—great ideas and strong teams mean nothing if no one knows about them.

Having great ideas and strong teams isn't enough—you need to showcase your work to the world. We're moving beyond excellent execution to masterful presentation, beyond good food to memorable dining experiences.

In this third and final section, we'll master five powerful capabilities that transform good habits into lasting influence:

11. **Storytelling—The Sizzle Factor**: Learn to present your ideas with the same precision a master chef uses to plate their signature dish. How you frame your message matters just as much as the message itself. Let's be honest—"Once upon a time, in a galaxy far, far away" beats "As per my last email" any day.

12. **The Power of Three—The Perfect Prix Fixe**: Master the art of structuring your message for maximum impact. Just as a well-balanced three-course meal leaves a lasting impression, a three-part message resonates more powerfully than an overwhelming flood of ideas.

13. **Sponsorship—The Executive Chef's Table**: Build relationships that elevate your visibility and accelerate your impact. Learn to find sponsors who showcase your talents to the right audiences—no car decals required.

14. **Personal Branding—Your Signature Dish**: Develop an authentic professional presence that makes you unforgettable and craft a reputation that keeps people coming back for seconds. Warning: may cause spontaneous LinkedIn profile updates.

15. **Diplomacy—The Balancing Act**: Navigate complex workplace dynamics with the grace of a seasoned maître d'. Turn potential conflicts into opportunities for connection and master the art of getting things done—without launching an office cold war.

Like a talented chef becoming a successful restaurateur, professional excellence must extend beyond technical skill. Everything we've covered—from gratitude to psychological safety—comes together here. Your internal mastery gives you confidence to present bold ideas. Your team skills transform into organizational influence. Your authentic voice finds its audience.

Think of these chapters as your guide to becoming a renowned restaurateur—someone who doesn't just create excellence, but knows how to showcase it. Whether you're pitching initiatives or building relationships, these skills help translate great ideas into lasting impact. After all, what good is the perfect recipe if you can't convince anyone to take a bite?

Ready to step out of the kitchen and into the limelight? Time to plate up something extraordinary.

STORYTELLING

APPETIZER

Facts make sense, but stories make impact. The right narrative doesn't just present ideas and insights—it makes people feel, remember, and act. We're about to dive into the art of storytelling and how it turns information into impact.

MAIN COURSE

Persuasion Trifecta: Balance pathos, ethos, and logos to craft stories that inspire and move
Neuroscience's Narrative: Tap into brain chemistry to make your stories engaging and unforgettable
Hero's Journey: Structure your narrative to mirror the universal cycle of challenge, growth, and transformation

DESSERT

The SPICE Formula: Turn up the heat and make your stories unforgettable
The Pixar Pitch: Use a proven framework to turn ideas into compelling stories
The Six-Word Story Challenge: Distill your narrative into its purest, most impactful form

PAIRS WELL WITH

Presenters who love slides more than stories
Teams lost in spreadsheets but missing the point
Leaders ditching jargon for unforgettable tales

CHAPTER 11

Storytelling—The Sizzle Factor

SPRING 2010. APPLE had just launched its first generation iPad, Instagram wasn't even a thing yet, and everyone was gaga for Gaga. You've been tasked with launching a brand-new sales division from scratch—in just ten weeks. The goal is ambitious—build a $100 million business in three years. And the subject? Ergonomics. Not exactly a topic that makes people sit up straighter (pun intended). And like many business challenges you'll face in your career, success wouldn't come from data alone.

This wasn't hypothetical—this was my actual job. The challenge seemed impossible at first. How do you make ergonomics sexy? Of course, with a growth mindset and some grit, you can do almost anything, but I knew we'd have to get creative. We had great products, an incredible new sales team, and a powerful distribution network. But to bring that all together, we needed something special.

We needed a story.

Ask any master chef: ingredients alone don't make the meal—it's how you bring them together that creates something unforgettable. Whether you're an emerging leader or a seasoned executive, the stories you tell shape not only how others perceive you, but also how you see yourself. Stories shape how we see the world, tackle challenges, and define our purpose within it. And effective communication starts with a simple but profound question: "What is my story?"

Every great story—whether a Hollywood blockbuster or your next board presentation—follows the same arc: challenge, struggle, transformation. As Adam Grant reminds us in *Originals*, stories have the power to challenge norms and ignite innovation when they're framed in ways that resonate with audiences.[165] And, while storytelling feels like an art, it's also a science. Joseph Campbell, in *The Hero with a Thousand Faces*, introduced the Hero's Journey—a universal narrative pattern that resonates because it mirrors the human experience.[166] We'll dive deeper into the Hero's Journey shortly.

Professional growth and storytelling science meet at this critical juncture. Paul Zak's research on oxytocin—the "trust hormone"—shows that compelling stories foster trust, build empathy, and drive engagement.[167] And these aren't just fun facts; they're tools for stronger relationships with colleagues, clients, and stakeholders. Just like a perfectly balanced sauce, these elements work together to create something greater than the sum of their parts. It's why the right narrative turns plain fare into a feast the whole town is still talking about.

Remember that whole "make ergonomics sexy" challenge from earlier?

Well, we did it.

In one pivotal client pitch, we passed around a bowling ball—not common in the commercial furniture business. "This weighs about as much as your head," I told the room of decision-makers. "Now imagine your spine balancing this—all day, every day—while hunched over staring at a screen." The narrative transport, the tactile experience, the smooth sultry voice—it all worked in tandem to create a moment that crystallized the problem. We defined the challenge, uncovered a struggle, and provided the desired transformation: a healthier, happier workplace experience through the ergonomic solutions we were providing.

That simple story shifted the conversation. Sure, I could have presented data on missed work days due to back pain, talked about anthropometric inches, or shared a simple total cost of ownership analysis. But that path offered little novelty, no pathos, and certainly didn't let me spend any corporate cash on a custom bowling ball—which was 100% against brand guidelines and, thus, totally worth it. The story we told wasn't about chairs or desks anymore. It was about human performance, productivity, and well-being. People could feel the strain we were describing, and more importantly, they understood why our ergonomic solutions mattered. Over three years, that narrative helped us turn a near start-up business into a $100 million-plus success.

This experience reflects a universal truth in business—facts alone won't drive change, but a compelling narrative will. When shared with others, storytelling becomes a bridge. It connects us to the world the storyteller often gets to create. It's how leaders inspire movements, brands connect with customers, and businesses turn visions into realities.

Jonathan Gottschall, in *The Storytelling Animal,* puts it best: "We are, as a species, addicted to story. Even when the body goes to sleep, the mind stays

up all night, telling itself stories."[168] It's woven into our DNA. From ancient myths to modern marketing campaigns to project update emails, narratives shape our emotions, decisions, and sense of identity. Even in sleep, our brains craft narratives to make sense of the world. This evolutionary wiring makes storytelling more than a tool—it's how humans connect, decide, and act.

Simply put: stories aren't just how we communicate. They're how we influence, inspire, and create change.

And you don't need to be Shakespeare to tell a good story. What you need is structure, purpose, and command of the three pillars of persuasion: ethos (credibility), pathos (emotion), and logos (logic). Like a well-balanced dish needs salt, acid, and heat, your story needs these three elements to come alive. Annette Simmons, in *The Story Factor*, describes storytelling as the ultimate tool for influence because it seamlessly blends these elements, making complex ideas relatable and compelling.[169]

In this chapter, we'll master the recipe for relatable and compelling storytelling with three delicious entrees. First up: the *Persuasion Trifecta*—ethos, pathos, and logos, which combine to form your secret sauce for crafting stories that persuade and inspire. Then, we'll explore *Neuroscience's Narrative*, uncovering why the brain loves stories and how to make your narratives stick. Finally, we'll guide you through the *Hero's Journey*, teaching you how to structure your stories so they resonate with your audience and drive action.

Whether you're chasing a promotion, leading a major initiative, or building your brand, tie on your metaphorical apron. In business, storytelling isn't an accoutrement. It's the main course.

Time to plate it perfectly!

THREE MAIN DISHES

1   **TWO THOUSAND YEARS** before PowerPoint decks and corporate storytelling workshops, Aristotle—the storytelling O.G.—was puzzling over why some speakers could move mountains while others couldn't budge a pebble. His conclusion? Persuasion isn't one thing, but three: pathos (emotion), ethos (credibility), and logos (logic). And it all starts with pathos—the emotional spark that activates the amygdala, our brain's center for processing emotions before logic. Experienced leaders know this truth: hearts open minds. We feel first, rationalize second.

Think of the last presentation that truly moved you to action. Chances are, it wasn't the data that sparked your interest—it was the story that made that data matter. As Miller explains in *Building a StoryBrand*, effective communication starts with understanding your audience's emotions, challenges, and desires.[170] This isn't emotional manipulation—it's human connection. Consider Nike's iconic "Just Do It" campaign. They don't just sell footwear—they sell triumph, determination, and the pursuit of greatness. Their messaging taps into pathos, transforming a shoe purchase into a statement of ambition.

Once emotions open the door, ethos builds the foundation of trust. Credibility makes your audience believe in you as much as your message. In *Made to Stick*, Heath & Heath show that credibility turns sticky ideas into actions—it's not just about sounding smart, it's about sounding trustworthy.[171] Sometimes, that means offering a clear, verifiable claim people can test for themselves. Other times, it's about what they call the Sinatra Test—if you've made it somewhere hard, like New York City, you don't need to say much more. One killer example can do all the heavy lifting.

Similarly, in *Talk Like TED*, communication expert Carmine Gallo explains that the most compelling speakers earn trust not by listing credentials, but by embedding credibility naturally within their narratives.[172] Through authentic storytelling, emotional transparency, and genuine passion, they connect on a human level. This authenticity, both authors argue, forms the bedrock of persuasive communication—trust gets built fast, and once people believe you, they're far more likely to act on your message, transforming it from merely informative to truly unforgettable.

The final element—logos—transforms interest into conviction. Facts, data, and logic provide structure, ensuring your narrative holds up under scrutiny. But as Cialdini notes in *Influence*, logic alone rarely persuades.[173] Just like precise measurements enhance flavor in cooking, numbers and details work best when they reinforce emotion—not when they drown it out.

The magic of the Persuasion Trifecta lies in its balance. Too much pathos feels manipulative. Too much ethos sounds self-important. Too much logos? Your audience tunes out. As Simmons explains in *The Story Factor*, persuasion is most effective when these three elements work together, creating a cohesive narrative that resonates and endures.[174]

This trinity of persuasion isn't just for formal presentations—it's your framework for every crucial conversation. Master this trifecta, and you'll transform how you communicate—whether leading a team, pitching an idea, or crafting the story of your own success.

And while understanding these three elements of persuasion gives us the framework for effective storytelling, modern neuroscience reveals exactly why they work…

Neuroscience's Narrative

2 **WHEN YOU SHARE** a story, you're not just transmitting information—you're literally rewiring brains. Beneath every compelling narrative lies a cascade of brain activity powered by chemicals like oxytocin, dopamine, and cortisol. A well-told story does more than inform—it triggers a reaction that builds trust, inspires action, and makes ideas unforgettable.

Oxytocin, often called the "trust hormone," plays a central role in this process. In *Immersion*, Zak explains how stories that evoke emotion and attention stimulate oxytocin production, fostering empathy and cooperation.[175] Whether you're delivering financial projections or outlining strategic vision, a well-told story can bring people together or move them to act. Like layering flavors in a complex dish, your brain choreographs a precise sequence of responses to story. As Zak later expands, dopamine reinforces

"We are, as a species, addicted to story. Even when the body goes to sleep, the mind stays up all night, telling itself stories."

— Jonathan Gottschall

HubSpot: Storytelling that Sells and Connects[176]

The Challenge: Transform traditional marketing software sales into an educational journey that builds lasting customer relationships.

The Approach: HubSpot crafted a narrative-driven strategy that went beyond typical software marketing. Through its "State of Marketing" reports, case studies, blog content, and HubSpot Academy, the company transforms complex marketing concepts into compelling stories. Their annual Inbound Conference serves as their flagship storytelling platform, where customer success stories and industry insights blend into a larger narrative about the future of marketing.

The Result:

- Strategic storytelling transformed HubSpot from a startup into a recognized industry thought leader.
- The company grew to over 150,000 global customers and achieved $1 billion in annual revenue by 2023.
- Story-driven content and resources, like HubSpot Academy, became industry standards.

The Take-Home Recipe:

- Turn data into narratives that resonate.
- Build community through shared stories.
- Let customers become your storytellers.

engagement by rewarding the brain during moments of suspense or resolution. Cortisol heightens focus during tension, keeping the audience hooked.[177] This neurochemical trio—oxytocin, dopamine, and cortisol—explains why stories are both captivating and memorable long after the facts fade.

In *Wired for Story*, Lisa Cron explains how stories engage sensory and emotional brain regions, making them far more memorable than raw data. She writes, "We think in story. It's hardwired in our brain. It's how we make strategic sense of the world around us."[178] A great narrative that resonates with audiences helps them process the world and make sense of their experiences.

In *You Have More Influence Than You Think*, Vanessa Bohns shows that even routine workplace interactions—a quick team update, a lunch conversation, or a simple email—shape how others see projects, problems, and possibilities.[179] Whether you're a new hire or a senior leader, your stories amplify your influence more than you think. Stories amplify influence by creating shared experiences that linger in the mind, achieving what data alone cannot.

Mastering this neuroscience turns storytelling from an art into a strategic advantage. By triggering the right neurochemical responses, you can craft narratives that captivate, inspire, and endure. Whether motivating teams, pitching ideas, or driving change, this biological blueprint transforms any message into a lasting experience.

Now that we understand why stories affect us so powerfully at a biological level, the question becomes: how do we structure them for maximum impact? The answer lies in a pattern so fundamental to human experience that it appears in everything from ancient myths to modern marketing campaigns.

Hero's Journey

3 BEHIND EVERY GREAT story is a hidden blueprint. This structure, famously defined by Joseph Campbell in *The Hero with a Thousand Faces*, is the Hero's Journey—a universal narrative arc that mirrors the cycles of human experience.[180] From myths to novels to blockbuster movies, the Hero's Journey captures the cycles of challenge, growth, and transformation that define us. For you, it provides a blueprint for creating narratives that drive real organizational change.

Now, before you start plotting an Odyssey-length epic about your company's journey to optimal supply chain management, let's break this down into business-friendly bites:

The Ordinary World: This is the "before" picture. In *Squirrel Inc.*, Steve Denning emphasizes how establishing the current state creates tension and urgency for change.[181] Maybe your company was struggling with outdated systems or your team faced a seemingly insurmountable challenge. The audience needs to see the status quo before they can appreciate the transformation.

The Call to Adventure: This is the moment of disruption—the challenge or opportunity that demands action. A market shake-up, a bold innovation, a crisis too big to ignore. In *Resonate*, Nancy Duarte highlights this as the turning point that shifts audience perspectives, sparking transformation.[182]

Trials and Allies: These are the obstacles faced and the partnerships formed along the way. Did you pivot your strategy? Collaborate with unexpected partners? As Jonah Sachs notes in *Winning the Story Wars*, these moments resonate because they show vulnerability and growth—two essential ingredients for building trust.[183]

The Ordeal: This is the big boss battle, the make-or-break moment. Perhaps it was a high-stakes product launch or a critical negotiation. Here Denning illustrates how this stage, framed around transformation, can align teams and inspire collective action.[184]

The Return: This is the moment of transformation—the point where lessons learned turn into lasting impact. Maybe your company reinvented its strategy, or your team emerged stronger than before. As Campbell describes, the hero returns with the "elixir"—the wisdom, innovation, or change that benefits the world.[185]

Mapping your narrative to this framework does more than tell a story—it invites your audience to step inside it. As Duarte emphasizes, in business storytelling, the audience—not the storyteller—is the true hero.[186] Your job is to act as their mentor, guiding them through their challenges and helping them emerge transformed.

The Hero's Journey works because it taps into universal truths about struggle, growth, and transformation. It mirrors the cycles of human life, creating stories that not only engage but inspire. Whether you're leading a team, pitching a bold idea, or rallying people around change, the Hero's Journey is a blueprint for action. When done right, it doesn't just engage your audience—it invites them to step into the story with you.

At the end of the day, every business challenge is just another hero's journey. So grab your metaphorical sword, rally your allies, and get ready—because the return trip is always where the real magic happens.

FIVE TASTE-TEST RECIPES

Great storytellers aren't born—they're built. These exercises are your training ground for mastering narrative impact. Start with one, mix and match, or use them as creative inspiration. Every small step refines your storytelling craft.

1 The SPICE Formula: Great stories don't just inform—they ignite action. Add SPICE: keep it Simple, tap into Perceived self-interest, embrace Incongruence, project Confidence, and convey Empathy. Master these elements, and your stories will captivate and compel.

2 The Pixar Pitch: Try Pixar's famous story framework: "Once upon a time... Every day... One day... Because of that... Until finally..." Whether you're presenting a strategy, launching an initiative, or inspiring a team, this formula distills complex ideas into compelling, easy-to-follow narratives.

3 The Empathy Map: Before crafting your story, map out your audience. Divide a page into four quadrants: Think, Feel, Say, Do. Fill in each section with insights about their mindset, emotions, words, and actions. The result? A story that speaks directly to them.

4 The Metaphor Game: Take a complex concept and create three metaphors to explain it. Is your team's rebrand a butterfly's metamorphosis? A home renovation? A '90s rom-com makeover? The more unexpected the metaphor, the more it sticks.

5 The Six-Word Story Challenge: Inspired by Hemingway's six-word classic ('For sale: Baby shoes. Never worn.'), try condensing your key message into six words. This forces clarity, sparks curiosity, and makes your story unforgettable.

LAST CALL

Storytelling isn't about performative presentations—it's about transforming information into experiences that drive action. Just as a chef knows that presentation enhances perception, great communicators craft messages that captivate as much as they inform.

In this chapter, you've learned how storytelling elevates communication through three essential elements: *Persuasion Trifecta*, which revealed how emotion, credibility, and logic combine to create impact; *Neuroscience's Narrative*, which showed how stories physically engage and align our brains; and *Hero's Journey*, which demonstrated how structure transforms messages into memorable experiences. You've discovered that strategic storytelling isn't just entertaining—it creates measurable improvements in engagement, understanding, and organizational buy-in.

As you craft your professional narratives, remember that every great dish tells a story of its origins. Your messages land more powerfully when wrapped in narrative structure. And the best communicators, like the finest chefs, know exactly how to plate their ideas.

CEREBRAL SOUS VIDE

- How do I use storytelling to influence others, and what results have I seen when I communicate through narrative?
- What story am I telling about myself in my work, and how does it shape the way others perceive me?
- When I think about my audience, how well do I tailor my stories to resonate with their challenges and aspirations?

THE SELF-SERVE STATION

Think storytelling is just for Hollywood? Think again. These resources reveal how narratives fuel influence and connection—whether you're rallying a team, pitching an idea, or strengthening key relationships:

- *The Storytelling Animal: How Stories Make Us Human* by Jonathan Gottschall (2012) – Dive into the science of why stories captivate our minds. Gottschall reveals how narrative shapes everything from decision-making to organizational culture. Essential reading for understanding the power of story in business.

- *Made to Stick: Why Some Ideas Survive and Others Die* by Chip Heath and Dan Heath (2007) – The Heath brothers crack the code on memorable ideas. Through compelling research and practical frameworks, they show exactly how to craft messages that resonate and endure.

- The Moth Podcast (available on all major platforms) – Want to experience storytelling at its finest? This series of live, unscripted narratives showcases the power of authentic storytelling. Observe how speakers use pacing, vulnerability, and structure to create unforgettable moments.

- *The Science of Storytelling: Why Stories Make Us Human and How to Tell Them Better* by Will Storr (2019) – Storr blends psychology, neuroscience, and narrative techniques to break down what makes stories truly compelling. A go-to for anyone serious about mastering storytelling at a deep level.

- *Building a StoryBrand: Clarify Your Message So Customers Will Listen* by Donald Miller (2017) – Miller's practical framework helps you clarify your message, connect with your audience, and transform how you communicate about your business. Perfect for leaders who want their stories to drive results.

A SWEET & SAVORY SHOUT-OUT

Nancy Duarte didn't just elevate storytelling—she redefined its role in the business world. As the CEO of Duarte, Inc., she has revolutionized how leaders and organizations communicate, proving that the most effective messages aren't crammed with data but powered by narrative. Her work has guided Fortune 500 CEOs and Silicon Valley innovators alike to craft presentations that inspire, persuade, and drive action.

What sets Duarte apart is her ability to make storytelling systematic and scalable. Through landmark books like *Resonate* and *Slide:ology*, she's shown that narrative isn't just an art—it's a learnable skill that drives business results. Like a master chef who can break down complex techniques into simple steps, Duarte has created frameworks that turn even the most analytical professionals into compelling storytellers.

Her revolutionary insight? The audience, not the speaker, is the hero of every story. Drawing from the Hero's Journey, Duarte developed practical tools that help leaders transform dry data into compelling narratives. Her methods guide audiences through meaningful trans-formation, create presentations that resonate emotionally and logically, and build messages that drive real action.

Perhaps most importantly, Duarte has proven that storytelling isn't just for creatives—it's essential for anyone who needs to communicate, persuade, or lead. Her methods have transformed how organizations approach everything from product launches to quarterly reviews, showing that structure and creativity aren't opposites—they're partners.

The next time you're crafting an important message, remember Duarte's core principle: great communication isn't about dazzling with complexity, but connecting with clarity. Her legacy isn't just better presentations—it's a fundamental shift in how business communicates.

10 QUICK BITES

- Storytelling isn't just a skill—it's a superpower that turns abstract concepts into compelling narratives that inspire, persuade, and connect.

- The stories we tell ourselves shape how we communicate, approach challenges, and define our role in the world.

- Effective storytelling balances the three pillars of persuasion: pathos (emotion), ethos (credibility), and logos (logic).

- Stories activate the brain's neurochemical trio—oxytocin for trust, cortisol for focus, and dopamine for engagement—making them unforgettable.

- The Hero's Journey framework mirrors human experience, turning challenges into relatable stories of transformation.

- Successful narratives begin with the audience's emotions, aligning their desires with the storyteller's message.

- Storytelling is a bridge between leaders and teams, fostering trust and connection by making messages personal and relatable.

- Science proves humans are hardwired for storytelling, with narratives shaping decisions and driving action.

- Great stories don't just inform—they ignite action and create shared experiences that last.

- Leaders who master storytelling unlock the potential to align, inspire, and move others toward collective success.

PREP CARD

Common Obstacle:

"Facts and data fall flat with no emotional impact."

Quick Fix:

Open with a story tied to audience challenges

Long-term:

Train teams to use a challenge-struggle-transformation format

---

Common Obstacle:

"Our team members don't see the bigger picture."

Quick Fix:

Use metaphors to link their work to goals

Long-term:

Create a shared team narrative connecting roles to outcomes

Common Obstacle:

"My presentations lack emotion and connection."

Quick Fix:

Frame content as problem-tension-solution

Long-term:

Use the Hero's Journey to craft stories that inspire action and highlight transformations

POWER OF THREE

APPETIZER

You know why great ideas stick? They're simple, snappy, and structured. That's the magic of the Power of Three—it cuts through noise, keeps people engaged, and makes your message impossible to ignore. And it's fun—I'm doing it now!

MAIN COURSE

Sweet Spot: Discover the cognitive science behind why three is the magic number for comprehension
Creating Cadence: Build natural rhythm and flow to keep your audience engaged
Memory Trifecta: Use chunking, repetition, and clarity to make your ideas stick

DESSERT

The Three-Word Challenge: Distill your message into three impactful words
The Power of Three Rewrite: Restructure your emails or memos into three key ideas
The Three-Act Storytelling: Frame your reports or case studies with a beginning, middle, and end

PAIRS WELL WITH

Data-swamped leaders hungry for clarity
Teams drowning in noise and craving alignment
Presenters who want their ideas to actually stick

CHAPTER 12

The Power of Three—
The Perfect Prix Fixe

LATE NIGHT AT the Globe Theatre. Shakespeare, quill in hand, stares at a blank parchment. The crowds arrive tomorrow, and he needs an opener that will land. "Hey, Romans, listen up?" More drunk toast than stately decree. "Friends and countrymen, gather round?" Sounds like a bad town crier. Then it hits him—three simple, rhythmic words. Friends. Romans. Countrymen. He scribbles furiously, crafting a line that will echo through centuries.

Shakespeare wasn't just lucky—he tapped into what cognitive scientists would later prove: the Power of Three is hardwired into our brains. Three isn't just a number—it's a communication powerhouse. Complete, satisfying, and, most importantly, unforgettable.

From "Life, Liberty, and the Pursuit of Happiness" to "Reduce, Reuse, Recycle," the Power of Three shapes our culture, communication, and yes, our boardrooms. It's the Swiss Army knife of persuasion, the triple shot of rhetoric, the holy trinity of getting your point across. Goldilocks had three bowls of porridge to choose from. The genie granted three wishes. And your favorite marketing campaign probably distilled its message into three memorable ideas (or at least should have).

But why does the Power of Three resonate so deeply? Because it's rooted in how people think and communicate. David Ogilvy, the father of advertising, put it best: "If you're trying to persuade people to do something or buy something, it seems to me you should use their language."[187] And one of the most effective patterns we think in? Threes. Structuring your ideas in sets of three mirrors the natural patterns of the human mind, making your message not just easy to understand but impossible to ignore.

And the Power of Three works at any scale—I've seen it firsthand. Throughout my career, three-word mantras have rallied teams around a shared vision. In 2017, "Make Business Noise" fueled our New York team. In 2020, during the pandemic, "True North Touch, True North Together" (#TNT) united our Canadian team. And in 2024, "The Obvious Answer" became the guiding principle for our Global Enterprise Management team. Each phrase wasn't just catchy—it created alignment, focus, and results. Why? Because three words stick. They resonate. They work.

Given the world of information overload we live in, the Power of Three isn't just a linguistic parlor trick. It's a fundamental principle of cognitive psychology, hardwired into the human brain. Between endless email threads, back-to-back meetings, and bloated slide decks, crucial messages often get lost in the noise. Strategies fail to gain traction not because they're bad ideas, but because they're buried under an avalanche of complexity. Daniel Kahneman, Nobel laureate and author of *Thinking, Fast and Slow*, explains that our working memory can only hold a few items at once. This cognitive limit makes simplification essential, as excessive complexity leads to mental fatigue.[188] By structuring your message in threes, you're not dumbing it down—you're making it impossible to ignore. When you use the Power of Three, you're crafting a communication strategy that fits the way our brains naturally work.

This mental shortcut, known as "chunking," is why we remember phone numbers in three parts and why classics like "Stop, Drop, and Roll" stick with us long after we stopped playing with matches. As Ann Handley reminds us in *Everybody Writes*: "No one will ever complain that you've made things too simple to understand." She goes on to emphasize that structuring ideas in a way that's easy for the brain to retrieve—often using the "Rule of Three"— enhances memorability.[189]

Now, I prefer "Power" over "Rule" as it conveys intention rather than limitation—a deliberate tactic to amplify clarity and retention, not just a guideline to follow. But regardless, whether you're crafting a pitch, presenting to stakeholders, or coaching a team, this "power" or "rule" ensures your message is not only heard, but remembered. Heck, I even used it in this book: three sections, Three Main Dishes, three this, three that. And I think we can all agree that this book is pretty unforgettable!

Now, it's not just about memory—it's about rhythm. There's a reason Julius Caesar's *"Veni, vidi, vici"* still gets quoted over two thousand years later. It's why slogans like Apple's "Thinner, Lighter, Faster," Nike's "Just do it," and McDonald's "I'm lovin' it" stick in our minds. When you present information in threes, you build rhythm and predictability into your message, which keeps audiences engaged. The Power of Three creates a cadence that feels complete and satisfying, like the final beat of a symphony. It's like serving your ideas in three perfectly plated courses—structured, engaging, and impactful.

In this chapter, we'll explore how the engaging and impactful nature of the Power of Three can become your secret weapon in communication through three main dishes: *Sweet Spot* dives into the cognitive science and universal appeal of three; *Creating Cadence* explores how rhythm and flow elevate your message's impact; and *Memory Trifecta* is a guide to making your ideas stick in the minds of your audience. Think of it as a professional recipe: three carefully chosen ingredients that come together to create something unforgettable.

And by the way, the enduring appeal of the Power of Three extends beyond oratory and psychology—it permeates how we make decisions *and* tell stories. Greg McKeown, in *Essentialism*, champions the practice of ruthless prioritization. He encourages readers to regularly identify just three top objectives—a practical, disciplined use of the Power of Three that cuts through distraction and brings clarity to complexity.[190] This isn't just minimalist productivity; it's strategic focus sharpened by constraint.

So no matter your role, whether you're leading a team, pitching an idea, or refining your communication, the Power of Three is a tool that's both practical and persuasive. Let's explore the science, art, and strategy behind it—and discover how it can transform the way you communicate, lead, and influence.

The table is set. Let's plate up the perfect prix fixe.

"I DON'T KNOW WHY, JEFFERSON, BUT THERE'S SOMETHING ABOUT THIS PLAN THAT REALLY SPEAKS TO ME."

THREE MAIN DISHES

1 **1956 WAS A** year of breakthroughs. Elvis had America swooning to *Heartbreak Hotel,* Velcro was about to replace zippers forever, and a cognitive scientist named George A. Miller made a discovery that changed how we understand memory. His now-famous study, *The Magical Number Seven, Plus or Minus Two* (clearly, George wasn't one for hard commitments), suggested a fundamental truth: our brains process information best in small, manageable chunks—typically between five and nine.[191] Decades later, communication experts confirmed what great storytellers had long intuited: three is the true sweet spot for human comprehension.

But Miller's discovery was just the beginning. The real magic of three goes beyond memory—it's about how we *think.* Dr. Carmen Simon, in *Impossible to Ignore,* explains: "The Rule of Three works because humans actively seek patterns to create meaning and make decisions. Three is the smallest number needed to create a pattern."[192] That's why three feels intuitive. It's stable, complete, and easy for our brains to grasp—like a tripod, always balanced.

You see it everywhere: in the scientific method (*observe, hypothesize, test*), in project management (*scope, execute, review*), and even in public speaking (*tell them what you'll tell them, tell them, tell them what you told them*). Why? Because three feels complete. Two is unfinished—like a joke missing its punchline. Four or more? Overwhelming. But three? It just works.

The magic of three isn't just psychological—it's also practical. Think about it: what's easier to remember—a long list of eight steps, or three core takeaways?

Nancy Duarte, in *Resonate,* explains why three is so effective: "We remember lists better when they have a natural flow and rhythm, like grouping information into three acts."[193] It's not just about storytelling or marketing slogans—it's about structuring ideas in a way that sticks. Donald Miller, in *Building a StoryBrand,* puts it even more simply: 'Simple ideas are easiest to share. That's why we prioritize three—it's digestible, efficient, and persuasive."[194]

Think about your next meeting or pitch. Instead of overwhelming people with details, focus on three: three key benefits, three core challenges, three next steps. The result? Your message doesn't just land—it sticks.

The Power of Three isn't just a pattern—it's a cheat code. It simplifies the complex, sharpens your message, and makes your ideas impossible to ignore. So next time you're tempted to add a fourth bullet point, stop. Ask yourself: which *three* of these things matter most? Stick to those, and let the Power of Three do the heavy lifting.

Because when it comes to communication, three is *magic*.

But memory is just one piece of the puzzle. If you want your message to truly land, it's not just what you say—it's how you say it.

Creating Cadence

GREAT COMMUNICATION HAS a rhythm—like a master chef plating a perfect dish or a musician landing the final note. It hooks you, pulls you in, and holds you there. That's the Power of Three.

Scott Berkun shares in *Confessions of a Public Speaker* that when you present information in threes, you build rhythm and predictability, keeping audiences engaged.[195] Without rhythm, ideas feel scattered. But with it, even complex concepts become effortless to follow. Carmine Gallo, in *Talk Like TED*, takes this further, tying cadence directly to the art of persuasion. He says language has a cadence, and three is a natural number for creating a rhythm that resonates. It keeps attention without overwhelming.[196]

Think of Martin Luther King Jr.'s "I Have a Dream" speech. His rhythmic repetition—delivering key phrases in sets of three—didn't just inspire. It pulled the audience into his vision, making his message unforgettable. At one point, he drives his point home with three escalating injustices: police brutality, travel discrimination, and forced migration from one ghetto to another. That triadic structure builds power, clarity, and emotional resonance—proof that threes don't just inform, they transform.

Long before George Miller's research, Aristotle understood the Power of Three—about 2,300 years earlier, in fact. In his work on rhetoric and drama, he emphasized that stories need a beginning, middle, and end—and, against all odds, he probably didn't need PowerPoint to make his point.[197] (You may remember his Ethos, Logos, Pathos trifecta from Chapter 11.)

"With this faith, we will be able to hew out of the mountain of despair a stone of hope.

With this faith, we will be able to transform the jangling discords of our nation into a beautiful symphony of brotherhood.

With this faith, we will be able to work together, to pray together, to struggle together, to go to jail together, to climb up for freedom together, knowing that we will be free one day."

— Martin Luther King, Jr.

Amtrak: All Aboard the Power of Three[198]

The Challenge: Enhance corporate communication to ensure clarity and alignment across a diverse, nationwide workforce.

The Approach: Amtrak adopted the Power of Three to distill its core values into three clear, memorable principles: "Do the Right Thing," "Put Customers First," and "Excel Together." This triadic structure simplifies decision-making and behavior expectations, making it easier for employees to internalize and act upon the company's mission.

The Result:

- Improved employee alignment through a straight-forward framework that fosters a unified company culture.
- Enhanced decision-making with three core values guiding consistent, value-driven actions.
- Strengthened brand identity by reinforcing Amtrak's commitment to integrity, customer focus, and teamwork.

The Take-Home Recipe:

- Simplify your message into three clear points.
- Use the Power of Three to drive alignment and clarity.
- Engage your audience with memorable, focused communication.

The Power of Three's impact lies in its elegance—simple yet profound, it invites focus without overwhelming. It's the same reason a well-crafted dish just works—balanced in flavor, satisfying in texture, and easy to digest. Whether you're giving a presentation or leading a meeting, structure your message in threes: past/present/future, or problem/solution/action. It pulls them into your ideas, keeps them engaged, and leaves them with a sense of resolution.

In the realm of storytelling, Robert McKee's seminal work *Story* underlines the timeless power of the three-act structure: setup, confrontation, and resolution. This framework—used in everything from ancient myths to modern screenplays—reflects our innate preference for triadic progression. It delivers emotional rhythm, narrative coherence, and a sense of closure. As McKee shows, the Power of Three isn't a gimmick; it's a storytelling blueprint embedded in human cognition.[199]

So, next time you need to communicate something important, ask yourself: does it flow? Does it engage? Does it guide your audience seamlessly from beginning to end? If not, trim the excess. Find the rhythm. And let the Power of Three do the work.

Now, the most powerful ideas aren't just heard; they're remembered. Up next, we'll dive into the science of making your ideas unforgettable—because if no one remembers what you said, did you really say anything at all?

Memory Trifecta

3 YOUR BRAIN IS like a cluttered kitchen—overstuffed shelves, messy counters, and a rogue stack of Tupperware lids with no matching containers. Now imagine a kitchen so organized that every item has its place, labeled and easy to grab. That's what the Power of Three does for your memory—it neatly shelves ideas so you can recall them instantly.

The Power of Three isn't just a trick—it's a cognitive blueprint for making ideas stick. By grouping information into threes, you help your audience process it more effectively, store it longer, and recall it more easily. And that matters. Decisions take time, attention is scarce, and complexity kills momentum. If you want your ideas to last, they need to be digestible, memorable, and repeatable.

Chunking alone isn't enough—repetition locks it in. Benedict Carey, in *How We Learn*, explains that repetition is key to memory, but how you organize that repetition—like grouping into threes—makes all the difference.[200] Try recalling eight random facts. Tough, right? Now break them into three categories. Suddenly, your brain has a framework—making retrieval effortless.

In a world drowning in information, clarity is your competitive edge. Dan Roam, in *The Back of the Napkin*, emphasizes that in a noisy landscape, the ability to communicate clearly and memorably sets you apart—and structuring your message around the Power of Three can be a powerful way to achieve that.[201] Whether you're leading a meeting, building out a deck, or summarizing the TPS reports, structuring your message in threes keeps it sharp and unforgettable.

Think about a product launch. Instead of dumping a laundry list of features on your audience, distill it to three: affordability, ease of use, and reliability. Now your message isn't just memorable—it's repeatable, which means it spreads. Or take a team meeting. Summarizing updates in three steps—what's done, what's in progress, what's next—keeps everyone focused, even with a packed agenda. The Power of Three makes ideas easy to share and act on. Again... you want that!

The memory trifecta—chunking, repetition, and clarity—turns abstract ideas into sticky, actionable insights.[202] The Power of Three doesn't just help people remember—it drives them to act. So before your next pitch, report, or meeting, ask yourself:

- Have I grouped my ideas into three?
- Have I repeated my key points enough to make them stick?
- Have I made it easy for my audience to recall and repeat?

Because in a world flooded with information, it's not about simplifying your ideas—it's about making them impossible to forget.

FIVE TASTE-TEST RECIPES

The Power of Three isn't just a trick—it's your shortcut to clearer, sharper, and more impactful communication. Use these ideas to structure your message with clarity and rhythm. Start with one, stack them up, or mix and match:

1 **The Three-Word Challenge:** Condense your company's mission statement into just three words. Think of it as a precision test— less fluff, more impact. Want an extra challenge? Try it for your personal mission, too.

2 **The Power of Three Rewrite:** Take a recent email or memo you've written and rework it into three clear points. It's like tailoring your communication with a three-piece suit—sharp, professional, and to the point.

3 **The Tricolon Workout:** In your next presentation, incorporate three tricola—phrases of three parallel ideas. For example, "We came, we saw, we conquered" those quarterly targets. Simple, rhythmic, and memorable!

4 **The Three-Act Storytelling:** Turn your next case study or project report into a three-act narrative. Act 1: The Challenge. Act 2: The Journey. Act 3: The Triumph. It's business storytelling that keeps everyone engaged—jazz hands optional.

5 **The Power of Three Brainstorm:** Try the "3-3-3" method in your next team meeting: brainstorm ideas in groups of three, discuss each for three minutes, then vote on the top three to pursue. It's like speed dating for ideas—minus the awkward icebreakers and even more awkward break-ups.

LAST CALL

The Power of Three isn't just about simplicity—it's about rhythm and resonance. Like a perfectly balanced three-course meal, effective messages need
structure that satisfies without overwhelming. Information served in threes
creates a natural cadence that audiences can digest and remember.

In this chapter, you've learned how the Power of Three enhances communication through three fundamental elements: *Sweet Spot*, which revealed why
three is the optimal number for human comprehension; *Creating Cadence*,
which showed how groups of three create natural rhythm and flow; and *Memory
Trifecta*, which demonstrated how three-part structure makes messages stick.
You've discovered that the Power of Three isn't just a technique—it creates
measurable improvements in message clarity, audience retention, and communication effectiveness.

As you structure your communication, remember that the finest menus don't
overwhelm with choices. Your messages resonate more deeply when organized
in threes. The most memorable ideas, like the most satisfying meals, leave your
audience neither overwhelmed nor wanting—but perfectly satisfied.

Because when it comes to communication, more isn't better—better is
better. And three? Well… three is just right.

CEREBRAL SOUS VIDE

✓ How do I leverage triads in my communication, and what
measurable impact does this have on audience engagement?
✓ When I reflect on my successful strategies, how often do they
naturally organize into three pillars, and why?
✓ Where could I apply the power of three more deliberately to
elevate my team's performance and results?

THE SELF-SERVE STATION

Not convinced yet that three is the magic number? These resources explore why the Power of Three resonates so deeply and how you can use it to make your communication clearer, sharper, and more impactful.

The Elements of Eloquence: How to Turn the Perfect English Phrase by Mark Forsyth (2013) – From Shakespeare to Steve Jobs, discover why history's greatest communicators worked in threes. Forsyth's masterful exploration of rhetoric reveals timeless patterns that make messages unforgettable.

Ultralearning: Master Hard Skills, Outsmart the Competition, and Accelerate Your Career by Scott H. Young (2019) – The Power of Three isn't just for communication—it's a cognitive shortcut for rapid skill acquisition. Young explores how chunking, pattern recognition, and repetition in threes drive mastery in any field.

Talk Like TED by Carmine Gallo (2014) – Behind the scenes of the world's most captivating presentations lies a powerful secret: the Power of Three. Gallo's analysis of over 500 TED talks reveals practical techniques for structuring information that resonates.

The Psychology of Persuasion: How To Persuade Others To Your Way of Thinking by Kevin Hogan (2010) – The Power of Three isn't just about clarity—it's a persuasion tool. Hogan breaks down how people absorb, process, and act on information, revealing why three-part structures consistently drive influence and decision-making.

Brain Rules: 12 Principles for Surviving and Thriving at Work, Home, and School by John Medina (2008) – Okay, it's not explicitly about the Power of Three—but Medina does lay out 12 brain-friendly truths that make life and work way easier. From why exercise supercharges cognition to how storytelling hijacks attention (in a good way), this neuroscience-meets-productivity guide helps you stop fighting your brain and start working with it.

A SWEET & SAVORY SHOUT-OUT

Let's raise our metaphorical glasses (in sets of three, naturally) to Dr. Carmen Simon, cognitive scientist extraordinaire and the mastermind behind the science of memorable content. While she didn't invent the Power of Three (that credit goes to, well, probably some ancient orator with a flair for the dramatic), Dr. Simon has been instrumental in explaining why our brains just can't get enough of that triple treat.

Dr. Simon's work, especially her book *Impossible to Ignore: Creating Memorable Content to Influence Decisions*, has transformed how we understand information-processing and memory in the business world. She's taken the Power of Three from a vague notion of "it just sounds good" to a scientifically-backed principle of cognitive psychology. And her influence extends across industries, from Fortune 500 companies to educational institutions, where her principles have revolutionized how we structure everything from presentations to strategic initiatives.

What sets Dr. Simon apart is her ability to bridge the gap between complex neuroscience and practical business applications. She's shown us that the Power of Three isn't just about catchy slogans or neat presentations—it's about fundamentally aligning our communication with how the human brain works.

Next time you craft a message that sticks like superglue, send a mental "thank you" to Dr. Simon. She's the reason we're all corporate trigonauts, navigating the sea of information overload with our trusty trident: clear, concise, and compelling communication.

In the spirit of Dr. Simon's work, let's commit to making our messages not just heard, but remembered. Here's to the Power of Three—may it inform, inspire, and impact everything we do!

10 QUICK BITES

- The Power of Three resonates because it aligns with the brain's natural preference for patterns, making ideas clearer and more memorable.

- Examples like "Life, Liberty, and the Pursuit of Happiness," "Stop, Drop, and Roll," and "Reduce, Reuse, Recycle" highlight the Power of Three's impact.

- Using three key points in communication simplifies complexity and reduces the risk of overwhelming your audience.

- Dr. Carmen Simon's research shows that grouping information into threes aligns communication with how the human mind processes and recalls data.

- Chunking information into threes helps people retain and retrieve ideas more effectively, especially in high-information environments.

- Famous slogans like Nike's "Just Do It" or speeches like MLK's "I Have a Dream" prove the Power of Three's ability to captivate and inspire.

- Structuring communication with rhythm and cadence—beginning, middle, and end—keeps audiences engaged and ensures a sense of completeness.

- The Power of Three transforms presentations, pitches, and reports by making key points stick and empowering audiences to act.

- Cognitive science, from Miller's chunking research to Kahneman's focus on simplicity, shows the Power of Three's impact on memory and understanding.

- In an overloaded world, three carefully chosen ideas cut through the noise, ensuring communication that informs, inspires, and leaves a lasting impact.

PREP CARD

Common Obstacle:

"Key messages are lost in complexity."

Quick Fix:

Group ideas into three clear points for better retention

Long-term:

Use the Power of Three to simplify communication

Common Obstacle:

"Ideas fail to engage or resonate with audiences."

Quick Fix:

Use rhythmic, three-part phrasing to build flow and connection

Long-term:

Develop a cadence-focused communication style that keeps audiences engaged

---

Common Obstacle:

"Teams struggle to remember or act on information."

Quick Fix:

Present content in three-part frameworks like past -present-future

Long-term:

Foster a culture of chunking information into threes to enhance memory and follow-through

today's special
PERSONAL BRANDING

APPETIZER

Notice how some people seem to attract opportunities effortlessly? That's not luck—that's a strong personal brand. It's not about being everywhere; it's about being in the right place, with the right reputation, at the right time.

MAIN COURSE

Signature Flavor: Define your unique strengths
and ensure they set you apart
Relevant Resonance: Align your brand with your
company's priorities to stay indispensable
Visible Value: Make your contributions seen
and trusted by those who matter most

DESSERT

The Expertise Audit: Map your skills to organizational
needs and identify growth areas
The Contribution Calendar: Make one visible,
high-impact contribution each week
The Feedback Loop: Gather honest insights
from colleagues to refine your brand

PAIRS WELL WITH

Professionals blending into the office wallpaper
The silent MVP who should be the headline act
The office ghostwriter for everyone else's success

CHAPTER 13

Personal Branding—
Your Signature Dish

TUESDAY MORNING ROLLS around, and you're in your usual Around-the-Horn meeting when someone pipes up: *"We need a subject-matter expert to lead this initiative."* You glance around, hoping your name will rise like a perfectly proofed sourdough. But nothing. Silence. Someone else volunteers, and you quietly stew in your lukewarm latte.

This Tuesday morning stinks, and you can't tell if you're mad at yourself, your over-confident colleague, or that $2,000 robot barista that still can't steam milk properly.

The answer: Mostly A... and definitely C. (I mean, it was two grand!)

Here's the thing: being skilled, hard-working, or reliable isn't enough to ensure your name gets served up at the right time. People need to know what you bring to the table—and they need to think of you as the go-to for something specific. That's personal branding. And no, it's not about flashy self-promotion or becoming the office loudmouth. It's about crafting a consistent and authentic story that communicates your unique value—the same way a chef's signature dish tells a diner exactly what they're about in one unforgettable bite. At its core, personal branding is just another form of communication.

When done right, personal branding transforms how others perceive you, how you communicate your expertise, and the opportunities that come your way. Dorie Clark, in *Reinventing You*, argues that personal branding is about taking control of your professional narrative and ensuring your unique strengths and contributions are visible to others.[203] Yet so many professionals fall into the trap of assuming that hard work alone will speak for itself. Spoiler alert: it doesn't.

I'll be vulnerable again (but only because you asked)—this is a subject where I have personally struggled. At times, I've ridden great waves—becoming a seating expert, the sales "culture guy," and a builder of high-performing teams. These moments helped define my brand and my career. But during leadership changes or shifts in company direction, I sometimes failed to project the strategic leadership skills I assumed were obvious. Instead of catching the next wave, I found myself drifting in frustration—stuck, stalled, and sinking.

One particularly sobering moment: A new CEO looked me in the eye and said, "You can't just be the funny guy on stage. You need more executive presence." Fifteen years of success, and suddenly, I felt like I was treading water.

But I was missing a key point: a strong brand isn't about riding waves of recognition; it's about building a foundation that lasts, about crafting a cohesive, authentic narrative that connects your skills, values, and impact over time. A strong personal brand isn't just what you do—it's who you are. It's showing up consistently as the leader you aspire to be, even when the tides of change try to pull you under. It's being trusted for the value you bring. And that trust isn't built on big moments. It's built on consistency, clarity, and showing up—especially when no one's watching.

That feedback made me realize my brand needed to be less reactive and more intentional. Past successes and natural charisma weren't enough (and to be fair, I barely had much of the latter). I had to deliberately shape a narrative that showcased my strategic thinking, adaptability, and leadership—no matter who the CEO was.

Here's something pretty cool: research backs this up. A study in the *Journal of Interactive Marketing* found that professionals who actively manage their personal brand generate higher engagement, greater trust, and more leadership opportunities.[204] Branding isn't just a buzzword—it's a measurable tool for career growth.

In this chapter, we'll break this career-catapult into three key elements. First, we'll help you identify your *Signature Flavor*, the unique skills, values, and attributes that set you apart. Forget being a jack-of-all-trades—it's time to master the art of specialization. Next, we'll dive into *Relevant Resonance*, which is all about aligning your personal brand with what matters most to your organization. After all, the most impressive skill set in the world won't matter if it's not solving a relevant problem. Finally, we'll tackle *Visible Value*—how

to ensure your expertise and contributions are consistently recognized and trusted. This is where we turn your brand into a magnet for opportunities.

Personal branding isn't just about what people see in meetings—it's about how they perceive you when you're not in the room. And today, that "room" extends far beyond the office. Your digital presence is an extension of your brand, shaping how colleagues, leaders, and industry peers engage with your expertise.

Dan Schawbel, in *Me 2.0*, highlights that professionals who actively shape their online presence stay more relevant and top-of-mind for opportunities.[205] While the book predates the widespread adoption of hybrid and remote work, its insights on online personal branding remain applicable in today's digital work environments. Whether through LinkedIn, internal company platforms, or industry forums, being intentional about your digital presence ensures that your expertise is seen, valued, and remembered.

Think of it this way: If your work speaks for itself, make sure it has a microphone.

As Jeff Bezos is purportedly famous for saying: "Your personal brand is what people say about you when you're not in the room."[206] Crafting your signature dish is what ensures your name is called in the moments that matter most.

So, what's on your personal branding menu? Time to cook up something unforgettable.

THREE MAIN DISHES

Signature Flavor

1 **TRYING TO BE** everything to everyone is like spinning a dozen plates. Eventually, something's going to crash—and when it does, no one remembers the effort, just the sound of breaking china. Instead of spreading yourself thin across countless skills, focus on defining what makes you truly stand out—the unique value you bring that no one else can quite replicate. This is your Signature Flavor, the essence of what makes you indispensable to your organization.

Personal branding isn't about being well-rounded—it's about being distinct, indispensable, and the natural first choice. Peter Montoya, in *The Personal Branding Phenomenon* explains that specializing in a specific area makes you memorable and irreplaceable.[207] Your goal isn't to be a jack-of-all-trades; it's to make sure that when a particular challenge arises, people immediately think, *"This is exactly who we need."*

Defining your Signature Flavor takes introspection and a clear understanding of your environment. Gorbatov, Khapova, and Lysova, in their systematic review of personal branding, emphasize that clarity comes through a combination of self-reflection and external feedback—seeing yourself through the eyes of your colleagues and mentors.[208]

To define your Signature Flavor, start with these three essential questions:

- What do people already rely on you for? The best indicator of your strengths is what colleagues repeatedly seek your help with.
- What do you do better than most? You don't need to be the world's top expert, but some sage wisdom I got years ago has really stuck: aim to be better than 75% of people at three things or 99% at one thing. (I chose the three things and am still working on it.)
- What aligns with your passions and long-term goals? A brand built around something you dislike is a shortcut to burnout. You need to choose something you enjoy and want to grow in.

Once you've identified your Signature Flavor, the next step is consistency. Cynthia Johnson, in *Platform*, reinforces that a strong personal brand stays aligned across all touchpoints.[209] This means that how you show up in meetings, communicate online, and interact with peers should all reinforce the same core message. For example, if you want to be known as an innovative problem-solver, make sure your work, LinkedIn presence, and team contributions consistently reinforce that reputation.

The best personal brands don't just stand out—they solve problems that matter. When you consistently showcase your unique strengths, you don't just add value—you become essential. But having a strong Signature Flavor isn't enough. You also need to make sure it's something people actually crave. Even the most perfectly crafted dish won't matter if it's not what's on the menu.

Relevant Resonance

2 BEING GREAT AT something doesn't matter if that "something" is not what's needed. (For example, I can tell exactly how long a microwave has left just by listening. My company, however, remains unimpressed.) That's because in today's workplace, talent alone isn't enough—your strengths have to be relevant. Your personal brand needs to align with your organization's priorities and address the challenges your industry is facing right now. Even the most decadent brownie will be ignored if everyone's in the mood for pie. (But no one can ignore the final buzz of the microwave... I'll take that promotion now, thank you!)

Dorie Clark, in *Stand Out*, explains that successful personal branding is about connecting your strengths with what your audience—or in this case, your organization—values most.[210] Personal branding is all about proving that your skills solve the right problems.

Research from Avery and Greenwald shows that aligning your personal brand with company goals builds trust, visibility, and career momentum.[211] But knowing this isn't enough—you need to take action.

Start by staying informed. Writing in the *Journal of Brand Management*, Manel Khedher highlights that personal branding enhances employability through dimensions like cultural capital, social capital, and authentic self-presentation. These elements help individuals better align with evolving

"People don't buy what you do; they buy why you do it. And what you do simply proves what you believe."

— Simon Sinek

SPANX: Shaping Success Through Personal Branding[212]

The Challenge: Sara Blakely wanted to establish SPANX as more than a shapewear brand—it had to become a symbol of innovation and empowerment, while positioning herself as a relatable and visionary entrepreneur.

The Approach: Blakely built her personal brand by embracing humor, vulnerability, and perseverance, openly sharing stories of rejection, mistakes, and triumphs. Blakely linked her personal brand to SPANX's corporate ethos, emphasizing creativity, problem-solving, and empowering women to feel confident in their skin.

The Result:

- SPANX became a billion-dollar company without spending money on traditional advertising in its early years.
- Sara Blakely was recognized as the world's youngest self-made female billionaire by Forbes.
- Blakely's personal brand built trust and loyalty, with millions of customers identifying with her mission of empowerment and authenticity.

The Take-Home Recipe:

- Share stories that build trust and connection.
- Tie your personal mission to your brand.
- Use platforms to amplify your impact.

market expectations and professional demands.[213] This supports the importance of understanding your company's strategic goals and emerging industry trends. So, take the time to read quarterly reports, attend town halls, and engage in team discussions. The better you understand your company's direction, the easier it is to align your brand with it.

Amplifying your alignment doesn't stop at understanding priorities—you need to demonstrate your contributions in visible, impactful ways. For example, if your company is pivoting toward sustainability, you can share articles, publish thought leadership posts, or volunteer for key projects. Show that you're not just part of the conversation—you're shaping it.

Worried you need to be the loudest voice in the room? (I got you, my introverted brethren.) You don't need to be!

Susan Cain, in *Quiet*, reminds us that powerful personal branding isn't about volume—it's about impact.[214] Focus on making thoughtful, targeted contributions. A single meaningful comment in a meeting can have more impact than hours of endless chatter.

Finally, remember that alignment isn't just about tactics—it's about purpose. In *Start with Why*, Simon Sinek explains that personal branding rooted in purpose resonates far more than superficial self-promotion. "People don't buy what you do; they buy why you do it," he writes. "And what you do simply proves what you believe."[215] When you communicate not just what you do, but *why* you do it, you build trust and inspire loyalty. Whether you're pitching an idea or leading a project, tie your contributions back to your core mission and values.

Relevant Resonance is about more than being noticed—it's about being needed. When your personal brand aligns with what your organization and industry value most, you become someone people can't imagine succeeding without. After all, the best dish on the table isn't just delicious—it's exactly what everyone's craving.

That said, even the perfect dish won't get ordered if it's hidden on the back page of the menu.

3 BUILDING YOUR PERSONAL brand isn't just about knowing your strengths (*Signature Flavor*) or aligning them with what matters (*Relevant Resonance*). It's about ensuring your contributions are seen, recognized, and valued by the people who matter most. If you've mastered the first two steps, *Visible Value* is what elevates your personal brand from quiet competence to tangible impact. Think of it as plating a signature dish—presentation isn't everything, but it's what draws attention to the substance behind your work.

As I.D.H. Shepherd explains in *From Cattle and Coke to Charlie*, visibility is most powerful when it's tied to meaningful contributions and results.[216] People trust professionals whose reputations are built on consistent value, not on tooting their own horn. Instead of just listing achievements, show how your work has solved problems, improved processes, or advanced company goals. Add a dash of gratitude, a layer of storytelling, and a sprinkle of humility—and voilà!

Herminia Ibarra, in *Act Like a Leader, Think Like a Leader*, argues that visibility is not just about showcasing your work, but about adopting leadership behaviors that demonstrate initiative and drive before you're formally recognized as a leader.[217] This could mean volunteering to lead a project, offering solutions in high-stakes meetings, or stepping into roles that push you outside your comfort zone. These actions don't just expand your influence—they signal to decision-makers that you're ready for more responsibility.

The best communicators aren't just heard—they're remembered. Visibility isn't just about showing up in meetings; it's about ensuring your contributions shape the conversations that matter. The way you communicate—verbally, in writing, in leadership moments—determines whether your ideas gain traction or get lost in the shuffle.

And today, that includes digital platforms.

Your ideas are only as powerful as the platforms that carry them. LinkedIn, internal company forums, and industry discussions can amplify your expertise far beyond your immediate team. Posting a short recap of lessons learned from a project, sharing insights, or participating in thought leadership conversations ensures your contributions don't just live in your head—or in last quarter's slide deck. If your work speaks for itself, make sure it has a microphone.

Your online presence isn't just an extension of your brand—it's one of the most powerful ways to communicate your expertise. Whether it's LinkedIn, internal company platforms, or industry discussions, your digital footprint tells a story about who you are, what you know, and how you contribute. And in a world where decisions get made in Slack threads, inboxes, and LinkedIn DMs, your ability to communicate your value online is just as critical as how you show up in the office.

Finally, visibility isn't about a one-time spotlight—it's about consistency. The best brands aren't built on one viral moment but on repeated, high-value contributions over time. Sponsors (more on that in Chapter 14!) play a key role in visibility, but they can only advocate for you if they know what you bring to the table. A sponsor can't amplify what they don't see.

Whether it's presenting at a quarterly meeting, mentoring junior colleagues, or sharing insights online, the goal is the same: stay visible, stay valuable, and ensure that when opportunities arise, your name is the first one that comes to mind.

FIVE TASTE-TEST RECIPES

Building a personal brand doesn't have to be complicated. These five simple ideas will help you craft an authentic and memorable brand that sets you apart, aligns with what matters most, and ensures your contributions are seen. Give some, none, or all a shot!

1. **The Expertise Audit:** Take a hard look at your skills and knowledge. Map them to your company's strategic goals. What are you known for? Where are the gaps? This isn't just a checklist—it's a treasure map to becoming the expert everyone turns to.

2. **The Value Proposition Pitch:** Craft a 30-second pitch that captures your unique value. What problems do you solve? How do you make things better? Deliver it with the precision of a Michelin-starred chef plating a signature dish. Share and tweak with a confidant willing to give you honest feedback.

3. **The Contribution Calendar:** Set a goal to make one high-impact contribution every week. Share insights, propose a fresh idea, or lead a quick session. Be consistent—people notice the colleague who adds value week after week.

4. **The Feedback Loop:** Ask 5–10 colleagues what they see as your strengths, what you can improve, and what comes to mind when they think of you. These insights are the secret ingredients for refining your personal brand.

5. **The Expertise Expansion Plan:** Identify (and confirm) one skill that will matter in your company's future. Dedicate the next three months to leveling up—whether it's through an online course, shadowing a colleague, or diving into industry research.

LAST CALL

Personal branding isn't about flashy self-promotion or becoming the office horn-tooter—it's about crafting a professional identity that's authentic, strategic, and impossible to forget. Like serving up your signature dish at a dinner party, it's what makes people remember you for all the right reasons. Because let's be real—a successful career isn't just about skill, but about how well you communicate that skill to the world.

In this chapter, you've explored how personal branding elevates your professional reputation through three key elements: *Signature Flavor*, which helped you identify the unique strengths that set you apart; *Relevant Resonance*, which showed you how to align your brand with your organization's goals and priorities; and *Visible Value*, which taught you how to ensure your contributions are recognized by the people who matter most.

And here's the truth: you already have a brand. The only question is whether it's intentional or accidental. So, what's it going to be? Will you be the best-kept secret in the office—or the obvious choice for the next big opportunity?

Your personal brand is the story people tell about you when you're not in the room. So make sure it's a story worth telling.

CEREBRAL SOUS VIDE

✓ Do I have a clear idea of the strengths and expertise I want to be known for?
✓ Am I focusing my energy on areas that align with my organization's most critical needs?
✓ Am I consistently finding ways to highlight my contributions?

THE SELF-SERVE STATION

Think personal branding is just for influencers or YouTube stars? Nope. These deep dives show you how to craft a brand so clear and compelling, your name will pop up in every meeting—in a good way:

- *Stand Out: How to Find Your Breakthrough Idea and Build a Following Around It* by Dorie Clark (2015) – Yes, Clark gets two mentions—she's that good. This one's all about standing out in crowded industries. From thought leadership to crafting your big idea, it's a masterclass in making your personal brand unforgettable.

- *Personal Branding For Dummies* by Susan Chritton (2014) – Still think personal branding is too complicated? Think again. Chritton breaks it down into bite-sized, actionable strategies to help you stand out at work without looking like you're trying too hard.

- *The Brand Called You* by Tom Peters (1997) – This iconic Fast Company article is the OG of personal branding. Peters was preaching the importance of "Brand You" before LinkedIn and TikTok existed. If you want to understand the roots of why personal branding is non-negotiable in corporate America, this is where it all began.

- *Promote Yourself: The New Rules for Career Success* by Dan Schawbel (2013) – Feel stuck in the shadows at work? Schawbel delivers a playbook for standing out in the modern workplace without looking like a self-promoter. Packed with real-world advice, this guide shows you how to align your brand with company goals, use social media strategically, and become the go-to person everyone remembers.

- "How to Craft Your Personal Brand Story," TEDx Talk by Tyrona Heath (2018) – Heath delivers an 18-minute crash course on turning your experiences, strengths, and values into a narrative that inspires trust and loyalty. Buckle up!

A SWEET & SAVORY SHOUT-OUT

Dorie Clark's *Reinventing You: Define Your Brand, Imagine Your Future* is a powerful guide for professionals ready to take control of how they're perceived and create opportunities on their own terms. Most people assume hard work is enough to advance their career, but Clark shows that success also depends on actively managing your personal brand. Whether you're aiming for a promotion, transitioning to a new industry, or simply refining your reputation, this book offers the tools to reshape your professional narrative and make it resonate.

Clark walks readers through a clear and actionable process to redefine their personal brand, starting with an honest audit of how others currently see them. She explains how to identify gaps between perception and reality and how to close those gaps through strategic communication and deliberate action. Her framework includes leveraging social proof, crafting a personal narrative, and building meaningful relationships that enhance visibility and trust. Throughout the book are real-world stories of professionals who successfully reinvented themselves, offering practical inspiration alongside her advice.

What makes *Reinventing You* stand out is its ability to blend strategy with accessibility. Clark writes with clarity and warmth, making her advice feel both actionable and authentic. Her approach is rooted in the idea that personal branding isn't about becoming someone you're not—it's about aligning your unique strengths with the opportunities you seek. Stuck in a career plateau or looking to redefine your role? This book provides a clear roadmap to transformation.

Reinventing You isn't just a guide to personal branding—it's a blueprint for redefining your professional identity and creating opportunities that align with your potential. Clark's legacy proves that career growth isn't about waiting to be noticed—it's about shaping a story so compelling that people can't help but pay attention.

Your career isn't just built on what you do. It's shaped by how you tell your story.

10 QUICK BITES

- Personal branding is about crafting an authentic story that highlights your unique value.

- Hard work alone won't get you noticed; visibility and strategic storytelling are key to ensuring your name comes up when it matters.

- Your Signature Flavor is the unique combination of skills that makes you indispensable—focus on being distinct, not well-rounded.

- To define your brand, ask: What do people rely on you for? What do you do better than most? What aligns with your goals?

- Dorie Clark explains that successful personal branding connects your strengths with what your organization values most.

- Research shows that aligning your personal brand with company goals builds trust, visibility, and career momentum.

- Susan Cain reminds us that powerful personal branding isn't about volume—it's about impact and thoughtful contributions.

- Herminia Ibarra argues that visibility means adopting leadership behaviors that demonstrate initiative before you're formally recognized as a leader.

- Your digital presence tells a story about who you are—LinkedIn and industry discussions amplify your expertise beyond your immediate team.

- As Jeff Bezos reportedly said: "Your personal brand is what people say about you when you're not in the room."

PREP CARD

Common Obstacle:

"My name isn't tied to any clear expertise."

Quick Fix:

Focus on one in-demand skill to really stand out.

Long-Term:

Aim to be better than 75% of people at three things or 99% at one thing, and consistently showcase them through impactful work.

Common Obstacle:

"Key decision-makers don't notice my work."

Quick Fix:

Share your wins directly with managers through concise updates.

Long-Term:

Volunteer for high-visibility projects that showcase your expertise.

Common Obstacle:

"My brand doesn't align with company priorities."

Quick Fix:

Tie your work to key organizational goals.

Long-Term:

Develop a reputation for solving relevant problems and driving organizational success.

SPONSORSHIP

APPETIZER

Ever wonder why some careers skyrocket while others stall? It's not just hard work—it's sponsorship. The right advocate doesn't just open doors; they make sure your name is in the room before you even step inside.

MAIN COURSE

Power Plays: Sponsors advocate for your ideas, amplify your achievements, and connect you to influential networks
Strategic Visibility: Position yourself intentionally so your work and potential are seen by decision-makers
Protégé Playbook: Build the traits sponsors value—reliability, ambition, and coachability—to make yourself sponsor-worthy

DESSERT

The Sponsor Wishlist: Identify three to five potential sponsors aligned with your goals
The Sponsorship Spark: Start the conversation to build trust and connection
The Visibility Boost: Take on stretch assignments to showcase your potential (Good for personal brand building, too!)

PAIRS WELL WITH

High performers stuck in the "great potential" loop
Invisible innovators watching others claim their ideas
Career climbers with talent but zero insider access

CHAPTER 14

Sponsorship—The Executive Chef's Table

YOUR CFO SCANS the presentation. "And who developed this market analysis framework?" she asks. Before you can speak, Sarah, your colleague, confidently responds: "Our team worked on it together, and I helped refine the final model." You nod along, knowing the truth: you built the framework—testing, iterating, and perfecting it. You've tried to present it three times in department meetings, but each time, the conversation moves on before you could make your case. Now here it is, getting the spotlight—without your name attached. Not because Sarah stole it, but because the right people never knew where it came from.

Six months and two promotions later, Sarah's leading the division while you're still being told you show "great potential." The missing ingredient? Sponsorship.

Beyond raw talent lives a career accelerant that separates the visible from the invisible: having someone who doesn't just believe in your potential but actively advocates for your success. Think of it as having an amplifier for your voice, someone who ensures that your message reaches the executive suite. The ultimate effective communication tool—a leader with influence telling your story, exactly the way you want it told.

This is true whether you're a seasoned professional or just starting your career. For early-career professionals, sponsorship often starts by demonstrating reliability in your first role—being the person who consistently delivers, learns quickly, and helps others succeed. Start by identifying leaders who actively develop talent, participate in cross-functional projects, and leverage programs like ERGs (Employee Resource Groups) to build visibility. Like a new chef mastering basic techniques before taking on complex dishes, you should focus on building your reputation through consistent, quality work. Convert mentors into sponsors by showing how you implement their advice and achieve measurable results. Your reliability and eagerness to learn can attract sponsors just as effectively as years of experience.

Drawing from decades of research, Dr. Sylvia Ann Hewlett, founder of the Center for Talent Innovation and author of *The Sponsor Effect*, emphasizes that sponsors advocate for individuals based on their potential for greatness, not out of a sense of obligation or because they need help. Additionally Hewlett goes on to say: "Mentors give, whereas sponsors invest."[218]

Capello and Sprunt (2020) elaborate on that Hewlett quote. Sponsorship, they add, goes beyond offering advice—it's about leaders putting their influence behind you. Sponsors open doors, place you in the right conversations, and ensure decision-makers see your impact.[219]

Fifteen years ago, I was stuck in "professional purgatory." Despite solid performance, my efforts went unnoticed, evaporating into the corporate void. My turning point came during an informal meeting between a partner principal and one of our product category VPs. After an impassioned, impromptu pitch for one of his products, I caught his attention—but what happened next changed everything.

Instead of just nodding along, he became an advocate. First, he put me in a position to contribute, assigning me to key projects where I could help the company and prove myself. When I delivered, he championed me for a cross-functional leadership role, making sure my name was in the right conversations. That opportunity became my launching pad—but only because his influence and my ability to deliver combined to make it happen.

My biggest takeaway: sponsorship isn't a gift. It's an investment in potential.

Now, let's replay that opening scenario—this time with sponsorship in action: The VP asks who led the analysis, and before Sarah can speak, another voice chimes in. "That was Alex's framework. She developed it after spotting a pattern in our APAC markets." Your sponsor—in this case, a senior director who's been advocating for your work—ensures your contributions are visible and credited. Instead of watching your ideas climb the ladder without you, you're climbing with them.

This hypothetical transformation is backed by actual data. According to a *Harvard Business Review* Research Report, professionals with sponsors are 23% more likely to advance in their careers than equally talented peers without advocacy. For women and underrepresented groups, the impact is even more profound—those with sponsors are 27% more likely to ask for raises and 22% more likely to seek out stretch assignments compared to those without.[220]

As author of *The Game Plan of Successful Career Sponsorship: Harnessing the Talent of Aspiring Managers and Senior Leaders*, Jovina Ang emphasizes that this type of advocacy creates a powerful symbiotic relationship. Sponsors amplify their protégés' careers while gaining influence and building organizational legacy themselves.[221] It's a total win-win.

In her groundbreaking work *Decoding Sponsorship*, sponsorship expert Maggie Chan Jones explains that sponsors are drawn to people who demonstrate reliability, coachability, and the ability to represent them well in critical moments.[222] It's not just about excelling at your job—it's about showing you're ready for the next level through clear, strategic communication.

Ursula Burns didn't just climb the corporate ladder—she redesigned it.

Starting as an intern, she rose to become the first Black woman to lead a Fortune 500 company as Xerox's CEO. She credits her ascent to her predecessor Anne Mulcahy—not just for mentorship, but for sponsorship.[223] Burns' success wasn't just because of her technical expertise; it was driven by alignment—ensuring her work and communication fit both Xerox's strategic goals and Mulcahy's vision. That made her not just a great employee, but the obvious choice for leadership.

But here's what most professionals miss: sponsorship isn't luck or favoritism. It's the result of strategic visibility and intentional communication. Every presentation, email, and interaction is an audition. Your gratitude practices (Chapter One) foster authentic relationships. Your ability to navigate challenges (Chapter Four) and manage energy (Chapter Nine) builds consistent, impressive performance. Paired with strong listening skills (Chapter Eight) and clear storytelling (Chapter 11), you make a compelling case for sponsorship—one that influential leaders can't ignore.

In this chapter, we'll explore three dynamics that transform potential into sponsorship gold. First, *Power Players* reveals why sponsors are career game-changers and how they operate behind the scenes. In *Strategic Visibility*, you'll learn to combine stellar performance with the art of being seen by the right people. Finally, *Protégé Playbook* shows you how to become the kind of professional sponsors fight to champion.

Sponsorship is your ticket to the Executive Chef's Table—where decisions are made, influence is built, and careers are accelerated.

The only question is: are you waiting for an invitation, or are you pulling up a chair?

THREE MAIN DISHES

Power Plays

1 **WHEN INDRA NOOYI** became CEO of PepsiCo, the world saw a visionary leader. What they didn't see was Roger Enrico, the former CEO who championed her from day one. Enrico didn't just give advice—he placed her in high-visibility roles, advocated for her in boardrooms, and made sure her strategic insights shaped PepsiCo's future.[224] This wasn't mentorship, it was sponsorship, clearing the path for her rise to the top. (Also, Indra was pretty badass in that role.)

Understanding the mechanics of sponsorship power means recognizing it's a strategic alliance, not a favor system. As Collett and Fenton demonstrate in their research on high-impact partnerships, effective sponsors operate as talent investors, carefully selecting individuals who offer strong potential returns on their reputational capital.[225] The most successful sponsorship relationships follow a clear framework: identify mutual value, establish clear expectations, and create consistent visibility for both parties' contributions.

This strategic power manifests in three distinct ways. And unlike your corporate headshots, these actually make you look good.

First, sponsors serve as your strategic amplifiers. They don't just speak about you—they speak for you, translating your achievements into language that resonates with decision-makers. When a sponsor says, "You need to put Shannon on this project," they're not just making a suggestion—they're putting their reputation behind your potential.

Second, sponsors plug you into what Collett and Fenton describe as the informal circles where real decisions get made.[226] I like to think of them as "power networks." These aren't just introductions—they're calculated invitations into rooms that shape careers. A sponsor who brings you to a private leadership dinner isn't just being nice—they're placing you where influence happens.

Third, sponsors act as your career strategists, identifying opportunities you might not even know exist. They don't just open doors; they tell you which doors are worth walking through. When a sponsor suggests you take a lateral move instead of a promotion, they're often seeing three moves ahead on your career chessboard.

The impact flows both ways. In *Decoding Sponsorship: The Secret Strategy to Accelerate Your Career and Launch Into Leadership*, Maggie Chan Jones found that successful sponsor-protégé relationships increased both parties' influence within their organizations.[227] Why? Because sponsors aren't just betting on talent—they're investing in them and their visibility.

Strategic Visibility

2 **IF YOU'VE BEEN** hiding your light under a bushel (or more likely, behind a stack of TPS reports), it's time to let it shine. The sponsorship equation is simple:

Performance + Visibility = Opportunity.

Sponsorship is a two-way street. The more a sponsor elevates you, the more their reputation as a talent spotter grows. It's a power exchange—visibility for credibility, influence for impact. But a sponsor's influence means nothing if no one knows about their great judgment. If you're great at what you do but no one knows it, you don't have a sponsor problem—you have a visibility problem.

First, let's talk performance. It's your baseline—your ticket to the sponsorship game. But here's the twist: being great at your job isn't enough. The world is full of talented people who never get discovered. Why? Because without visibility, performance is just potential waiting to be recognized.

That's where visibility comes in. As Sylvia Barber emphasizes in *The Visibility Factor*, visibility isn't about shameless self-promotion—it's about standing in your power and showing up authentically in ways that align with your strengths and goals.[228] This means deliberately positioning yourself where your efforts and results are seen by the right people. Think of it this way: you might be serving up a Michelin-worthy dish, but if it's hidden in the kitchen, no one's ordering it off the menu.

Seek out and volunteer for high-profile projects that align with organizational priorities and showcase your capabilities. When in meetings, contribute meaningful insights that demonstrate both your expertise and commitment to collective success. Share your wins and—equally important—what you've learned from setbacks with both your immediate team and senior leadership. Build relationships beyond your department by taking on cross-functional initiatives that expand your network while delivering measurable impact.

"Mentors give, whereas sponsors invest."

— Sylvia Ann Hewlett

Santander: Sparking Careers and Championing Leaders[229]

The Challenge: Santander aimed to foster leadership diversity by accelerating the development of women and underrepresented groups within the organization.

The Approach: To achieve this, Santander introduced the SPARK program (Sponsorship, Prosperity, Advancement, Retention, Knowledge), a nine-month initiative designed to invest in emerging female and diverse talent. The program pairs participants with senior leaders who act as sponsors, providing advocacy, guidance, and opportunities for visibility within the company.

The Result:

- Many participants advanced into leadership roles during or shortly after the program.
- Retention rates among diverse talent improved significantly compared to the company average.
- The program enhanced the diversity and strength of the leadership pipeline.

The Take-Home Recipe:

- Pair high-potential employees with senior leaders to drive growth.
- Support underrepresented groups to foster inclusivity.
- Track outcomes and share successes to boost impact.

This strategic visibility matters because, as Herminia Ibarra, Professor of Organizational Behavior at London Business School, observes, people are more likely to become sponsors when they perceive in your traits or potential that echo their own experiences or resemble those they've supported successfully in the past.[230]

Visibility isn't just about being seen—it's about being seen as sponsor-able. Joel Garfinkle explains in *Getting Ahead* that combining consistent performance with strategic visibility is the key to creating career-accelerating opportunities.[231] This idea is further reinforced in Edward Evarts' *Raise Your Visibility & Value*, which argues that visibility isn't just about individual success, but making yourself indispensable to your organization by demonstrating value consistently and authentically.[232]

Finally, as Cathy Benko and Molly Anderson observe in *The Corporate Lattice*, building visibility in today's evolving workplace means navigating non-linear paths.[233] Success comes from embracing collaboration and adaptability—essential ingredients in fostering strategic relationships, including sponsorship. Because let's be real: no one's sponsoring the office ghost. If your biggest workplace achievement is sneaking out early without anyone noticing, you're not getting a sponsor—you're getting replaced by an AI chatbot.

Protégé Playbook

3 **WANT TO KNOW** the true secret to attracting a sponsor? Be someone worth sponsoring. Simple in theory, frustrating in execution—like trying to fold a fitted sheet with dignity.

First and foremost—and again—be excellent at what you do. This is non-negotiable. Scott Keller and Colin Price, in *Beyond Performance*, emphasize that consistent high performance isn't just a career baseline—it's a prerequisite for gaining trust and credibility in the eyes of leaders who can influence your advancement.[234]

But beyond performance, sponsors look for key traits:

Reliability: Deliver every time. No drama, no excuses. In the corporate world, reliability is the ultimate flex.

Ambition: Be hungry for growth. Chase challenges. Good energy is contagious.

Loyalty: Demonstrate that you'll have your sponsor's back, just as they have yours. Sponsorship runs both ways.

Coachability: As Adam Grant explains in *Think Again*, the ability to rethink, adapt, and embrace feedback is a hallmark of successful professionals and a key trait sponsors seek in protégés.[235]

Value Add: Bring something unique to the table. Maybe it's a skill, a perspective, or a network.

Remember, sponsorship is a meaningful deposit into the Bank of You. Your job is to ensure that investment yields returns for your sponsor. As Hewlett et al. emphasize in *The Sponsor Effect: Breaking Through the Last Glass Ceiling*, sponsorship is most effective when protégés deliver measurable results that enhance their sponsor's credibility and influence within the organization.[236] By performing at a high level, you not only accelerate your own advancement but also contribute to your sponsor's standing—making the relationship mutually reinforcing.

So, cultivate these traits, showcase your potential, and become the kind of protégé sponsors brag about. Who knows? That next big opportunity might already have your name on it.

FIVE TASTE-TEST RECIPES

Sponsorship isn't just networking—it's career rocket fuel. These five strategies will help you build real connections that open doors and put your name in the right rooms. Start with one, stack them like layers of a perfect dish, or go all in for maximum impact.

1   **The Value Proposition Pitch:** Craft a sharp, concise statement of your unique value—what you bring to the table that no one else does. Think of it as your professional tagline, minus the cheesy jingle. Practice until it's smoother than a buttered slide.

2   **The Strategic Visibility Plan:** Map out key players in your organization and plan how to get on their radar. Volunteer for cross-functional projects, speak at events, or strike up small talk by the coffee machine (pro tip: know their coffee order). Remember, you're going for "rising star," not "stalker."

3   **The Sponsor Wishlist:** Identify 3-5 potential sponsors in your organization. Research their backgrounds, current projects, and interests. Look for alignment with your own goals and values. Think of it as building a corporate dream team—minus the awkward icebreakers.

4   **The Reciprocal Value Exchange:** For each sponsor, brainstorm ways to add value to their work or goals. Maybe you have a skill they need or market knowledge they lack. The best protégés don't just receive—they give back.

5   **The Sponsorship Spark:** Once you've done your homework, start the conversation. Share your goals, seek their insights, and explore ways to collaborate. Don't rush—sponsorship is built on trust, not cold pitches.

LAST CALL

Sponsorship isn't corporate favoritism—it's a strategic alliance that turns potential into opportunity. Like an executive chef handpicking a line cook for a promotion, a great sponsor doesn't just notice talent—they advocate for it in the rooms that matter. Every successful career needs both exceptional performance and powerful champions.

In this chapter, you've learned how sponsorship drives career advancement through three critical elements: *Power Players*, which revealed how sponsors actively champion your success behind closed doors; *Strategic Visibility*, which showed how to combine excellence with the art of being seen by decision-makers; and *Protégé Playbook*, which demonstrated how to become someone worth sponsoring. You've discovered that sponsorship creates measurable improvements in career trajectory, professional opportunities, and organizational influence.

So, as you cultivate sponsorship, remember—great dishes don't just speak for themselves. Someone has to bring them to the table. And the right advocate doesn't just put your name on the menu—they make sure it's the house special.

CEREBRAL SOUS VIDE

✓ Who has advocated for my growth in the past, and how can I show gratitude or pay it forward?

✓ What steps can I take to make my contributions more visible to potential sponsors and who needs to see it?

✓ How can I align my goals with the priorities of leaders who could champion my career?

THE SELF-SERVE STATION

Think sponsorship is just about who you know? These resources will show you how to attract the right advocates, build career-changing relationships, and turn influence into real opportunities—no favoritism required:

- *(Forget a Mentor) Find a Sponsor* by Sylvia Ann Hewlett (2013) – Tired of well-meaning advice but no actual opportunities? Hewlett reveals why the best career currency isn't just knowledge—it's having someone powerful in your corner. Think of it as your guide to turning coffee chats into corner offices.

- "The Sponsor Effect"–Center for Talent Innovation Report (2019) – For the data nerds who need proof that relationships trump resumes. This research doesn't just tell you sponsorship matters—it shows you exactly why, how, and what it means for your next promotion. Warning: Contains enough stats to make your MBA jealous.

- "Sponsors Need to Stop Acting Like Mentors" – *Harvard Business Review* Article by Kennedy & Jain-Link (2021) – Finally, someone says what we're all thinking: mentorship is nice, but sponsorship gets results. Like a relationship intervention for well-meaning leaders who think another coffee chat is the answer. (Spoiler: it's not.)

- "How to Find the Person Who Can Help You Get Ahead at Work" – TED Talk by Carla Harris (2021) – 18 minutes of career truth bombs from someone who's actually been in the C-suite trenches. Harris drops the kind of insights that make you want to totally rebuild your network. Perfect for your commute.

- *The Game Plan of Successful Career Sponsorship* by Jovina Ang (2019) – Ever wonder what your sponsor is really thinking? Ang spills the tea from both sides of the desk. Essential reading for anyone who's ever wondered why some colleagues seem to effortlessly climb the ladder while you're still waiting for someone to notice your PowerPoint skills.

A SWEET & SAVORY SHOUT-OUT

Sponsorship, the ultimate career game-changer, owes its spotlight to the groundbreaking research of Sylvia Ann Hewlett. Through her seminal work at the Center for Talent Innovation and her landmark book *(Forget a Mentor) Find a Sponsor*, Hewlett proved that while mentorship matters, sponsorship is what truly propels careers forward.

What sets Hewlett apart is her masterful mix of rigorous data and actionable insights. She didn't just theorize about sponsorship—she quantified its impact. Her research showed that men with sponsors are 23% more likely to advance, and women with sponsors are 19% more likely to take on stretch assignments. In *The Sponsor Effect*, she expanded on this, showing that while many professionals assume hard work alone will get them noticed, real career acceleration happens when a senior leader actively champions their success.

Her game-changing insight? Sponsorship isn't just about good advice—it's about having powerful advocates who fight for your advancement. Through research at major corporations, she revealed that while mentors guide, sponsors do three vital things: believe in you, bet on you, and fight for your success.

Perhaps most importantly, Hewlett has proven that sponsorship isn't just beneficial for protégés—it's essential for leaders who want to build strong teams and leave lasting legacies. Her work at the Center for Talent Innovation revealed that when leaders actively sponsor others, they themselves are 23% more likely to advance and 53% more likely to receive a promotion.

The next time you're in a position to seek or offer sponsorship, remember Hewlett's core principle: real career advancement isn't just about what you know or who you know—it's about who's ready to champion what you can do. Her legacy isn't just about career advice— it's a reimagining of how talent gets its seat at the table.

10 QUICK BITES

- Sponsorship ensures your contributions are visible and credited, helping you climb the ladder with your ideas.

- *Harvard Business Review* research shows professionals with sponsors are 23% more likely to advance and 27% more likely to request raises.

- As Dr. Sylvia Ann Hewlett explains: "Mentors give, whereas sponsors invest"—sponsors actively advocate, not just advise.

- Sponsorship is a mutual investment that amplifies both the protégé's career and the sponsor's influence.

- Sponsors look for five key traits: reliability, ambition, loyalty, coachability, and unique value-add contributions.

- Strategic visibility—through high-profile projects and cross-functional work—makes you sponsor-worthy.

- Every interaction, from emails to meetings, is a chance to showcase leadership potential.

- Sponsors plug you into "power networks"—the informal circles where real decisions get made.

- Maggie Chan Jones found that successful sponsor-protégé relationships increased both parties' influence within their organizations.

- The sponsorship equation is simple: Performance + Visibility = Opportunity.

PREP CARD

Common Obstacle:
"I get overlooked for sponsorship opportunities."
Quick Fix:
Highlight your value with clear, measurable contributions
Long-Term:
Use the Power of Three to consistently communicate your impact

---

Common Obstacle:
"Sponsors struggle to advocate for me effectively."
Quick Fix:
Arm them with ready-to-go soundbites—examples of your "what" and "why"
Long-Term:
Build an open feedback loop so they understand your goals, strengths, and what doors you want opened

---

Common Obstacle:
"I'm unsure how to position myself for sponsorship."
Quick Fix:
Demonstrate coachability and a willingness to take on stretch work
Long-Term:
Develop a reputation as someone who delivers results and aligns with organizational priorities

Notes

DIObjective DIPLOMACY

APPETIZER

Ever feel like the workplace is more Game of Thrones than team effort? That's where diplomacy comes in. The right approach turns tension into trust, influence into impact, and office politics into actual progress—no dragon needed.

MAIN COURSE

Perspective Mastery: View conflicts from all angles
to foster understanding and spark innovation
Authority-Free Influence: Lead with trust,
credibility, and collaboration—not titles
Constructive Conflict: Turn disagreements into solutions
that build relationships and drive creativity

DESSERT

The Perspective Swap: Articulate the opposing
view to build empathy and trust
The Alliance Audit: Identify key allies
and influencers in your network
The Conflict Reframe: Treat disagreements
as shared puzzles, not battles

PAIRS WELL WITH

Professionals drained by toxic office politics
High achievers who want to lead with influence, not authority
Teams seeking to turn conflicts into collaborative breakthroughs

CHAPTER 15

Diplomacy—The Balancing Act

ONDAY MORNING ROLLS around... again! The weekly
strategy meeting is in full swing, and the tension is thick enough to
spread on a stale bagel. A passive-aggressive jab lands across the table,
followed by an audible sigh and an expertly timed eye roll. The conversation
is teetering on disaster when, seemingly out of nowhere, Grahm—the team's
unspoken diplomat—steps in. He acknowledges the different viewpoints,
reframes the issue, and shifts the tone from combative to collaborative.

Everyone breathes a collective sigh of relief, and the meeting finds its footing.
Grahm's subtle yet masterful handling of the situation? That's office diplomacy
in action. And if you've ever seen what happens in its absence—when office
politics take over—you know how rare and essential it truly is.

As we've explored throughout this book, effective communication takes many
forms. We started with understanding how we communicate with ourselves,
moved to direct communication with others, and now we arrive at the most
nuanced communication challenge: navigating organizational dynamics.
Diplomacy represents the culmination of all our communication skills. It's
where self-awareness, interpersonal skills, and organizational savvy converge.

Unfortunately, office politics are the silent saboteur of communication,
eroding trust, inflaming tension, and making collaboration about as appealing
as last week's tuna sandwich. Patrick Lencioni, in *The Five Dysfunctions of a*

Team, explains that dysfunctions like lack of trust and accountability weaken team cohesion by encouraging guarded behavior and fear of conflict.[237] In such environments, office politics often thrive—fueled by ambiguity, avoidance, and a focus on individual agendas over collective goals. Diplomacy, on the other hand, is the secret ingredient to creating a workplace where communication thrives. It's about building bridges, not walls, and fostering an environment where even the stickiest conflicts can be transformed into opportunities.

And when it comes to getting out of sticky situations, few know the game better than Chris Voss. In *Never Split the Difference*, the former FBI negotiator breaks down how understanding and addressing emotions can turn tense standoffs into productive conversations, explaining, "He who has learned to empathize with the irrational also has the ability to be a master influencer."[238] So next time your coworker flips out over printer toner, just remember: you're not stuck—you're one empathic question away from Jedi-level diplomacy.

And it's not just for hostage and toner crises—these tactics work just as well in budget meetings, project debates, and everyday office drama. Diplomacy isn't just about smoothing things over—it's how real influence happens.

Take me, for example. Early in my career, I thought the key to getting ahead was winning arguments. If someone presented an idea I didn't agree with, I'd counter with data, wit, and all the finesse of a bull in a china shop. I didn't realize that my relentless "proving my point" approach made others dig in their heels or run in the other direction.

One particular Dealer Partner Quarterly Review in 2009 was a masterclass in what *not* to do. My bosses—both my direct manager and a senior leader—were meeting with a critical dealer partner about underperformance. As the Dealer Sales Development Manager, I saw this as my moment to shine. Instead, halfway through the meeting, after listening to what I thought were excuses and empty promises, I let loose. Armed with data, anecdotes, and a tone that read more angry than assertive, I laid into the dealer principal.

After the meeting, my boss pulled me aside. "You're not here to win. You're here to work *with* people to solve problems. You were right on the facts—but wrong on the timing and tone." The senior leader sealed the deal: "We want them seeing green, not red."

That conversation was a gut punch—but it was also my initiation into real influence. Winning an argument means nothing if you lose the room. From that moment on, I focused less on proving a point, and more on moving conversations forward. I traded debate tactics for diplomacy—and that's when I started actually winning.

Daniel Goleman, in *Emotional Intelligence: Why It Can Matter More Than IQ*, highlights how empathy and self-awareness foster trust and collaboration—skills I sorely lacked at the time of this conversation.[239] Diplomacy doesn't mean avoiding conflict or always agreeing, but it's all about how you navigate those

conflicts when they arise. When done well, it makes you someone people want to collaborate with—a trusted colleague who can tackle challenges without leaving scorched earth in their wake.

Consider the quiet power of introverts in this context. As Jennifer Chen writes in *Smart, Not Loud*, introverts can use their listening skills and thoughtful communication to navigate workplace dynamics diplomatically.[240] Diplomacy isn't about loud gestures or grandstanding; it's about calm, intentional action. Whether you're the loudest or the quietest person in the room, this skill is accessible to anyone willing to refine their communication approach.

In this chapter, we'll explore the art of office diplomacy through three critical lenses. First, we'll dive into *Perspective Mastery*, the ability to see a situation from every angle—even when it's uncomfortable. Next, we'll tackle *Authority-free Influence*—because in today's cross-functional workplace, your ability to lead doesn't depend on your position but on how effectively you can bring others on board. Finally, we'll delve into *Constructive Conflict*, transforming disagreements into stepping stones for progress rather than roadblocks.

So, sharpen your negotiation skills and grab your metaphorical oven mitts, because done right, diplomacy isn't just damage control. It's how you turn tension into traction, debates into deals, and workplace landmines into career goldmines.

And if things still get heated? At least your mitts are on.

THREE MAIN DISHES

Perspective Mastery

1 UNDERSTANDING DIFFERENT PERSPECTIVES requires the same careful attention as mastering any complex skill—you need to slow down, observe, and appreciate each distinct element. In the high-stakes world of office dynamics, the ability to see multiple perspectives isn't just a nice-to-have; it's a strategic superpower. Whether you're navigating a team conflict, responding to feedback, or pitching a bold idea, seeing the situation from all sides allows you to act with clarity, creativity, and credibility. Stephen R. Covey, in *The 7 Habits of Highly Effective People*, lays out a fundamental rule of influence: "Seek first to understand, then to be understood."[241] When people feel heard, they're more open to listening in return—a skill that transforms difficult conversations into productive ones.

Mastering perspective means moving beyond your own biases and assumptions. It's about recognizing that what seems obvious to you may be invisible—or even irrelevant—to someone else. In *Hit Refresh*, Satya Nadella illustrates how fostering empathy and curiosity at Microsoft helped break down silos and create a culture where collaboration thrived.[242] Empathy isn't a soft skill—it's a tactical one. When you can demonstrate genuine understanding of others' motivations and concerns, you reduce resistance, build trust, and open the door to more innovative solutions.

Mastering perspective doesn't mean becoming a corporate bobblehead, nodding along to keep the peace. This is where diplomacy kicks in—balancing respect for differing views with the confidence to challenge ideas without burning bridges. Deborah Tannen, in *The Argument Culture*, explains that seeing value in opposing viewpoints isn't about conceding your position—it's about shifting from a combative mindset to one that values problem-solving over point-scoring.[243] This approach allows you to challenge ideas constructively without alienating your peers.

Practical tools can help you sharpen this skill. For instance, practice active listening—focusing on understanding, not just responding (reminder: re-read Chapter 8 for a refresher on listening). Ask clarifying questions. Paraphrase to confirm what you've heard. You could even reframe their perspective in a way that highlights common ground, making collaboration feel like a shared win rather than a debate to be won. These techniques not only enhance your understanding but also signal to others that their perspectives are valued. As Oliver Burkeman notes in *Four Thousand Weeks*, prioritizing relationships and meaningful interactions is key to navigating complex dynamics effectively.[244]

Work isn't a zero-sum game—it's a shifting puzzle, and perspective helps put the right pieces together. Master it, and you won't just navigate workplace dynamics—you'll shape them. This deeper understanding fundamentally changes how we communicate. Instead of broadcasting our message and hoping it lands, we can tailor our communication to resonate with different audiences, making our words more meaningful and effective.

Of course, seeing the whole picture is only half the battle. The real challenge? Getting others to see it too—especially when you don't have a fancy title to back you up. That's where influence without authority comes in.

Authority-free Influence

2 **LEADERSHIP ISN'T FOUND** in a title—it's the ability to inspire action, build trust, and rally others around a vision. The most effective professionals don't wait for authority; they cultivate influence through strategic communication and strong relationships. Real influence isn't instant. It's built over time through trust, thoughtful engagement, and a willingness to learn from feedback. John Maxwell, in *The 21 Irrefutable Laws of Leadership*, argues that the "The Law of Influence" is the core of real leadership: "Leadership is influence, nothing more, nothing less."[245] Your ability to align others with your vision, rather than your position power, determines your impact.

Consider PepsiCo's Indra Nooyi, who famously navigated resistance when introducing healthier product lines to an organization built on soda and snacks. She didn't wield her CEO title as a weapon. Instead, she built coalitions, aligned her vision with long-term business goals, and used persuasion to rally support.[246] This is the essence of authority-free influence: creating alignment without coercion.

"Leadership is influence, nothing more, nothing less."

— John Maxwell

Pixar: Diplomacy in Action, One Frame at a Time[247]

The Challenge: Even in a company full of world-class talent, navigating strong opinions and managing creative differences is no easy feat. With high stakes in every project, maintaining a culture of collaboration without succumbing to office politics or ego-driven clashes was crucial for Pixar to sustain their dominance.

The Approach: At the heart of Pixar's success is the "Braintrust" meeting—an environment designed to foster honest, productive dialogue. The Braintrust gathers the studio's top minds, including directors, writers, and producers, to review works-in-progress. The secret? No one, not even the most senior leader, has formal authority in these sessions. Feedback focuses on improving the work, not criticizing the person.

The Result:

- Pixar produced iconic films like Toy Story, Cars, and Inside Out.
- Their Braintrust model became a benchmark for constructive collaboration.
- The company built a culture of trust, mutual respect, and innovative problem-solving.

The Take-Home Recipe:

- Separate feedback from hierarchy to foster honest, productive dialogue.
- Focus on improving ideas, not critiquing individuals.
- Use diverse perspectives to turn disagreements into innovation.

This isn't about manipulation—it's about understanding what truly drives people. Robert Cialdini, in *Influence: The Psychology of Persuasion*, explains how motivation and reciprocity shape decision-making. When you understand what resonates with people, you can present ideas in ways that inspire action, not resistance.[248] The goal isn't to dictate or demand, but to inspire collaboration through meaningful engagement.

But influence isn't just about knowing what others want; it's also about showing what you stand for. Adam Grant, in *Think Again*, explains how intellectual humility and openness to feedback make leaders more approachable and trustworthy.[249] When people see you as adaptable and willing to question your own assumptions, they're more likely to follow your lead.

Authority-free influence also thrives on credibility. In *On the Edge*, Nate Silver illustrates how taking calculated risks—whether by championing an unpopular idea or stepping into a challenging project—can solidify your reputation as someone worth following.[250] People don't follow titles; they follow credibility. When colleagues see you take smart risks and deliver results, they'll trust your judgment—no title required.

Finally, Theresa West, in *Job Therapy*, emphasizes the importance of clear, empathetic communication in navigating workplace dynamics without formal power.[251] The way you present ideas—respectfully, logically, and with genuine regard for others—can transform skeptics into allies and opponents into advocates.

Authority-free influence ultimately creates lasting organizational impact through relationship-building and trust. By combining strategic communication with authentic engagement, you develop influence that carries weight regardless of your position.

Like cooking, influence is all about the right mix of ingredients. But sooner or later, you're going to set off the office smoke alarm. The key isn't avoiding the heat—it's knowing how to control the fire.

Constructive Conflict

3 CONFLICT IN THE workplace is as inevitable as a "quick meeting" running over time. But the difference between a thriving team and a toxic one isn't whether conflict happens—it's how it's handled. Do

disagreements spark silent resentment, passive-aggressive emails, or fruitless shouting matches? Or do they become catalysts for innovation, trust, and stronger collaboration?

Adam Grant, in *Originals*, argues that challenging the status quo doesn't have to be disruptive—it can be done diplomatically, fostering progress without alienating others.[252] Sunita Sah, in *Defy: The Power of No*, emphasizes that pushing back effectively is about balancing authenticity with respect—challenging ideas without steamrolling people.[253] This nuance separates skilled communicators from workplace arsonists. (You know the ones... Cheryl!)

The best teams create cultures where disagreement isn't feared—it's leveraged. At Pixar, Ed Catmull designed Braintrust meetings—spaces where candid feedback fuels creativity, but personal attacks are off the table.[254] This approach, described in *Creativity, Inc.*, ensures that strong opinions lead to stronger work, not bruised egos.

Conflict isn't the problem—defensive, unproductive reactions are. In *Difficult Conversations*, Douglas Stone, Bruce Patton, and Sheila Heen argue that shifting from blame to curiosity—seeking to uncover motivations rather than assign fault—transforms conflict from a battle to win into a problem to solve.[255] This mindset turns tense meetings into conversations that actually go somewhere.

And here's an underrated truth: Introverts are a secret weapon in conflict resolution. While they're often overshadowed by louder voices, their ability to listen, reflect, and respond thoughtfully makes them ideal at de-escalating heated discussions. Susan Cain, in her book *Quiet*, highlights how introverts' measured approaches to disagreement often lead to deeper, more creative solutions.[256]

Even high-stakes situations benefit from these principles. Todd Stern, lead negotiator for the Paris Climate Agreement, didn't resolve one of the most complex global conflicts by shouting the loudest—he built consensus through patient diplomacy.[257] Whether at a world summit or a Tuesday team meeting, the key to navigating disagreement is the same: focus on shared interests, not just opposing positions.

When handled well, conflict isn't destructive—it's transformative. Organizations that cultivate strong conflict-resolution cultures often experience enhanced communication, streamlined processes, and increased innovation.

By addressing disagreements constructively, these organizations turn potential obstacles into opportunities for growth and collaboration.[258] Instead of creating landmines, disagreements become launchpads.

Mastering constructive conflict means viewing every tough conversation as an opportunity—to improve outcomes, strengthen relationships, and drive progress. Success doesn't come from avoiding conflict—it comes from knowing how to navigate it with skill, diplomacy, and a well-timed deep breath.

And if all else fails, do what we all do: let Sam think it was his or her idea.

FIVE TASTE-TEST RECIPES

Office diplomacy might sound about as thrilling as watching water boil, but don't be fooled—this is where careers get cooked or overcooked. These recipes will help you turn down the heat on conflict, stir up collaboration, and dish out solutions everyone can actually digest.

1. **The Perspective Swap:** In your next disagreement or conflict, challenge yourself to articulate the other person's point of view as clearly and convincingly as possible. Think of it as putting on their "mental apron"—understanding their recipe for the situation.

2. **The Interest Investigation:** Before your next high-stakes meeting, consider the key players and what drives them. What's their end-game? Their biggest fear? Their "currency"whether it's recognition, resources, or influence? It's part detective work, part corporate chess match.

3. **The Diplomacy Diary:** For one week, keep a journal of all your workplace interactions. Record when diplomacy worked and where it could have helped. Think of it as creating your personal playbook for professional communication.

4. **The Alliance Audit:** Map your professional network within your organization. Who are your allies? Who are the influencers? Where are the gaps? Then, strategize on strengthening those relationships, turning your network into a high-performing coalition.

5. **The Conflict Reframe:** Next time you're facing a conflict, try re-framing it as a shared problem to solve rather than a battle to win. Use language like "How can we..." instead of "I think..." or "You should..." Imagine turning a tug-of-war into a group problem-solving session.

LAST CALL

Office diplomacy isn't about tiptoeing around issues or nodding politely while secretly updating your resume—it's about navigating workplace dynamics with finesse, fairness, and foresight. It's the difference between orchestrating meaningful change and letting office politics fester into dysfunction. When mastered, diplomacy transforms tension into productive dialogue and creates environments where ideas (and careers) flourish.

In this chapter, you've explored three critical elements of workplace diplomacy: *Perspective Mastery*, which laid out the art of seeing challenges through multiple lenses to foster creative solutions; *Authority-Free Influence*, which showed the power of leading and inspiring action without relying on formal titles; and *Constructive Conflict*, transforming disagreements into opportunities for innovation and growth. Together, these diplomatic tools help you communicate with impact, strengthen workplace relationships, and rise above office politics to drive real results.

Whether you're navigating a heated project discussion or trying to unite departments that get along about as well as cats and cucumber slices, remember: diplomatic communication builds bridges that office politics can't burn down. And while those passive-aggressive break room notes might be entertaining, your diplomatic skills will prove far more valuable in the long run.

CEREBRAL SOUS VIDE

- ✓ How can I approach workplace disagreements as shared problems to solve rather than battles to win?
- ✓ How often do I influence without authority by building trust and aligning goals with colleagues across teams?
- ✓ When was the last time I took the time to understand all perspectives in a disagreement, and how did it change the outcome?

THE SELF-SERVE STATION

Down to master the art of workplace diplomacy? These resources will help you navigate office dynamics with the savvy of a world-class negotiator—minus the secret service escort (sadly).

- *Never Split the Difference* by Chris Voss (2016) – From FBI hostage negotiator to business consultant, Voss shows how the same principles that defuse crises can transform workplace conflicts into collaborative wins. Because, let's face it—that budget meeting can feel just as intense.

- *Difficult Conversations: How to Discuss What Matters Most* by Stone, Patton, & Heen (1999) – A must-read for anyone who's ever dreaded a feedback session or tough conversation. This guide equips you with tools to tackle awkward discussions diplomatically and productively.

- *The Argument Culture* by Deborah Tannen (1998) – Discover how shifting from debate to dialogue transforms workplace dynamics. Tannen reveals why winning arguments often means losing opportunities, and how to go about building bridges instead of proving points. An oldie but goodie.

- *The Culture Code* by Daniel Coyle (2018) – Through fascinating case studies of high-performing teams, Coyle reveals the hidden language of successful collaboration. Learn why psychological safety matters more than power plays, and how trust builds stronger teams than authority.

- *Creativity, Inc.* by Ed Catmull (2014) – The Pixar co-founder shares how to build a culture where honest feedback flourishes without bruising egos. Perfect for anyone wondering how to turn creative tensions into breakthrough innovations.

A SWEET & SAVORY SHOUT-OUT

Adam Grant transforms workplace psychology from academic theory into actionable wisdom. Through groundbreaking research and compelling storytelling, he's redefined how we think about leadership, creativity, and success. His work isn't just about understanding workplace dynamics—it's about revolutionizing them with evidence-based insights that feel like career revelations.

In *Think Again*, Grant shows why intellectual humility drives success. *Give and Take* reveals how generosity can become a competitive advantage. *Originals* demonstrates how challenging conventions sparks innovation, while *Hidden Potential* explores how untapped talent flourishes. Each book combines rigorous research with unforgettable stories, making complex ideas accessible and impossible to ignore.

What distinguishes Grant is his ability to challenge workplace assumptions with data-driven insights. He proves that productive disagreement beats artificial harmony, that givers can outperform takers, and that the best leaders prioritize lifting others. His research consistently shows that effective communication—whether expressing dissent, sharing credit, or fostering collaboration—underpins every successful organization.

As a Wharton professor and influential thought leader, Grant has guided organizations from startups to Fortune 500s in transforming their cultures. His impact stems from a simple but powerful premise: the best workplaces thrive on curiosity, constructive challenge, and unleashing everyone's potential. In a world obsessed with quick fixes, Grant offers something better—evidence-based strategies that actually work.

Grant's ultimate lesson for workplace diplomacy? The best leaders don't just navigate office politics—they transform them through honest dialogue and genuine collaboration. In today's workplace, that might be the most valuable insight of all.

10 QUICK BITES

- Diplomacy in the workplace prioritizes collaboration, trust, and shared success, while politics often thrives on self-interest and competition.

- Stephen R. Covey's fundamental rule of influence: "Seek first to understand, then to be understood"—when people feel heard, they're more open to listening.

- John Maxwell argues that "Leadership is influence, nothing more, nothing less"—your ability to align others with your vision determines your impact.

- Constructive conflict turns disagreements into opportunities for growth by focusing on shared goals and respectful dialogue.

- Daniel Goleman highlights how empathy and self-awareness foster trust and collaboration—essential skills for navigating workplace dynamics.

- Clear and consistent communication prevents misunderstandings and reinforces your credibility as a collaborative problem-solver.

- Diplomacy requires patience and strategic thinking, emphasizing long-term value over quick wins or political maneuvering.

- Building alliances and cultivating relationships across teams and hierarchies creates a network of support for achieving shared objectives.

- Douglas Stone, Bruce Patton, and Sheila Heen argue that shifting from blame to curiosity transforms conflict from a battle into a problem to solve.

- Pixar's Braintrust meetings demonstrate constructive conflict—honest feedback focuses on improving work, not criticizing people.

Common Obstacle:

"Conflicts escalate into unnecessary tension."

Quick Fix:

Reframe disagreements as shared problems to solve collaboratively

Long-Term:

Practice active listening and adopt a mindset of curiosity during conflicts

---

Common Obstacle:

"My influence is limited without formal authority."

Quick Fix:

Connect your proposals to others' priorities

Long-Term:

Build a cross-functional stakeholder map and relationship plan

---

Common Obstacle:

"My perspective is misunderstood or ignored."

Quick Fix:

Summarize others' points before sharing yours

Long-Term:

Develop the habit of seeing situations from multiple perspectives to bridge gaps

DIGESTIF

Washing It All Down

FOR OBVIOUS REASONS, I wanted to call this section the *Pousse-café*. But I'm an "adult," and most of you don't know French, so here we are.

In the years since this book was first conceived, the business world has undergone seismic shifts. The global pandemic accelerated remote work trends, artificial intelligence went from sci-fi to boardroom staple, and terms like "quiet quitting" and "the great resignation" became part of our everyday lexicon. Yet amidst all this change, the fundamental truths we've explored have only become more relevant. Effective communication—how we talk to ourselves, our peers, and the world—truly slaps.

Consider, again, the rise of Microsoft under Satya Nadella's leadership (yes, again—at this point, he should be paying me). Nadella's approach embodies many of the principles we've discussed. His emphasis on a growth mindset (Chapter 3) transformed Microsoft's culture from "know-it-all" to "learn-it-all."[259] His focus on empathy and emotional intelligence in leadership reflects the importance of gratitude (Chapter 1) and mindfulness (Chapter 2) in the workplace.[260] Under his guidance, Microsoft has not only rekindled its innovative spirit but has also become a leader in corporate responsibility and ethical AI development, showcasing the power of aligning personal values with corporate goals (Chapter 14 on Personal Branding).[261]

Want more examples? Classic you—love that! Let's talk about how Airbnb navigated the pandemic crisis. When travel collapsed in 2020, CEO Brian Chesky demonstrated the power of gratitude (Chapter 1) by publicly thanking hosts who supported travelers during the crisis, psychological safety (Chapter 10) by encouraging open dialogue about challenges, and storytelling (Chapter 11) to pivot the company's entire business model while maintaining team cohesion.[262] Their successful transformation wasn't just about strategy—it was about how they communicated that strategy with appreciation at every level.[263]

Or take Shopify's CEO, Tobi Lütke, and how he handled their 2023 reorganization. By combining gratitude for team members' contributions (Chapter 1) with humility (Chapter 7) and clear storytelling (Chapter 11), he turned a challenging situation into an opportunity for deeper team alignment. His consistent acknowledgment of the impact made by both departing and remaining employees' demonstrated how authentic appreciation can transform even the most difficult business decisions.[264] And how did that reorg work for Shopfiy? In 2024, their revenue increased by 26% year-over-year, reaching $8.88 billion, up from $7.06 billion in 2023.[265] Not too shabby.

Speaking of badass leadership transformations, let's distill the essential takeaways from this obvious masterpiece. Each chapter provides a crucial ingredient in your recipe for professional excellence:

The Prep Station (Chapters 1-5)

- Gratitude: Your foundation that transforms workplace relationships from transactional to transformational.
- Mindfulness: Your gathering place for mental clarity and focused decision-making.
- Growth Mindset: Your rising agent that turns challenges into opportunities.
- Do Hard Better: Your high-heat technique for handling pressure with grace.
- Momentum Mirage: Your slow-cooking method that yields breakthrough results.

The Cooking Line (Chapters 6-10)

- Humor: Your seasoning for building authentic connections.
- Humility: Your mindset that keeps learning fresh.
- Listening: Your taste test for understanding others deeply.
- Energy Management: Your kitchen flow for sustainable success.
- Psychological Safety: Your perfect temperature for innovation.

The Perfect Plating (Chapters 11-15)

- Storytelling: Your plating technique for memorable impact.
- Power of Three: Your prix fixe approach to clear communication.
- Personal Branding: Your signature dish that sets you apart.
- Sponsorship: Your seat at the executive chef's table.
- Diplomacy: Your balancing act for workplace harmony.

These skills build upon each other like layers in a complex dish. The internal work we do (Section One) creates the foundation for team dynamics (Section Two), which in turn enables our external impact (Section Three).

As we look to the future, these skills will become even more crucial. In a world increasingly mediated by technology, the ability to build genuine human connections through gratitude, humor, and humility will be more valuable than ever. The future belongs to professionals who can combine technical expertise with the uniquely human capabilities shared in this book—things like listening, storytelling, and not sending passive-aggressive Slack messages.

Here's your challenge: choose one principle from this book and commit to practicing it for the next week. Maybe it's starting each day with gratitude, applying the Power of Three to your next presentation, or bringing more diplomatic finesse to your team interactions. Document what changes. Notice what shifts in your relationships and opportunities. And remember, if you don't see an immediate change, quit. Give up entirely. This stuff is clearly impossible, and it's definitely not the book's fault. (You've gotten this far in the book, so I'm assuming you've learned to recognize my sarcasm.)

So, as we close this bad boy out, think of the journey ahead like preparing for a Michelin-starred service—or at least a dinner party where you actually clean your apartment first. Your professional kitchen is stocked with:

- THREE MAIN DISHES (your essential ingredients)
- FIVE TASTE-TEST RECIPES (your well-maintained tools)
- 10 QUICK BITES (your time-tested techniques)
- A PREP CARD (your daily practices)

The key isn't perfection on day one—it's consistent refinement of your craft.

This book is not the end of your journey, merely a delicious tasting menu in a lifetime of professional growth. Every day brings new opportunities to practice these skills, refine your approach, and create something extraordinary. Plan on making a mess, having some fun, and getting 1% better every day.

You've got this. Now go burn an omelet. And yes, that was officially the last food reference. I promise. No more. Not even a tiny morsel. Not even a crumb.

Okay, I'm done...

For real this time.

Wait—one last thing. What's your stance on the sandwich feedback method?

...Bon appétit!

MERCI MILLE FEUILLES

WRITING *THE BUSINESS Buffet*—a book about communication, leadership, and the messy, meaningful work of bringing people together—has been an exercise in practicing exactly what I preach. It has reminded me, again and again, that none of us communicates or leads in isolation. Our voices are echoes of the conversations, challenges, and communities that shape us. This book is my attempt to bring those voices together, and I'm grateful beyond measure to the people who made it possible.

To my wife, Vicki, and our son, Easton: thank you for being my grounding force and my daily reminder of what matters most. Vicki, your steady wisdom and uncanny ability to know when to say "keep going" and when to say "maybe sleep on it" were invaluable. Plus, let's be honest—you were thrilled when I disappeared into my office to write because it meant you could finally watch your "shows" in peace with the dog. Easton, at 16, you think I'm an idiot, and that's probably fair. But someday you'll realize I'm doing all of this to be a good example for you and maybe leave you some money... maybe. Your questions and eye rolls reminded me that great communication starts with listening—and often with accepting that teenagers communicate primarily through sighs. And to Coby, our dog, who doesn't care about me at all and only has eyes for Vicki—thank you for keeping my ego in check and reminding me daily that not all audiences can be won over, no matter how hard you try.

Graham, Shannon, and John, your feedback was both generous and surgical. You didn't just point out what worked or didn't—you helped me sharpen my message and clarify my intent. You reminded me that feedback, like leadership, is a gift when delivered with respect and purpose. More importantly, you reminded me that good colleagues and good friends will tell you the truth even when it stings—and that's exactly what makes them invaluable.

Ashley, this journey started with our conversations. You were the original thought partner in this wild idea of writing a book. You're hilarious, multi-talented, and have this uncanny ability to make me laugh while making me want to be a better leader. You helped me see that good communication isn't about saying more—it's about saying what matters. I still hope we'll co-write something someday. Maybe a sequel? *The Dessert Table*?

To my publishing team at Gordon Publishing and Streamline Books—you deserve hazard pay. Andrew Blackburn, my copy editor, somehow turned my grammatical disasters and complete ignorance about how books work into something readable. That's either dedication or masochism, but I'm grateful either way. Huge thanks to my co-sherpas, Mandi Reed and Becca Blackburn, who guided me through the entire publishing journey with equal parts patience, grace, and good humor. Every panicked text, every silly question, every "wait, what's a galley?" moment—you both responded with kindness when I probably deserved exasperation. And to Will Severns and Alex Demczak—thank you for seeing something in this quirky idea and taking a chance on a guy who thought "business meets food metaphors" was a viable concept.

To Rachel Royer of Rachel Royer Design—thank you for making this book look as good on the outside as I hope it reads on the inside. Your design instincts and ability to make sense of my scattered ideas made all the difference. And to Alice Brigg—your interior design work brought this book to life from the inside out. Every layout detail, flourish, and thoughtful choice made the pages feel like a real experience. I'm beyond grateful for your creativity and care.

To the generous souls who wrote blurbs for this book—thank you for lending your names, your words, and your reputations to something that, at the time, only existed as a Google Doc full of bad food puns and semi-coherent leadership advice. Your encouragement gave this project credibility before it had a cover, a title, or any real business existing in the world. You showed up at the buffet line before the food was even hot—and still managed to say something kind.

And to the readers who will bring these ideas to life in their own workplaces and communities—thank you for trusting me with your time and attention. This book only matters if it helps you communicate more effectively, lead more authentically, and connect more meaningfully with the people around you. If it doesn't, well, at least you'll have some good stories about that time you read a business book written by a guy who thinks food metaphors are the height of literary sophistication.

Finally, this book is dedicated to my mother. My first and finest example of leadership. You led with courage, strength, and an unmatched sense of humor. You cheered the loudest and listened the closest. I owe you more than I can say—but I've tried to say some of it here. Thank you for showing me that effective leadership always begins with compassion, and that the best communication happens not just with words, but with presence.

Like the delicate layers of a mille-feuille, this book has been built on countless thin, beautiful sheets of encouragement, feedback, and fuel from those I respect and love the most.

Merci.

THE CULINARY CREDITS

CHAPTER 1

1 Gallup & Workhuman. (2024). *Unleashing the Human Element at Work: Transforming Workplaces Through Recognition.* Gallup.

2 Bersin, J. (2012, June 13). *New Research Unlocks the Secret of Employee Recognition.* Forbes.

3 Quantum Workplace. (2023). *The Benefits of Employee Engagement to Your Business, Culture, & People.* Retrieved from

4 Harter, J. (2018, August 26). *Employee Engagement on the Rise in the U.S.* Gallup.

5 Korb, A. (2015). The Upward Spiral: Using Neuroscience to Reverse the Course of Depression, One Small Change at a Time. New Harbinger Publications.

6 Diniz, G., Korkes, L., Tristão, L. S., Pelegrini, R., Bellodi, P. L., & Bernardo, W. M. (2023). The effects of gratitude interventions: a systematic review and meta-analysis. einstein (São Paulo), 21, eRW0371.

7 Kini, P., Wong, J., McInnis, S., Gabana, N., & Brown, J. W. (2016). The effects of gratitude expression on neural activity. *Social Cognitive and Affective Neuroscience,* 11(5), 693-700.

8 Cortini, M., Converso, D., Galanti, T., Di Fiore, T., Di Domenico, A., & Fantinelli, S. (2019). *Gratitude at Work Works! A Mix-Method Study on Different Dimensions of Gratitude, Job Satisfaction, and Job Performance. Sustainability,* 11(14), 3902.

9   Emmons, R. A. (2007). *Thanks!: How the new science of gratitude can make you happier.* Houghton Mifflin Harcourt.
10 Blanchard, K. H. (n.d.). *The key to successful leadership today is influence, not authority.*
11 Bartlett, M. Y. (2015). Warm thanks: Gratitude expression facilitates social affiliation in new relationships via perceived warmth. *Emotion,* 15(1), 1.
12 Zappos. (2021). Employee Satisfaction and Retention Report. Zappos Insights. Feloni, R. (2016, July 26). A Zappos employee had the company's longest customer-service call at 10 hours, 43 minutes. *Business Insider.* Taylor, B. (2008, May 19). "Why Zappos Pays New Employees to Quit—And You Should Too." *Harvard Business Review.* Chafkin, M. (2009, May 1). "The Zappos Way of Managing." *Inc. Magazine*
13 Sinek, S. (2014). *Leaders Eat Last: Why Some Teams Pull Together and Others Don't.* Penguin.
14 Grant, A. M. (2013). Give and Take: A Revolutionary Approach to Success. Viking.
15 Gallup & Workhuman. (2024). The Human-Centered Workplace: Building Organizational Cultures That Thrive. Gallup.
16 Deloitte Insights. (2023). Future of Total Rewards: Trends and Strategies. Deloitte.
17 Adair, K. C., Rodriguez-Homs, L. G., Masoud, S., Mosca, P. J., & Sexton, J. B. (2020). *Gratitude at Work: Prospective Cohort Study of a Web-Based, Single-Exposure Well-Being Intervention for Health Care Workers. Journal of Medical Internet Research, 22(5),* e15562.

CHAPTER 2

18 World Health Organization. (2019). Burn-out an "occupational phenomenon": International Classification of Diseases.
19 Creswell, J. D., Lindsay, E. K., & Chin, B. (2020). *Mindfulness training and cognitive performance in the workplace: A randomized controlled trial. Journal of Occupational Health Psychology,* 25(2), 123–135.
20 Gelles, D. (2015). *Mindful Work: How Meditation Is Changing Business from the Inside Out.* Houghton Mifflin Harcourt.

21 Minda, J. P., Cho, J., Nielsen, E. G., & Zhang, M. (2017). *Mindfulness and Legal Practice: A Preliminary Study of the Effects of Mindfulness Meditation and Stress Reduction in Lawyers.* Department of Psychology & Brain and Mind Institute, The University of Western Ontario.

22 Watson, J. M., & Strayer, D. L. (2010). *Supertaskers: Profiles in extraordinary multitasking ability. Psychological Science,* 21(4), 470–477

23 Medina, J. (2008). *Brain Rules: 12 Principles for Surviving and Thriving at Work, Home, and School.* Pear Press.

24 Clear, J. (2018). *Atomic Habits: An Easy & Proven Way to Build Good Habits & Break Bad Ones.* Penguin Random House LLC.

25 *Harvard Business Review* article: "The Busier You Are, the More You Need Mindfulness" (2015).

26 *Harvard Business Review* article: "The Busier You Are, the More You Need Mindfulness" (2015).

27 Li, Y., Yang, N., Zhang, Y., Xu, W., & Cai, L. (2021). *The Relationship Among Trait Mindfulness, Attention, and Working Memory in Junior School Students Under Different Stressful Situations.* Frontiers in Psychology, 12, 558690.

28 Schaufenbuel, K. (2015). "Why Google, Target, and General Mills Are Investing in Mindfulness." *Harvard Business Review*

29 Mindful Staff. (2014, April 9). *Intel to Launch Mindfulness Program.* Mindful.org.

30 Unilever. (2022). Unilever Annual Report and Accounts 2022. Chhabra, E. (2017, February 14). Former Unilever CEO Paul Polman Believes Purpose Is The Best Business Strategy. *Fortune.*

31 Brown, B. (2015). *Rising Strong: The Reckoning. The Rumble. The Revolution.* Spiegel & Grau.

32 Colzato, L. S., Ozturk, A., & Hommel, B. (2012). Meditate to create: The impact of focused-attention and open-monitoring training on convergent and divergent thinking. *Frontiers in Psychology,* 3, 116.

33 Google's "Search Inside Yourself" Program: Mindful.org, 2012; SIYbook. com, 2017

34 Tan, C.-M. (2012). *Search Inside Yourself: The Unexpected Path to Achieving Success, Happiness (and World Peace).* HarperOne

CHAPTER 3

35 Dweck, C. S. (2006). *Mindset: The New Psychology of Success.* Random House.

36 Syed, M. (2018). *You Are Awesome: Find Your Confidence and Dare to Be Brilliant at (Almost) Anything.* Wren & Rook.

37 Galef, J. (2021). *The Scout Mindset: Why Some People See Things Clearly and Others Don't.* Portfolio.

38 Dweck, C., & Hogan, K. (2020). Growth Mindset Culture in Organizations: Impact on Employee Trust and Commitment. *Journal of Organizational Behavior,* 41(2), 135–150.

39 McKinsey & Company. (2023). In the spotlight: Performance management that puts people first. McKinsey & Company. (2023). Courageous growth: Six strategies for continuous growth outperformance.

40 Achor, S. (2010). *The Happiness Advantage: How a Positive Brain Fuels Success in Work and Life.* Crown Business.

41 Moser, J. S., Schroder, H. S., Heeter, C., Moran, T. P., & Lee, Y. H. (2011). *Mind Your Errors: Evidence for a Neural Mechanism Linking Growth Mindset to Adaptive Post-Error Adjustments.* Psychological Science, 22(12), 1484-1489.

42 Blackwell, L. S., Trzesniewski, K. H., & Dweck, C. S. (2007). Implicit Theories of Intelligence Predict Achievement Across an Adolescent Transition: A Longitudinal Study and an Intervention. *Child Development,* 78(1), 246-263.

43 Geller, T. (2022). Postmortem Culture: Learning from Failure at Google. Communications of the ACM, 65(4), 33-35.

44 Buchanan, L. (2013, November). *Innovation by celebrating mistakes: NixonMcInnes's "Church of Fail."* Inc.

45 Reuter, M. (2021, August). A real example of living a growth mindset, individually and collectively. Siemens AG. (2021). Siemens fosters a growth mindset to build a resilient and innovative workforce.

46 Mueller, C. M., & Dweck, C. S. (1998). Praise for Intelligence Can Undermine Children's Motivation and Performance. *Journal of Personality and Social Psychology,* 75(1), 33-52.

47 Kerr, J., & Winograd, K. (2022). The Transformation of Performance Management at Microsoft. *Harvard Business Review Digital Articles,* 2-8.

CHAPTER 4

48 Clear, J. (2018). *Atomic Habits: An Easy & Proven Way to Build Good Habits & Break Bad Ones.* Penguin Random House

49 Zhou, H., & Li, Y. (2022). The Impact of Challenge-Hindrance Stress on Innovation Performance: The Mediating Role of Intrinsic Motivation and Knowledge Acquisition. *Frontiers in Psychology*, 13, 745259.

50 McKinsey Global Institute. (2023). Performance and Health: Sustaining Superior Organizational Performance Through People Practices. McKinsey & Company.

51 Menkes, J. (2023). Leadership Under Pressure: The Importance of Building Resilience in High-Pressure Work Environments. *Harvard Business Review.* Harvard Business Publishing.

52 Willink, Jocko. "Good." *Jocko Podcast*, Episode 3, 21 December 2015

53 Cole, R. E., "What Really Happened to Toyota?" *MIT Sloan Management Review*, 2011. "Toyota's Safety Recall Involves Record 3.8 Million Cars." *Wired*, 30 Sept. 2009. Kiley, D. "Toyota: $2 Billion Hit from Recall, Profit Outlook Slashed." *CNNMoney*, 4 Feb. 2010. Inman, P. "Toyota Profits Crash after Safety Recall." *The Guardian*, 4 Feb. 2010.

54 Netflix Q3 2011 Earnings Report. Pepitone, Julianne. "Netflix loses 800,000 subscribers." *CNNMoney*, 24 Oct. 2011. "Netflix Stock Plunges After 800,000 Members Quit." *ABC News*, 25 Oct. 2011. Tuttle, Brad. "Netflix Admits It 'Messed Up,' Will Split DVD and Streaming Into Two Businesses." *TIME*, 19 Sept. 2011

55 Cowan, N. (2001). "The Magical Number 4 in Short-term Memory." Behavioral and Brain Sciences

56 Weinberger, S. (2017). "The Imagineers of War: The Untold Story of DARPA." Knopf. *National Academy of Sciences.* (2022). "DARPA: Creating Breakthrough Technologies for National Security" Dugan, R., & Gabriel, K. J. (2021). "Special Forces Innovation: How DARPA Attacks Problems." *Harvard Business Review*, 99(2) Schoeni, D. (2023). "DARPA's Role in the Development of mRNA Vaccines." *Revista de la Escuela Jacobea de Posgrado*, No. 24, June 2023, pp. 1–16.

57 Project Management Institute. (2021). "Pulse of the Profession: Beyond Agility." *Agile Genesis.* "Agile vs. Waterfall: Comparing Success Rates in Project Management."

58 Gerstner, L. V. (2002). "Who Says Elephants Can't Dance?: Inside IBM's Historic Turnaround." HarperBusiness

59 Project Management Institute. (2017). *Pulse of the Profession: Success Rates Rise: Transforming the High Cost of Low Performance*

60 McKinsey & Company. (2021). *Transformation with a Capital T*

61 Gibbons, S., & Gibbons, S. (2018). *Applications of Performance Psychology: Performance Enhancement and Nonclinical Populations.* In: Tenenbaum, G., & Eklund, R.C. (Eds.), *APA Handbook of Sport and Exercise Psychology,* Vol. 2. American Psychological Association.

62 Gardner, H. K. (2017). *Smart Collaboration: How Professionals and Their Firms Succeed by Breaking Down Silos.* Harvard Business Review Press.

CHAPTER 5

63 World Economic Forum. (2020). The Future of Jobs Report 2020. Geneva: World Economic Forum.

64 Amazon. (2022). Annual Report 2022. Seattle: Amazon.com, Inc.

65 Duckworth, A. (2016). *Grit: The Power of Passion and Perseverance.* New York: Scribner.

66 Xu, T., Yu, X., Perlik, A. J., Tobin, W. F., Zweig, J. A., Tennant, K., & Zuo, Y. (2009). Rapid formation and selective stabilization of synapses for enduring motor memories. *Nature,* 462(7275), 915–919.

67 Boyke, J., Driemeyer, J., Gaser, C., Büchel, C., & May, A. (2008). Training-induced brain structure changes in the elderly. *The Journal of Neuroscience,* 28(28), 7031–7035.

68 Chima, C. (2011, October 25). *How Airbnb failed its way through "the trough of sorrow" to a $1B valuation.* VentureBeat.

69 Butterfield, S. (2019). The Slack origin story. *TechCrunch.*

70 Lunden, I. (2019, September 26). Peloton raises $1.16B in IPO, valuing at $8.1B, after pricing at $29/share. TechCrunch. PYMNTS. (2023, May 4). Peloton CEO Says App Subscriptions Are Path to 'The Promised Land'. Wall Street Zen. (n.d.). Peloton Interactive (PTON) Revenue.

71 Emmons, R. A., & McCullough, M. E. (2003). Counting blessings versus burdens: An experimental investigation of gratitude and subjective well-being in daily life. *Journal of Personality and Social Psychology*, 84(2), 377–389.

72 Hardy, D. (2010). *The Compound Effect: Jumpstart Your Income, Your Life, Your Success*. Vanguard Press

73 Liker, J. K. (2004). *The Toyota Way: 14 Management Principles from the World's Greatest Manufacturer*. McGraw-Hill.

74 Clear, J. (2018). *Atomic Habits: An Easy & Proven Way to Build Good Habits & Break Bad Ones*. Avery.

75 Mann, S., & Cadman, R. (2014). Does Being Bored Make Us More Creative? *Academy of Management Discoveries*, 1(2), 162–176.

76 First Round Review. (2015, January 28). *From 0 to $1 Billion: Slack's Founder Shares Their Epic Launch Strategy*.

77 Duckworth, A. (2016). *Grit: The Power of Passion and Perseverance*. Scribner.

78 Jha, A. P., Morrison, A. B., Parker, S. C., & Stanley, E. A. (2017). Practice is associated with increased attentional stability: Theoretical and applied implications of mindfulness training in high-stress contexts. *Cognitive, Affective, & Behavioral Neuroscience*, 17(6), 1212–1223.

CHAPTER 6

79 De Gruyter. (2016). The impact of positive humor on workplace outcomes: A meta-analytic review. De Gruyter.

80 SHRM. (2021). *How humor can keep employees engaged and productive*. Society for Human Resource Management (SHRM).

81 World Economic Forum. (2019). Humor in the workplace: Enhancing collaboration and preventing burnout. World Economic Forum.

82 Giordano, C., Giromini, L., & Bazzanella, C. (2023). *Humor as a Moderator Between Coping Strategies and Perceived Stress: A Cross-Sectional Study on the Italian General Population During the COVID-19 Lockdown. Healthcare*, 11(2), 306.

83 Blodgett, L. (2021). *Humor: Serious Business*. Stanford Graduate School of Business.

84 Riggio, R. E. (2023). The Psychological Benefits of Humor in the Workplace. *Psychology Today*. Retrieved from Psychology Today

85 Mayo Clinic. (2022). *Stress relief from laughter? It's no joke.*

86 Robinson, C. (2025, March 9). *Laughter In Leadership: How Humor Enhances Workplace Performance*

87 Andrade, C. (2020). Dopamine and the Neuroscience of Creativity: The Biological Foundations of Innovative Thinking. *Indian Journal of Psychiatry*, 62(3), 231–234.

88 Mammano, D. (2025, May 20). *Laughing Your Way to the Top: Humor and Success at Work*. Rochester Business Journal.

89 Aaker, J., & Bagdonas, N. (2021, January 26). Humor is such an important leadership trait we teach it at Stanford's business school. *Fast Company*.

90 Liu, D., Liao, H., & Loi, R. (2012). The dark side of leadership: A three-level investigation of the cascading effect of abusive supervision on employee creativity. *Academy of Management Journal*, 55(5), 1187–1212. Kong, D. T., Cooper, C. D., & Airen, O. (2020). The relationship between leader humor and employee innovative behavior: The mediating role of work engagement. *Frontiers in Psychology*, 11, 592999. Edmondson, A. (1999). Psychological safety and learning behavior in work teams. *Administrative Science Quarterly*, 44(2), 350–383.

91 Eisenhower, D. (1954). *A sense of humor in leadership*. Public Papers of the Presidents of the United States: Dwight D. Eisenhower.

92 The Motley Fool. (2022, November 19). Company culture tips, vol. 10: Greatest hits. Gusto. (n.d.). 10 of the most creative employee handbooks. MeridianLink. (2025, May 20). MeridianLink announces 2025 MeridianLink LIVE keynote speakers. Cult Branding Company. (n.d.). Core values: The heart of your brand. FasterCapital. (n.d.). Boosted employee morale and job satisfaction. Culture Amp. (n.d.). The Motley Fool case study: A winning culture.

93 NeuroLeadership Institute. (2020). *The Neuroscience of Laughter at Work: How Humor Triggers Dopamine, Oxytocin, and Endorphins*. NeuroLeadership Institute.

94 Mesmer-Magnus, J., Glew, D. J., & Viswesvaran, C. (2012). A Meta-Analysis of Positive Humor in the Workplace. *Journal of Managerial Psychology*, 27(2), 155-190

95 León-Pérez, J. M., Cantero-Sánchez, F. J., Fernández-Canseco, Á., & León-Rubio, J. M. (2021). Effectiveness of a Humor-Based Training for Reducing Employees' Distress. *International Journal of Environmental Research and Public Health*, 18(21), 11561.

CHAPTER 7

96 Chen, L., Liu, S., Wang, Y., & Hu, X. (2021). Humble leader behavior and team creativity: The team learning perspective. *Journal of Managerial Psychology*, 36(3), 272-284.

97 Owens, B. P., & Hekman, D. R. (2012). *Modeling how to grow: An inductive examination of humble leader behaviors, contingency factors, and outcomes.*

98 Krumrei-Mancuso, E., & Begin, M. R. (2022). *Cultivating Intellectual Humility in Leaders: Potential Benefits, Risks, and Practical Tools*

99 Catmull, E., & Wallace, A. (2014). *Creativity, Inc.: Overcoming the Unseen Forces That Stand in the Way of True Inspiration.* Random House. Cited in *The Mind Tools*. (2023). Book Summary: Creativity, Inc. by Ed Catmull.

100 Owens, B. P., & Hekman, D. R. (2012). Modeling how to grow: An inductive examination of humble leader behaviors, contingency factors, and outcomes. *Academy of Management Journal*, 55(4), 787-818.

101 Argandoña, A. (2015). Humility in management. *Journal of Business Ethics*, 132(1), 63-71.

102 Nielsen, R., Marrone, J. A., & Slay, H. S. (2010). The role of humility in leadership: A meta-analytic review. *Leadership Quarterly*, 21(5), 925-941.

103 Liu, H., Ahmed, S. J., Kakar, A. S., & Durrani, D. K. (2023). Creative Performance and Conflict through the Lens of Humble Leadership: Testing a Moderated Mediation Model. *Behavioral Sciences*, 13(6), 483.

104 Dalio, R. (2017). *Principles: Life and Work.* Simon & Schuster.

105 Liu, H., Ahmed, S. J., Kakar, A. S., & Durrani, D. K. (2023). Creative Performance and Conflict through the Lens of Humble Leadership: Testing a Moderated Mediation Model. *Behavioral Sciences*, 13(6), 483.

106 Edmondson, A. C. (2018). *The Fearless Organization: Creating Psychological Safety in the Workplace for Learning, Innovation, and Growth*. Wiley.

107 Gelles, D. (2022). Billionaire No More: Patagonia Founder Gives Away the Company. The New York Times. O'Connor, S. (2023). Patagonia: Revenue and Financial Metrics. Forbes Business Analysis. Great Place to Work Institute. (2022). Patagonia Workplace Culture Analysis. Annual Report. Chouinard, Y. (2016). Let My People Go Surfing: The Education of a Reluctant Businessman. Penguin Books. Lowitt, E. (2011). The Triumph of Patagonia's Marketing Strategy of 'Don't Buy Our Products'. The Guardian.

108 Wang, L., Owens, B. P., & Li, J. (2020). The impact of leader humility on team effectiveness: A meta-analytic review. *Journal of Organizational Behavior*, 41(6), 587-611.

109 Chandan, P. (2020). *From Breakdown to Breakthrough: How Coaching Saved Ford's Future*. Medium

110 Gino, F. (2018). The Business Case for Curiosity. *Harvard Business Review*.

111 Hu, J., Erdogan, B., Jiang, K., Bauer, T. N., & Liu, S. (2018). Leader humility and team creativity: The role of team information sharing, psychological safety, and power distance. *Journal of Applied Psychology*, 103(3), 313-323.

112 Owens, B. P., Johnson, M. D., & Mitchell, T. R. (2013). Expressed humility in organizations: Implications for performance, teams, and leadership. *Organization Science*, 24(5), 1517-1538.

113 Nadella, S. (2017). Hit Refresh: The Quest to Rediscover Microsoft's Soul and Imagine a Better Future for Everyone. *Harper Business*.

CHAPTER 8

114 Steil, L. K., Barker, L. L., & Watson, K. W. (1983). *Listening: Our Most Used Communication Skill*. Allyn & Bacon. Flynn, J., Valikoski, T. R., & Grau, J. (2008). Listening in the Business Context: Reviewing the State of Research. *The International Journal of Listening*, 22(2), 141–158. Hargie, O. (2011). *Skilled Interpersonal Interaction: Research, Theory, and Practice* (5th ed.). Routledge

115 Zenger, J., & Folkman, J. (2016). *The Power of Listening Leadership: A Leader's Secret Weapon for Building Trust.* Zenger Folkman Insights.

116 Gallup. (2023). *State of the American Workplace Report.* Gallup, Inc.

117 Deloitte. (2017). Global Human Capital Trends: Rewriting the rules for the digital age.

118 Marriott International. (2023). *Serve 360: Doing Good in Every Direction.* Great Place to Work. (2023). *100 Best Companies to Work For.* Marriott International. (2018). *Serve 360 Report.* (2021). Marriott International Named One of Fortune's 100 Best Companies to Work For—A Record 24th Year.

119 Fey, T. (2011). *Bossypants.* Reagan Arthur Books.

120 Hasson, U., Ghazanfar, A. A., Galantucci, B., Garrod, S., & Keysers, C. (2012). Brain-to-brain coupling: A mechanism for creating and sharing a social world. *Trends in Cognitive Sciences*, 16(2), 114–121.

121 Stephens, G. J., Silbert, L. J., & Hasson, U. (2010). Speaker–listener neural coupling underlies successful communication. Proceedings of the National Academy of Sciences, 107(32), 14425-14430.

122 Kluger, A. N., & Zaidel, K. (2013). Are listeners perceived as leaders? *International Journal of Listening*, 27(2), 73–84.

123 Zak, P. J. (2017). The neuroscience of trust. *Harvard Business Review*, 95(1), 84–90.

124 Brownell, J. (2013). Listening: Attitudes, Principles, and Skills. Pearson.

125 Covey, S. R. (2020). *The 7 Habits of Highly Effective People: Powerful Lessons in Personal Change.* Simon & Schuster.

126 Zenger, J., & Folkman, J. (2016). What Great Listeners Actually Do. *Harvard Business Review*, 94(7), 81–88.

127 Chief Learning Officer. (2023). Case Study: How Lincoln Financial Uses Employee Listening to Strengthen Their Employee Experience. Chief Learning Officer.

128 Schwarz, R. (2013). The Skilled Facilitator: A Comprehensive Resource for Consultants, Facilitators, Managers, Trainers, and Coaches. Jossey-Bass.

129 Covey, S. R. (2020). *The 7 Habits of Highly Effective People: 30th Anniversary Edition.* Simon & Schuster.

130 Pentland, A. (2012). "The new science of building great teams." *Harvard Business Review*, 90(4), 60–69.

131 Newman, A., Donohue, R., & Eva, N. (2017). Psychological safety: A systematic review of the literature. *Human Resource Management Review*, 27(3), 521–535

132 Duhigg, C. (2016). What Google Learned From Its Quest to Build the Perfect Team. *The New York Times Magazine.*

133 Edmondson, A. C., & Lei, Z. (2014). Psychological safety: The history, renaissance, and future of an interpersonal construct. *Annual Review of Organizational Psychology and Organizational Behavior*, 1(1), 23-43.

134 Bernstein, E., & Turban, S. (2018). *The impact of the 'open' workspace on human collaboration.*

CHAPTER 9

135 *Microsoft.* (2022, March 16). Great Expectations: Making Hybrid Work Work.

136 The Energy Project. (n.d.). Reinventing the Workplace: Meeting Employee Mental Needs.

137 Hoomans, J. (2015, March 20). *35,000 Decisions: The Great Choices of Strategic Leaders.* Roberts Wesleyan College

138 Loehr, J., & Schwartz, T. (2003). *The Power of Full Engagement: Managing Energy, Not Time, Is the Key to High Performance and Personal Renewal.* HarperCollins.

139 *Forbes Human Resources Council.* (2023, October 5). How To Focus On Energy Management Instead Of Time Management.

140 *World Health Organization.* (2019, May 28). Burn-out an "occupational phenomenon": International Classification of Diseases.

141 Johnson & Johnson. (n.d.). Position on Employee Development and Total Health and Well-Being. Johnson & Johnson. (2018, November 19). Strengthen your body, expand your mind: Energy for performance® training at Johnson & Johnson. Johnson & Johnson. (2017, June 28). New Findings Show Sustained Improvement in Employee Quality of Life 18 Months After Training. Johnson & Johnson. (n.d.). Workplace Wellness: Johnson & Johnson's Healthiest Employees Goal.

142 *Upstartist.* (n.d.). The 4 Dimensions of Energy: Physical, Emotional, Mental and Spiritual.

143 *Arootah.* (n.d.). How to Balance Your 4 Sources of Energy.

144 *Mindfulness with Kiran.* (n.d.). *The Four Body System.*

145 *The Energy Project.* (n.d.). *Employee Wellbeing and Performance.*

146 *American Psychological Association.* (n.d.). *Workplace Burnout.*

147 *American Psychiatric Association.* (2024). Preventing Burnout: A Guide to Protecting Your Well-Being. Wiens, K. (2024, April). "How Burnout Became Normal — and How to Push Back Against It." *Harvard Business Review.*

148 *Forbes.* (2024, September 6). "Understanding and Addressing Burnout in the Workplace."

149 American Psychological Association. (n.d.). Workplace Burnout.

CHAPTER 10

150 Duhigg, C. (2016). What Google Learned From Its Quest to Build the Perfect Team. *The New York Times Magazine.*

151 Covey, S. R. (1989). *The 7 Habits of Highly Effective People.* Free Press.

152 Brown, T. (2009). *Change by Design: How Design Thinking Creates New Alternatives for Business and Society.* Harper Business.

153 Edmondson, A. C. (2019). *The Fearless Organization: Creating Psychological Safety in the Workplace for Learning, Innovation, and Growth.* Wiley.

154 Teller, A. (2016). *The Unexpected Benefit of Celebrating Failure* [Video]. TED Conferences

155 Sabel, R., Gerstel, H., & Wöhrmann, A. (2023). *Celebrating Failure: The Effects of Failure Awards on Risk-Taking and Escalation of Commitment.* SSRN.

156 McCord, P. (2018). *Powerful: Building a Culture of Freedom and Responsibility.* Silicon Guild.

157 Play4Business. (2023). LEGO® SERIOUS PLAY® Method and Innovation in Teams. Leadership Storybank. (2025). Unlock Team Innovation with the LEGO® SERIOUS PLAY® Method. Innovation Training. (2024). LEGO® Workshops for Organizations and Business with LEGO® SERIOUS PLAY® Boston University. (2016). Exploring Positive Psychology with LEGO® SERIOUS PLAY®. Edmondson, A. (2019). The Fearless Organization:

Creating Psychological Safety in the Workplace for Learning, Innovation, and Growth. Wiley.

158 Goleman, D. (2013). *Focus: The Hidden Driver of Excellence*. Harper.

159 Forbes Coaches Council. (2022). *The Critical Link Between Psychological Safety And Innovation*. Forbes.

160 McKinsey & Company. (2022). *Psychological Safety and the Critical Role of Leadership Development*. McKinsey Insights.

161 Brown, B. (2018). *Dare to Lead: Brave Work. Tough Conversations. Whole Hearts*. Random House.

162 Hsieh, T. (2010). *Delivering Happiness: A Path to Profits, Passion, and Purpose*. Business Plus.

163 Brown, B. (2018). *Dare to Lead: Brave Work. Tough Conversations. Whole Hearts*. Random House.

164 Zak, P. J. (2017). *Trust Factor: The Science of Creating High-Performance Companies*. AMACOM. Breathe. (2020). *The Culture Economy Report 2020*. Breathe HR.

CHAPTER 11

165 Grant, A. (2016). *Originals: How Non-Conformists Move the World*. Viking.

166 Campbell, J. (2008). *The Hero with a Thousand Faces*. New World Library.

167 Zak, P. (2012). *The Moral Molecule: How Trust Works*. Dutton.

168 Gottschall, J. (2012). *The Storytelling Animal: How Stories Make Us Human*. Houghton Mifflin Harcourt.

169 Simmons, A. (2006). *The Story Factor: Inspiration, Influence, and Persuasion through the Art of Storytelling*. Basic Books.

170 Miller, D. (2017). *Building a StoryBrand: Clarify Your Message So Customers Will Listen*. HarperCollins Leadership.

171 Heath, C., & Heath, D. (2007). *Made to Stick: Why Some Ideas Survive and Others Die*. Random House.

172 Gallo, C. (2014). Talk Like TED: *The 9 Public-Speaking Secrets of the World's Top Minds*. St. Martin's Griffin.

173 Cialdini, R. B. (2006). *Influence: The Psychology of Persuasion*. Harper Business.

174 Simmons, A. (2006). *The Story Factor: Inspiration, Influence, and Persuasion through the Art of Storytelling*. Basic Books.

175 Zak, P. (2022). *Immersion: The Science of the Extraordinary and the Source of Happiness*. Wiley.

176 HubSpot's Storytelling Approach HubSpot. (n.d.). The ultimate guide to storytelling in marketing & business. HubSpot. HubSpot. (2024, February 13). HubSpot reports Q4 and full year 2023 results. HubSpot Investor Relations. R Wikipedia contributors. (n.d.). HubSpot. Wikipedia.

177 Zak, P. (2022). *Immersion: The Science of the Extraordinary and the Source of Happiness*. Wiley.

178 Cron, L. (2012). *Wired for Story: The Writer's Guide to Using Brain Science to Hook Readers from the Very First Sentence*. Ten Speed Press.

179 Bohns, V. K. (2021). *You Have More Influence Than You Think: How We Underestimate Our Power of Persuasion, and Why It Matters*. Norton.

180 Campbell, J. (2008). *The Hero with a Thousand Faces* (3rd ed.). New World Library. (Original work published 1949)

181 Denning, S. (2004). *Squirrel Inc.: A Fable of Leadership Through Storytelling*. Jossey-Bass

182 Duarte, N. (2010). *Resonate: Present Visual Stories that Transform Audiences*. Wiley.

183 Sachs, J. (2012). *Winning the Story Wars: Why Those Who Tell (and Live) the Best Stories Will Rule the Future*. Harvard Business Review Press.

184 Denning, S. (2011). *The Leader's Guide to Storytelling: Mastering the Art and Discipline of Business Narrative*. Jossey-Bass.

185 Campbell, J. (2008). *The Hero with a Thousand Faces* (3rd ed.). New World Library. (Original work published 1949)

186 Duarte, N. (2010). *Resonate: Present Visual Stories that Transform Audiences*. Wiley.

CHAPTER 12

187 Ogilvy, D. (1983). *Ogilvy on Advertising*. Vintage Books.

188 Kahneman, D. (2011). *Thinking, Fast and Slow*. Farrar, Straus and Giroux.

189 Handley, A. (2014). *Everybody Writes: Your Go-To Guide to Creating Ridiculously Good Content*. Wiley.

190 McKeown, G. (2014). *Essentialism: The Disciplined Pursuit of Less.* Crown Business.

191 Miller, G. A. (1956). "The Magical Number Seven, Plus or Minus Two: Some Limits on Our Capacity for Processing Information." *Psychological Review*, 63(2), 81–97.

192 Simon, C. (2016). *Impossible to Ignore: Creating Memorable Content to Influence Decisions.* McGraw Hill.

193 Duarte, N. (2010). *Resonate: Present Visual Stories that Transform Audiences.* Wiley.

194 Miller, D. (2017). *Building a StoryBrand: Clarify Your Message So Customers Will Listen.* HarperCollins Leadership.

195 Berkun, S. (2010). *Confessions of a Public Speaker.* O'Reilly Media.

196 Gallo, C. (2014). *Talk Like TED: The 9 Public-Speaking Secrets of the World's Top Minds.* St. Martin's Press.

197 Aristotle. *Poetics.* Translated by S.H. Butcher, Part VII.

198 Ragan Communications. (n.d.). "Applying the Rule of Three to Corporate Communications." The Wall Street Journal. (2023). "Amtrak's New Marketing Strategy: It's Not a Train, It's a Hotel on Wheels."

199 McKee, R. (1997). *Story: Substance, Structure, Style, and the Principles of Screenwriting.* HarperCollins.

200 Carey, B. (2014). *How We Learn: The Surprising Truth About When, Where, and Why It Happens.* Random House.

201 Roam, D. (2008). *The Back of the Napkin: Solving Problems and Selling Ideas with Pictures.* Portfolio.

202 Brown, P. C., Roediger, H. L., & McDaniel, M. A. (2014). *Make It Stick: The Science of Successful Learning.* Belknap Press.

CHAPTER 13

203 Clark, D. (2013). "Reinventing You: Define Your Brand, Imagine Your Future." *Harvard Business Review*

204 Labrecque, L. I., Markos, E., & Milne, G. R. (2011). Online Personal Branding: Processes, Challenges, and Implications. *Journal of Interactive Marketing*, 25(1), 37–50

205 Schawbel, D. (2010). *Me 2.0: Build a Powerful Brand to Achieve Career Success*. Kaplan Publishing.

206 This quote is widely attributed to Jeff Bezos in various media and business literature, but no original source has been definitively confirmed.

207 Montoya, P., & Vandehey, T. (2002). *The Personal Branding Phenomenon*. Peter Montoya Incorporated.

208 Gorbatov, S., Khapova, S. N., & Lysova, E. I. (2018). "Personal Branding: Interdisciplinary Systematic Review and Research Agenda." *Frontiers in Psychology*, 9, 2238.

209 Johnson, C. (2019). *Platform: The Art and Science of Personal Branding*. W. W. Norton & Company.

210 Clark, D. (2017). *Stand Out: How to Find Your Breakthrough Idea and Build a Following Around It*. Portfolio.

211 Avery, J., & Greenwald, R. (2023). "Personal Branding: What It Is and Why It Matters." *Harvard Business School Online*

212 Blakely, S. (2012). How I Built This [Audio podcast episode]. In G. Raz (Host), How I Built This. NPR. O'Connor, C. (2012, March 12). How SPANX Became A Billion Dollar Business Without Advertising. Forbes. Forbes. (2012, March 26). Global Billionaires 2012: Sara Blakely - American Booty. Santi, A. (2022, March 10). 3 Publicity Lessons Women Founders Can Learn From SPANX's Sara Blakely. Entrepreneur. Coogan, J. (n.d.). How Sara Blakely Built SPANX. JohnCoogan.com.

213 Khedher, M. (2019). "Conceptualizing and Researching Personal Branding Effects on Employability." *Journal of Brand Management*, 26(2), 99–109.

214 Cain, S. (2012). *Quiet: The Power of Introverts in a World That Can't Stop Talking*. Crown Publishing Group.

215 Sinek, S. (2009). *Start with Why: How Great Leaders Inspire Everyone to Take Action*. Portfolio

216 Shepherd, I. D. H. (2005). From Cattle and Coke to Charlie: Meeting the Challenge of Self-Marketing and Personal Branding. *Journal of Marketing Management*, 21(5-6), 589–606.

217 Ibarra, H. (2015). *Act Like a Leader, Think Like a Leader*. Harvard Business Review Press.

CHAPTER 14

218 Hewlett, S. A. (2019). *The Sponsor Effect: How to Be a Better Leader by Investing in Others.* Harvard Business Review Press.

219 Capello, M. A., & Sprunt, E. (2020). *Mentoring and Sponsoring: Keys to Success.* Springer.

220 Hewlett, S. A., Peraino, K., Sherbin, L., & Sumberg, K. (2010). *The Sponsor Effect: Breaking Through the Last Glass Ceiling. Harvard Business Review* Research Report.

221 Ang, J. (2019). *The Game Plan of Successful Career Sponsorship: Harnessing the Talent of Aspiring Managers and Senior Leaders.* Emerald Publishing.

222 Jones, M. C. (2021). *Decoding Sponsorship: The Secret Strategy to Accelerate Your Career and Launch Into Leadership.* Tenshey, Inc.

223 Hewlett, S. A. (2013, October). "How I Did It: Xerox's Former CEO on Why Succession Shouldn't Be a Horse Race." *Harvard Business Review.*

224 Nooyi, I. (2021). *My Life in Full: Work, Family, and Our Future.* Portfolio.

225 Collett, P., & Fenton, W. (2011). *The Sponsorship Handbook: Essential Tools, Tips and Techniques for Sponsors and Sponsorship Seekers.* Wiley.

226 Collett, P., & Fenton, W. (2011). *The Sponsorship Handbook: Essential Tools, Tips and Techniques for Sponsors and Sponsorship Seekers.* Wiley.

227 Jones, M. C. (2021). *Decoding Sponsorship: The Secret Strategy to Accelerate Your Career and Launch Into Leadership.* Tenshey, Inc.

228 Barber, S. M. (2021). *The Visibility Factor: Break Through Your Fears, Stand In Your Own Power and Become the Authentic Leader You Were Meant to Be.* Balboa Press.

229 Santander. (2022). 2022 ESG Report. FairyGodBoss. (2022). Companies With Great Mentorship, Sponsorship, and Other Career Development Programs

230 Ibarra, H. (2015). *Act Like a Leader, Think Like a Leader.* Harvard Business Review Press.

231 Garfinkle, J. A. (2011). *Getting Ahead: Three Steps to Take Your Career to the Next Level.* Wiley.

232 Evarts, E. (2015). *Raise Your Visibility & Value: Uncover the Lost Art of Connecting On the Job.* CreateSpace Independent Publishing.

233 Benko, C., & Anderson, M. (2010). *The Corporate Lattice: Achieving High Performance in the Changing World of Work.* Harvard Business Review Press.

234 Keller, S., & Price, C. (2011). *Beyond Performance: How Great Organizations Build Ultimate Competitive Advantage.* Wiley.

235 Grant, A. (2021). *Think Again: The Power of Knowing What You Don't Know.* Viking.

236 Hewlett, S. A., Peraino, K., Sherbin, L., & Sumberg, K. (2010). *The Sponsor Effect: Breaking Through the Last Glass Ceiling.* Center for Work-Life Policy.

CHAPTER 15

237 Lencioni, P. (2002). *The Five Dysfunctions of a Team: A Leadership Fable.* Jossey-Bass.

238 Voss, C. (2016). *Never Split the Difference: Negotiating As If Your Life Depended On It.* Harper Business.

239 Goleman, D. (1995). *Emotional Intelligence: Why It Can Matter More Than IQ.* Bantam Books.

240 Chen, J. (2019). *Smart, Not Loud: How to Leverage Quiet Influence for Leadership Success.* HarperCollins.

241 Covey, S. R. (1989). *The 7 Habits of Highly Effective People: Powerful Lessons in Personal Change.* Free Press.

242 Nadella, S. (2017). *Hit Refresh: The Quest to Rediscover Microsoft's Soul and Imagine a Better Future for Everyone.* Harper Business.

243 Tannen, D. (1998). *The Argument Culture: Stopping America's War of Words.* Ballantine Books.

244 Burkeman, O. (2021). *Four Thousand Weeks: Time Management for Mortals.* Farrar, Straus and Giroux.

245 Maxwell, J. C. (1998). *The 21 Irrefutable Laws of Leadership: Follow Them and People Will Follow You.* Thomas Nelson.

246 World Finance. (2015). How Indra Nooyi changed the face of PepsiCo.

247 Catmull, E., & Wallace, A. (2014). *Creativity, Inc.: Overcoming the Unseen Forces That Stand in the Way of True Inspiration.* Random House Catmull, E. (2008). "How Pixar Fosters Collective Creativity." *Harvard Business Review.*

248 Cialdini, R. B. (1984). *Influence: The Psychology of Persuasion.* Harper Business.

249 Grant, A. (2021). *Think Again: The Power of Knowing What You Don't Know.* Viking.

250 Silver, N. (2024). *On the Edge: The Art of Risking Everything.* Penguin Random House.

251 West, T. (2024). *Job Therapy: Finding Work That Works for You.* Penguin Random House.

252 Grant, A. (2016). *Originals: How Non-Conformists Move the World.* Viking.

253 Sah, S. (2025). *Defy: The Power of No in a World That Demands Yes.* One World.

254 Catmull, E. (2014). *Creativity, Inc.: Overcoming the Unseen Forces That Stand in the Way of True Inspiration.* Random House.

255 Stone, D., Patton, B., & Heen, S. (1999). *Difficult Conversations: How to Discuss What Matters Most.* Penguin Books.

256 Cain, S. (2012). *Quiet: The Power of Introverts in a World That Can't Stop Talking.* Crown Publishing Group.

257 Stern, T. (2020). *Negotiating for the Future: The Paris Climate Agreement and Global Diplomacy.* Yale University Press.

258 Pollack Peacebuilding Systems. (2023). Top 5 Benefits of Conflict Resolution Training for Employees.

DIGESTIF

259 Mehta, S. (2023, September 29). Satya Nadella changed Microsoft's culture: how leaders can learn. *Fast Company.*

260 Nelson, N. (2023, September 29). Empathy and listening: The two strongest superpowers of leadership in times of change. *Fast Company.*

261 Wired Staff. (2024, November 21). Relevance! Relevance! Relevance! At 50, Microsoft Is an AI Giant, Open-Source Lover, and as Bad as It Ever Was. *Wired.*

262 Chesky, B. (2020, May 5). A Message from Co-Founder and CEO Brian Chesky. Airbnb Newsroom. Chesky, B. (2021, February 9). Brian Chesky: Managing Through Crisis and Uncertainty. *Stanford Graduate School of Business.*

263 Lagorio-Chafkin, C. (2020). How Airbnb Survived the Pandemic: The Power of Storytelling. *Inc.*

264 Ross, S. (2023, May 4). Important team and business changes. *Shopify News.*

265 Shopify Inc. (2025, February 13). Fourth-Quarter and Full-Year 2024 Financial Results.

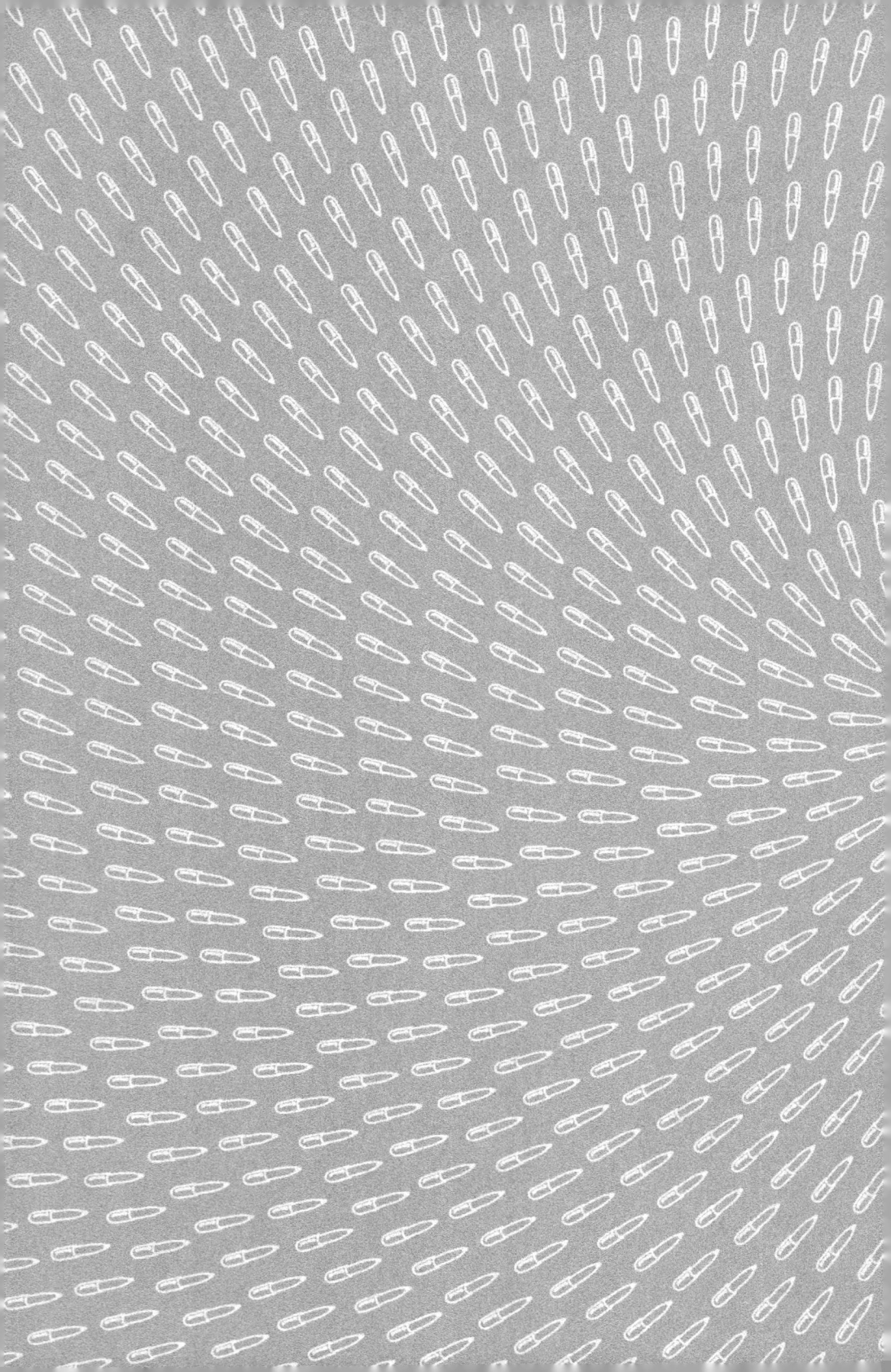